EXPLORING MORMON THOUGHT: GOD'S PLAN TO HEAL EVIL

Volume 4

Blake T. Ostler

Greg Kofford Books
Salt Lake City, 2020

Copyright © 2020 Blake T. Ostler
Cover design copyright © 2020 Greg Kofford Books, Inc.
Cover design by Loyd Isao Ericson

Published in the USA.

All rights reserved. No part of this volume may be reproduced in any form without written permission from the publisher, Greg Kofford Books. The views expressed herein are the responsibility of the author and do not necessarily represent the position of Greg Kofford Books.

ISBN 978-1-58958-191-3 (hardcover); 978-1-58958-648-2 (paperback)
Also available in ebook.

Greg Kofford Books
P. O. Box 1362
Draper, UT 84020
www.gregkofford.com
facebook.com/gkbooks
twitter.com/gkbooks

Library of Congress Control Number: 2020946099

GOD'S PLAN TO HEAL EVIL

Also by
BLAKE T. OSTLER

EXPLORING MORMON THOUGHT:
The Attributes of God
The Problems of Theism and the Love of God
Of Gods and Gods

Fire on the Horizon: A Meditation on the Endowment and Love of Atonement

CONTENTS

PREFACE ix

Chapter 1
WHAT WE LEARN FROM THE PROBLEM OF EVIL 1
  Radical Evils 2
  The Problem of Evil: The Argument 4
  Human Cognitive Limitations 9
  The Problem of Moral Quietude for Skeptical Theism 15
  The Problem of Moral Quietude and Meticulous Providence 18

Chapter 2
THE NO MINIMUM EVIL DEFENSE 29

Chapter 3
THE FREE WILL DEFENSE 37

Chapter 4
THE LESS EVIL OPTIONS ARGUMENT 47
  Objection #1 50
  Objection #2 51
  Objection #3 55
  Objection #4 56
  Objection #5 58

Chapter 5
NATURAL LAW THEODICIES 61
  God's Relation to Natural Regularities in
    the Tradition of Creation Out of Nothing 63
  Prospects of a Natural Law Theodicy in
    the Tradition of Ex Nihilo Creation 66

Chapter 6
A MORMON FINITISTIC THEODICY   71

Chapter 7
A MORMON PROCESS THEODICY   83
  Precedents in Mormon Thought for a Process Theodicy   83
  Basic Commitments of a Mormon Process Theodicy   90
  An Outline of a Mormon Process Theodicy   102
  Criticisms of Process Theodicy   105

Chapter 8
A RELATIONAL AGAPE THEODICY   113
  The Nature of God's Providence   117
  An Outline of the Agape Theodicy   135

Chapter 9
THE PLAN OF AGAPE   141
  Can Radical Evils Benefit the Victims as
    an Essential Feature of God's Plan of Agape?   148

Chapter 10
IS IT JUSTIFIABLE TO PERMIT CONSENT
TO PERSONALITY-DESTROYING EVILS?   155
  Is General Consent Sufficient or Must There Be Specific Consent
    to the Particular Evils That We Will Actually Experience? 164
  How Can the Purpose of Life be to Become United with God
    When Most Never Hear of Christ in this Lifetime?   170

Chapter 11
ARE RADICAL EVILS ESSENTIAL TO THE PLAN OF AGAPE?   173
  God and Natural Evils   176

Chapter 12
ATONEMENT IN MORMON THOUGHT — 185
   A. Desiderata for a Theory of Atonement — 186
   B. Does Mormonism Add Anything to the Penal-Substitution Theory? — 191
   C. Mormon Theories of Atonement — 194
   D. A Brief Summary of the Compassion Theory of Atonement — 203
   E. Response to Critiques of the Compassion Theory — 209

HEALING EVIL: A CONCLUSION — 223

Appendix
SELECT BIBLIOGRAPHY FOR PROCESS THEODICY — 227

Bibliography — 233
Index — 239

PREFACE

The problem of evil is perhaps the greatest challenge to belief in a loving and personal God. At least for those in the Abrahamic traditions—Christians, Jews, and Muslims—the existence of evil in the world is a major challenge to the acceptance of a God who both cares about us and is in some sense responsible for the way that the world is. The challenge naturally leads us to ask, "Why, God, has this happened to me, to my loved ones, to my enemies?" Or, to ask with the Psalmist, "Where art thou God?" Or, to perhaps echo Jesus, "My God, my God, why hast thou abandoned me?"

The problem with attempting to give an answer to these questions is that the only real answer we can give is that we just do not know. Lacking any clear revelation on the matter, we are left to struggle, to doubt, and to suffer through this challenge. Perhaps even worse, when we attempt to provide an answer, we often just end up justifying and even defending the evils that occur in the world.

I remember a woman standing to bear her testimony in our church meeting and thanking God that her son was not harmed in a recent car accident. Just two pews away sat the mother of another son who did not survive that same accident. I was spiritually embarrassed. The gratitude of the mother whose son survived was both real and understandable. However, the grief and additional thoughtless pain caused by this expression of thanksgiving struck me as remarkably insensitive and obtuse. But who was I to judge?

This book is the result of an existential struggle with my own commitments and experiences. My life has been remarkably blessed. But even remarkably blessed lives have challenges and heartaches, losses and kicks in the gut. Evil is not just pain and suffering, it is our own evil and the vile things that we do to each other—and especially to those that we say we love the most. Sometimes humans are just truly and irrefutably evil. However, we do not need to look at others who are examples of true evil; the real revelation comes when we look at our own hearts. We have all done things that we are ashamed of and that in context are truly evil. We know it better than anyone.

This book delves into the problem from an analytic perspective that seeks to transcend mere analysis and make the problem both personal and existential. The cases of evil that I cite have been true struggles and challenges for me. My own experiences have forced me to my knees, where I have spent hours questioning, writhing in anguish, crying, begging, pleading, and imploring God for answers, insights, comfort, enlightenment, and solace.

The way I have approached the issue is not the only way to do so. It is just the most responsible way I know how to discuss it. Over the years, I have had many, many conversations with David Paulsen—an incredible Latter-day Saint philosopher and one of the greatest men I have encountered. We discussed the issues at length, and our conversations are often reflected in what we each wrote on the subject. This book is in many ways the fruit of those discussions. In particular, the agape theodicy reflected in this book is a result of hours of creative musings and assessments. However, I emphasize that any deficiencies in the theory are my own and not attributable to David.

I also discussed the issues related to the problem of evil with Truman Madsen. His book *Eternal Man* first introduced me to the fact that the restored gospel has a very unique and powerful perspective to put our experiences of evil into perspective. Truman was one of the most creative and entertaining thinkers I have spoken with. He would often just stop mid-discussion with some breakthrough or insight that got him excited to see it in a new way. I loved that about him.

I also discussed the issues at length with Sterling McMurrin. He did not approach the issue from a believing perspective. However, he took an interest and emphasized to me that he still had a sense of God even if he was an agnostic. I never figured out how one could hold that stance, but God's existence remained an existential question for him (even if he detested existentialism!). My assessment of finitist Mormon thought owes much to my discussions with Sterling.

But most of all, this book is the result of being a son, sibling, husband, father, and grandfather. What I have learned from the challenges and blessings of the basic nuclear family astounds me. My father passed away last year, and I still find myself suddenly tearing up when I remember him, the things he did and said to me, and his personal idiosyncrasies that bring a smile to my face. The sense of loss is profound and at times overwhelming. The weight of mortality has fallen on me, and the promise of continued life after death has gained more meaning. Watching my mother and father take care of each other in their health challenges inspired me and taught me what it is to see real and lasting love.

I can never adequately put into words what I feel about my wife and children. They are everything to me. This poem that I wrote for my wife expresses the love that I have gained the capacity to know through them:

> There are times when I wonder,
> How it is we came to be,
> At such times of wonder,
> There is you and there is me,
> But in the times we have together,
> You and me have become we,
> And over time this we has grown,
> So that you and me are not just we two,
> But now the time has come,
> That we are all of our children too.
> And at times tears come to my eyes,
> At the wondrous image of loving embrace,
> That includes all of the times we shared together,
> Not just me and not just you,
> But also all of these that are ours forever,
> With whom we are no longer just you and me,
> WE are everything that I ever wished to be.

1

WHAT WE LEARN FROM THE PROBLEM OF EVIL

> From a distance we all have enough,
> and no one is in need.
> And there are no guns, no bombs, and no disease,
> no hungry mouths to feed . . .
> From a distance there is harmony,
> It's the hope of hopes, it's the love of loves.
> This is the song of every man.
> And God is watching us, God is watching us,
> God is watching us from a distance.
> Oh, God is watching us, God is watching.
> God is watching us from a distance.
> —Julie Gold

I have always disliked the song "From a Distance" made popular by Bette Midler, where the evils of the world look like a pleasant cosmic harmony if one just backs up far enough and assesses it in the abstract. I dislike the notion that God is so aloof that He views us from a distance and doesn't notice the evils that confront us because everything is really just fine from His distance. Such a view is totally consonant with the view that God ordained virtually everything that occurs. Everything that we think is evil is really a part of the harmony and thus all for the best. There can be no logical problem of evil, because the observation that, for all we know, God may just have his reasons, shows that God may be justified in allowing whatever merely apparent evils occur.

I prefer the Christian notion that God did not stand aloof "at a distance" but participated directly with us in the mud and blood of human horror—up close and personal. It's only when we get closer and look at particular instances of evil that the harmony disappears. If we take concrete instances of evil in all of their particularity, the notion that such evils can plausibly be explained by some abstract possibility of a greater harmony dissipates. It is in light of such concrete instances of evil that it becomes apparent that either our every attempt to explain how God could ordain them to produce some greater good is a complete failure, or our explanations themselves are morally abhorrent.

Radical Evils

There are a few instances of radical evil that I am going to focus on to address the problem of evil. Each is, terribly, too real. These events still rip the heart out of my chest every time I think about them.

1. In 1982, a three-year-old girl was kidnapped from a park in Utah. She was playing with her two brothers, ages five and one-and-a-half years old, as well as other children from the area. According to the witnesses, a twenty-five- to thirty-five-year-old male offered the little girl some gum. They last saw the perpetrator put her in a car and drive away. Twenty-four days later, her body was found with her hand tied behind her neck. The three-year-old had been brutalized before her death. This case remains unsolved.

2. My good friend had an eight-year-old son and a five-year-old daughter who had just returned from church. As they went out to play, a car in their neighbor's driveway inexplicably began to roll backward. The brother saw that his sister was in the car's path and rushed to try to stop it. Unable to save her, he watched the car roll over his little sister, crushing her head. My friend has since gone through a divorce from his wife, who was never able to get past the devastating events of that day. His son suffered psychological trauma from the incident and has been essentially nonfunctional since this tragedy.

3. Until its declared eradication on December 9, 1979, smallpox was the most virulent killer in the recorded history of the world. The advent of smallpox in the New World nearly wiped out existing Native

American populations, with several distinct tribes being completely decimated by the contagion. In Europe, near the end of the eighteenth century, the disease accounted for nearly four hundred thousand deaths each year, including five kings. Of those surviving, on-ethird were blinded. Between 20 and 60 percent of all those infected—and over 80 percent of infected children—died from the disease. During the twentieth century alone, it is estimated that smallpox caused the death of three hundred million to five hundred million people. Survivors were almost always left with severe disfiguring pox scars. Throughout human history, smallpox killed at least several billion people, vastly exceeding the combined total of deaths in all world wars.[1]

These are instances of moral and natural radical evils. Radical evils are those that appear to us, for all that we can grasp, to be unjustifiable because they destroy the very humanity of the victims and have no fathomable good to which they are necessary. The three-year-old girl's death resulted presumably from the depraved free acts of moral evil. It is an instance of radical moral evil. My friend's daughter's death resulted from what appears to be sheer random happenstance of a confluence of fairly innocent negligence and inexplicable operation of natural laws that result in overwhelming trauma to those involved. It is an instance of a mix of mild human negligence and natural evils—those that result from the operation of natural laws. Smallpox is an instance of radical natural evil. All are radical evils because the immediate victims of these events cannot benefit from the experiences of evil and because their very dignity and personhood were destroyed by the events involved.[2]

---

1. Allsdair M. Geddes, "The History of Smallpox," 152–57.

2. This kind of argument from particular evils owes much to William Rowe. See William Rowe, "The Problem of Evil and Some Varieties of Atheism," 335–41; William Rowe, "Evil and the Theistic Hypothesis: A Response to Wykstra," 95–100; William Rowe, "The Evidential Argument from Evil: A Second Look," 262–85; William Rowe, "Skeptical Theism: A Response to Bergmann," 297–303; and William Rowe, "Friendly Atheism, Skeptical Theism, and the Problem of Evil," 79–92. See also Bruce Russell, "The Persistent Problem of Evil," 121–39; Bruce Russell, "Defenseless," 193–206; Bruce Russell, "The Problem of Evil: Why is there So Much Suffering?" 207–13; Bruce Russell and Stephen Wykstra, "The Inductive Argument from Evil: A Dialogue," 133–60; Paul Draper, "Pain and Pleasure: An Evidential Problem for Theists," 331–50; and Paul Draper, "Probabilistic Arguments from Evil," 303–17.

The Problem of Evil: The Argument

Each of these radical evils is something that any decent person would prevent if possible. We cannot fathom how any of these events is necessary to the attainment of some greater good. It seems fairly obvious that the moral fabric of the universe would not be put at risk, the value of agency for humanity would not be destroyed, and the natural order of the universe and its laws would not be thrown into chaos if these events had been prevented from happening.

Do these events demonstrate that God is either not good or cannot exist? For purposes of this argument, "omnipotence" means roughly that there are no non-logical constraints on the exercise of divine power. An "omniscient" being is one who knows all truths. A "perfectly good" being is one who is essentially good in the sense that, if it were supposed to do something less than what is optimally good, it would either (a) not exist or (b) freely choose to cease to be divine. The argument goes as follows:

1. Necessarily, any being that is God is a perfect being.
2. Necessarily, a perfect being is omnipotent.
3. Necessarily, an omnipotent being could unilaterally prevent any instance of evil of which it is aware.
4. Necessarily, a perfect being is omniscient.
5. Necessarily, an omniscient being is aware of all events that have, are now, or will occur.
6. Necessarily, a perfect being is morally perfect.
7. Necessarily, a morally perfect being would prevent all evils that it could of which it is aware.
8. Therefore, if there is any evil in the world, then there is no perfect being. (From 1-7)
9. There is evil in the world.
10. Therefore, there is no perfect being. (From 8 and 9)
11. Therefore, there is no God. (From 1 and 10)

This argument is logically valid. However, it is not a logical proof that God cannot exist. It is merely a persuasive argument that, if all the premises are true, shows that God does not exist. Are the premises true? Those who believe in a deity with all power, all knowledge, and perfect goodness (which I shall call the "omni-god") may question both premises 7 and 9. Premise 7 is false because a perfectly good being does not necessarily prevent all evils;

it needs only to prevent those evils that are not necessary for the realization of some greater good. Further, premise 9 is not logically necessary—it depends on the way the world is and, as such, is an empirical premise that must be demonstrated by evidence. Thus, premise 7 also is not necessarily true. Premise 9 is, at best, a value judgment that can only be assessed based on the evidence available to us coupled with a sound moral judgment. For all we know, all evils may be justified by some greater good. For example, a loving mother may justifiably subject her daughter to a series of very painful vaccination shots because the benefits of being protected from painful, crippling, or deadly illnesses outweigh the momentary pain. Thus, while there is some bad in experiencing the pain of receiving a vaccination, the pain is justified by the benefits of preventing diseases that are much worse.

If we take a step back and view the world from "a distance," as the song suggests, we can ask whether all evils are like the pain of a vaccination and merely apparent evils. In itself such pain is bad, but given the great benefits of immunity against diseases that, if unvaccinated, could result in much greater pain and even death, and which cannot be obtained in any other way that is less painful, the vaccination is really good—all things considered. Of course, if there were no benefit from the painful shots (say we just stuck needles into little children for the fun of it), such actions would be an unjustifiable evil. Further, if we could obtain the same benefit with less pain (say by having the child swallow a sugar cube), we would be unjustified in inflicting the pain of multiple shots on the child. The good to be realized must be necessary for the benefit in the sense that it cannot be achieved in some less painful way and must be sufficient in its good effects to justify the pain.

What kinds of greater goods could justify allowing the radical evils I have outlined? To begin, the interests and consent of the victim are crucial to whether such events could be justified. For example, if a doctor decided to perform painful experiments that could result in long-lasting and undesirable side-effects on a patient without their consent in order to further the cause of science, we would view the doctor as a criminal. However, if the mature patient consented to the experiment after being fully informed of the pain and health risks, then the experimentation is sometimes justified—if the risks are not too great and the benefit to be achieved is considerable. Nevertheless, the patient is entitled to assess the risks and benefits for themself. If the patient consents that the experimental operation is worth it, then we do not fault the physician if the operation does not turn out as planned. It is a risk inherent in the experimental procedure that the patient freely chooses to confront.

Based on these considerations, among others,[3] I suggest, just as Immanuel Kant asserts with his second formulation of the categorical imperative, that it is not appropriate to treat a person as a mere means and not also as an end in and of themself. Such dehumanizing treatment makes a person a mere thing—an object that is used to appropriate something that always had less value than any person.

I propose that there are at least three conditions that must be met for the "greater goods" to count as Justifying Goods (JG) in response to the argument from the problem of evil:

> (JG) In order to constitute a Justifying Good, the benefit derived from allowing an evil must be such that (a) it outweighs the magnitude of the evil; (b) the evil is necessary to achieve the benefit in question; and (c) the evil furthers the interests of the victim—not merely as a means to achieve the benefit but also as a Thou—an intrinsically valuable person whose own interests are also furthered.[4]

Any evil that is not justified by some Justifying Good may be referred to as an Unjustified Evil (UE).

> (UE) An Unjustified Evil is such that (a) its magnitude of dis-value outweighs the value of any possible good to which the evil is necessary to achieve; or (b) it is not necessary to realizing the value of any outweighing good; or (c) its occurrence cannot result in some benefit to the victim of the evil sufficient to justify its dehumanizing effects.

Note that these conditions are disjunctive in the sense that each is in itself sufficient to show that a suggested good is not truly justified. Demonstrating any one of these conditions in relation to some suggested Justifying Good is sufficient to undermine the justification of the supposed good. All three conditions need not be demonstrated. So the question for the problem of evil is whether there are any Unjustifiable Evils. If there are

---

3. I discussed the reasons for adopting the view that it is immoral to treat others as a mere means or objects in Blake T. Ostler, *Exploring Mormon Thought: The Problems of Theism and the Love of God*, ch. 1.

4. On experiencing other persons as a Thou, see Blake T. Ostler, *Fire on the Horizon: A Meditation on the Endowment and Love of Atonement* 7–11.

WHAT WE LEARN FROM THE PROBLEM OF EVIL

Unjustified Evils, then there are events occurring that, all things considered, would be better that they not occur.

Thus, the following premises of the argument must be adjusted to accommodate these requirements:

7*. Necessarily, a morally perfect being would prevent all *unjustified* evils that it could of which it is aware.

8*. Therefore, if there is any *unjustified* evil in the world, then there is no perfect being. (From 1-7)

9*. There is *unjustified* evil in the world.

The three instances of radical evils I discussed appear to meet the criteria of Unjustified Evils. The kidnapping, rape, and brutal murder of a little girl is an instance of a radical moral evil. It results from the supposedly free acts of an as yet unknown murderer. It seems impossible that the little girl herself could possibly benefit from these events because she did not survive. Allowing the murder does not appear to be necessary to the realization of any good of sufficient value that would justify this murder. It is true that freedom to act and the exercise of free will are valuable. However, the freedom of the girl's murderer to carry out this reprehensible murder is not of sufficient value to justify allowing him to exercise his freedom. For example, no one would fault any person who interfered with the freedom of the little girl's murderer to prevent him from carrying it out. While freedom is valuable, her murderer's freedom to carry out his reprehensible acts just does not count in the moral considerations we take into account to determine whether to allow such events to occur. Nor would we consider it appropriate to just stand by and watch as the murderer assaulted and killed her because it may give *us* the opportunity to become more compassionate. We would still judge it as obligatory to stop the murderer every time we could without risking harm to ourselves—even though we may ourselves derive some benefit from allowing it to happen.

If any one of us were present and had the capacity to stop this murder without risk of harm to ourselves, we would be obligated to stop it. The world is not a better place, as far as we can assess matters, because a three-year-old girl was murdered. Yet God was there and had the capacity to stop it without risk to Himself. He could have sent angels to overpower the murderer—like He stopped Abraham from sacrificing Isaac (Gen. 22:10–12) or like He stopped

Laman and Lemuel from beating Nephi to death (1 Ne. 3:28–29). He could have revealed to any adult around what was happening or the whereabouts of the murderer shortly after the kidnapping. If it is suggested that such obvious intervention would have made his existence obvious and obviated the need for faith, then it is easy to come up with other scenarios where there is no risk of rendering God's existence obvious. God could have stopped the entire series of events leading to her murder by causing the murderer to suffer an aneurysm or stroke—and no mortal would have even known of the intervention. He could have interfered with the function of the neurons in the murderer's brain to cause him to be repelled by the thought of kidnapping and murdering little girls. In fact, if God caused such desires, then the murderer is still free in a compatibilist sense of free will to choose to not murder even though his desires were immediately caused by God.[5]

It seems to me that unless we make God the exception to all moral rules that apply to us (such that everything we know about good and evil and moral obligation does not apply to God), then we must admit that there is nothing we know of that is both necessary and sufficiently good that it would justify God in not intervening in the ways I have suggested, among many others, to stop these events from occurring. The instances of natural evil and pointless evil that I have discussed are similar. We know of no good that has sufficient value that it is even plausible to suggest that allowing these events to occur is both necessary to the attainment of that good and also benefits the victims of these events. The death of my friend's little girl from a freak car accident could surely have been prevented by just making the brake catch or preventing it from starting to roll until just a few minutes later. Moreover, the accident could have been prevented by a man of usual strength who was present and observed what was occurring.

I submit that it is obvious on its face that the natural order of the universe would not be upset by divinely intervening to stop the car from starting to roll for just a few minutes. Nor is there any benefit to the little girl or her family that we can fathom from allowing her to be crushed by the car. Preventing this type of event is not necessary to prevent some greater good from obtaining. An omnipotent being who foreknew the dehumanizing and crushing effects of the little girl's death on her brother and parents cannot be justified in allowing an evil of this sort by referring to anything

---

5. Blake T. Ostler, *Exploring Mormon Thought: The Attributes of God*, 202–13.

less than a very great good that cannot be accomplished in any other way than by allowing this particular event to occur.

I also submit that we know that preventing natural evils of great magnitude, such as smallpox and the black plague, did not throw our universe into chaos, truncate human moral freedom, or prevent anyone from developing valuable moral attributes through soul-building. If smallpox had been cured before the eighteenth century, either through a revelation of medical means or by divine fiat, no greater good would have been prevented. I submit that we are in a cognitive position to know that curing smallpox did not upset the natural order or prevent the world from functioning as a place where we can make important moral decisions in the face of real challenges necessary for our moral growth as persons.

So is the argument from evil a good argument? From the standpoint that it would be some justification for doubting the omni-god's existence, the argument is a resounding success. Remember that arguments are merely attempts at persuasion. The argument is logically valid as an evidential argument. The premises of the argument appear to us to be true for all we can assess. However, whether it is persuasive is a person-specific kind of assessment regarding whether, in fact, Unjustified Evils exist. Can a person reasonably believe that there are not any Unjustified Evils?

Human Cognitive Limitations

It seems to me that at least three observations must be admitted with respect to the challenge to God's existence from evil: (a) we cannot be expected to know what God's actual purposes in allowing these particular evils in fact are (absent particular revelation); (b) we are often not in a very good cognitive position to make decisions about "all things considered" judgments; and (c) God's glory and vast knowledge are such that His possible reasons for allowing particular events may very well be beyond our ability to grasp.

If we cannot make "all things considered" judgments, such as assessing all of the relevant variables of how changing an event would impact all of the interrelated concerns a divine being may have, then it is difficult to see how the argument from evil can be persuasive. Premise 9* must be shown by evidential or empirical considerations. However, as I believe my discussion demonstrates, premise 9* enjoys a good deal of *prima facie* credibility. Nevertheless, consideration of our cognitive limitations vis-a-vis God may suggest that we simply are not in a position to judge. The argument requires us to assess whether there are plausible greater goods that are both necessary to attain the greater good and sufficient in value to justify God's allowing the kinds of evils that actually occur. However, assessing such greater goods requires us to assess what the effect would be of disallowing the radical evils for such concerns as human moral development, prospects to realize the value of free will, developing truly loving relationships through circumstances that call us to compassionate response, the effect on the natural order, what God's purposes for creation could be, and the possibility that God just may have His reasons that we cannot begin to fathom. Are we really in a cognitive position to assess such things—given all of the various variables at issue?

The Skeptical Theist (ST) answer to the problem of evil suggests that we are justified by considerations such as (a) through (c) above in concluding that:

> (ST) Given our cognitive limitations, it is likely that if there were goods known to God that were necessary for a greater good, then it would be beyond our ability to either (a) grasp what they are; or (b) assess how it is necessary to allow the evils that actually occur in order to obtain these goods.

The analogy is often used that we stand in terms of cognitive capacities like a dog stands to its master. If I take my dog to a veterinarian for a worms shot, my dog may well feel that I have delivered him up to a stranger to inflict pain on him. My dog cannot begin to fathom the science of germ theory necessary to grasp why I would do such a thing. The analogy suggests that my dog can no more grasp why I would subject him to a shot to cure worms than I can grasp God's reason for allowing evil. There may be goods that we simply cannot begin to fathom, and God could not explain them to us because they are so far beyond our cognitive capacity to grasp.

The strength of this suggestion is that it is immune to criticism. By supposition, we are not in a cognitive position to assess whether it is true or not. If something is beyond our grasp, how could we know what it is that is beyond our grasp in order to assess whether we cannot fathom what it would be? Thus, as a response to the problem of evil it is a complete defense. The proponent of the argument from evil, in principle, cannot show that there are no goods that are beyond our cognitive capacities that would justify the evils that occur.

However, I don't believe that the Skeptical Theist defense is fully persuasive. I suggest that the problem of evil arises not from what is beyond our cognitive grasp but from what is within our grasp to assess. We can see that we ourselves have acted to prevent specific instances of evil and what the consequences of doing so have been. When we prevent small children from running into the street when there are cars speeding about, we know that we prevent possible radical evils and don't worry about the effects on some greater good—precisely since we don't know of any greater good that could be achieved by allowing little children to die. We know that overpowering a child and taking away its freedom of action is justified to save its life. In exercising such coercive power with regard to children, we have every reason to believe that we don't thereby prevent some greater good that is unknown to us. After all, if the omni-god exists, then it allowed us to prevent these radical evils! Then why doesn't the omni-god apply coercive power to stop similar radical events from occurring? The omni-god could have easily overpowered the little girl's murderer. The omni-god could have stopped the car from rolling that killed my friend's little girl. Then why didn't He?

In applying vaccinations and antibiotics to completely eradicate aggressive infections and diseases such as smallpox and bubonic plague, we know that we haven't upset the natural order to such a degree that the natural order becomes unstable or that the development of moral courage thereby becomes impossible. Thus, we have very good reason to believe that the instances of particular radical evil that actually occur could also be prevented without endangering the moral order or the natural order of the universe.

I suggest a principle that I shall dub the Principle of Relevant Similarity (PRS):

> (PRS) If humans have successfully prevented events from occurring that are relevantly similar to other events that have occurred that could have been prevented by an omni-god (if He exists), and one rationally believes that preventing those events did not deprive the world of some greater good (because the omni-god, if He exists, allowed us to prevent them from occurring), then we also have strong reason to believe that preventing the events that actually occur would not deprive the world of some greater good.

I suggest that PRS is intuitively compelling. Take, for example, that we have successfully eradicated smallpox—the most deadly contagion known in human history. We have every reason to believe that, if the omni-god exists, then the omni-god would not have allowed us to cure smallpox were the actual occurrence of smallpox necessary to the realization of a greater good. We now know that the actual occurrence of smallpox cases is not necessary to such goods as the stability of the natural order, moral responsibility, the exercise of free will, and so forth. We know these things because we have done just fine without smallpox to plague us. By PRS we also can rationally generalize that curing the AIDS virus would not deprive the world of some essential, more valuable goods (if the omni-god is supposed to exist) or lead to catastrophe regarding the natural and moral order of the world.

Indeed, the AIDS virus either didn't exist as such or was inactive until the first case of AIDS in 1959.[6] Approximately 32 million people have died from AIDS-related illness since 1980, and at present about 1.5 million people die each year. Young children and women in sub-Sahara Africa are the most common victims of AIDS at present.[7] We know that AIDS is not essential to some greater good because it didn't even exist until 1959. If we cure it now, the world will be no worse off than in was before 1959. Indeed, the world would be considerably better if we cured AIDS.

We can thus also define a class of natural evils that are intransigent to explanation as necessary to some greater good. We can refer to them as *intransigent evils*. They are "intransigent" because they resist explanation in terms of being necessary for a greater good. They are known to not be necessary to a greater good by the fact that they either no longer exist or only began to exist a short time ago. Smallpox and AIDS are excellent candidates for such intransigent evils. For example, it may be necessary to allow the painful polio shots necessary to inoculate against polio. However, if polio were to cease to exist as a virus, then enduring the pain of polio shots is no longer necessary to achieve such goods. In fact, polio shots would not be necessary to achieve any possible greater good because the very reason for the shots has ceased to exist. By parity of reason, if polio were to cease to exist, and we suppose that the omni-god exists, then we would be in a position to infer that polio (a) was never necessary to any greater good; (b) the nature of the greater good has changed; or (c) the omni-god found some less evil

---

6. Although the AIDS virus was first recognized in 1981, it appears that the first case was identifed in 1959. See "Origin of HIV & AIDS."

7. "Global HIV and AIDS Statistics."

means to achieve the greater good for which polio was necessary. However, if (c) is true, then the omni-god is not omniscient and is therefore not an omni-god. That is, if the omni-god *discovers* some fact about the means of eradicating evils that it didn't know before, it follows that the omni-god was not omniscient. If (b) is true, then the nature of good is not objective and unchanging. It is difficult to imagine any viable ethical theory that would accommodate such change in the nature of what is good. Perhaps matters have changed so much that what once was logically necessary to achieve God's purposes to realize the good has changed, but I cannot imagine how the nature of what is good and right could change in this manner. It is a strange theory of ethics that suggests that today it is morally permissible to purposely infect a person with AIDS but that it wasn't morally permissible yesterday. If (a) is true, then the omni-god isn't perfectly good and thus is not the omni-god. The existence of intransigent evils, then, seems to defeat the Skeptical Theist response to the problem of evil.

Of course, it can be argued that it is only by allowing diseases such as smallpox and AIDS that humans could be inspired to find cures for diseases. Diseases must exist to be cured and cause humans to endeavor to benefit others through their research to cure those diseases. Yet who among us would suggest that it would be a good thing to release a deadly mutant strain of smallpox that is immune to the smallpox vaccination because then it may allow us to look for a further cure? Such suggestions are implausible on their face. Any person who released a new strain of smallpox is properly regarded as a bioterrorist. The reason that such suggestions aren't plausible is that we can see that the potential cost in terms of human suffering does not justify allowing a mutant strain of smallpox to run rampant just so that we can find a cure.

I submit that we also can see that allowing a little girl to be kidnapped and murdered is not necessary to a greater good—for we have prevented similar events from occurring by apprehending and stopping criminals who perpetrate such atrocities. We know quite enough to know, even given our cognitive limitations, that allowing these atrocities does not make the world a better place—even if we cannot assess all of the variables that may be affected. We know that stopping such events from occurring saves little girls from unspeakably reprehensible evil and spares their family the pain of such immense loss. We also know from our experience that the moral order continues to function, the natural world is not thrown into chaos, and that the only person's freedom that would be truncated of which we are aware (i.e., the murderer's) is one whose freedom should have been truncated.

We also know that the omni-god could have Himself prevented the occurrence of any smallpox or AIDS virus—and no one would have ever known that the omni-god did so. We also can see with pellucid clarity that if the omni-god had made us smarter, even omniscient, we could have found a cure for smallpox much sooner—or even eradicated it before it ever mutated to its deadly form. We could eradicate AIDS now if we were omniscient. It is also clear that making us smarter doesn't render us unfree. Indeed, the omni-god is, if He exists, both omniscient and significantly free (at least that is what its proponents claims). Thus, it is evident that the omni-god had alternatives open to it, even without limiting human freedom in any way, that didn't require the suffering and death of literally hundreds of millions from smallpox—which in ironic cruelty often was carried by Catholic missionaries to Native Americans in an effort to help them and save their souls.[8]

It is true that God may know of goods that are beyond our grasp for allowing smallpox and other similar viruses to wreak havoc on human lives (and animals). Nevertheless, we know that these radically evil events are relevantly similar to acts that the omni-god (if He exists) has allowed us to prevent. Thus, we can conclude from relevantly similar events that we have prevented, that the omni-god did not need them to accomplish some greater good. If He did need them for the greater good, and if the omni-god did exist, then we would not have been allowed to prevent similar atrocities from occurring, because the omni-god would have assured that we did not prevent the atrocities in order to preserve the greater good to which they are somehow necessary. Of course, it can still be argued that there is some significant difference between smallpox that we have eradicated and other infectious diseases (such as Covid-19) that we have not that is relevant to some greater good, and that it is just beyond our ability to grasp this difference.

Thus, it seems to me that the skeptic is right to this extent: we cannot assess an exact percentage of probability that the omni-god wouldn't allow these radical and intransigent evils. We cannot assign a "75 percent probability" or other specific number of judgment to premise 9*. The crucial premise thus cannot be proven with precision or accuracy. Does that mean

---

8. Kristine B. Patterson and Thomas Runge, "Smallpox and the Native American," 216–22.

that the argument is defeated? Hardly. A rational person is well within his or her rights to conclude that, given the particular evils that occur and the fact that we could prevent them without any evident loss of significant value, the likelihood is extremely high that the omni-god could do at least the same with respect to any particular instance of evil that we identify. We know enough to see very clearly that we do not know of any particular greater good that meets the criteria of a Justified Good for the radical evils I have identified. We can see that any goods we can imagine are not quite good enough to justify the evils in question, or that allowing the evils is not necessary to attain any greater good we can imagine, or that the victim is not themself benefitted by allowing such evils to occur. *We are thus justified in concluding that, so far as we can see given our cognitive capacities, the existence of the omni-god assumed in the argument from evil does not exist.* That is a pretty significant conclusion—and it is more than enough to justify the rationality of disbelief in such an omni-god. We are also justified in concluding that *intransigent evils are not now necessary to the realization of a greater good.* Indeed, it seems to me that such a conclusion requires us to provide a theodicy—a reasonable explanation of how God could possibly be justified in allowing the radical evils and intransigent evils that occur.

The Problem of Moral Quietude for Skeptical Theism

The believer in the omni-god cannot adopt Skeptical Theism as outlined in ST without significant revision to our moral beliefs. It seems to me that if we really believe that the omni-god exists, so that there are no unjustified evils, then we are justified in moral quietude—in believing that no matter what we do, the particular events of so-called evils that we confront are in reality justified because they are necessary to the realization of some greater good that may well be beyond our cognitive capacity to grasp. If a little girl is raped and bludgeoned to death, it is all for the best, because otherwise the omni-god wouldn't allow it to happen. If we had stopped this event from happening, then we would have prevented a necessary condition for some good so great in value that it outweighs the disvalue of this radical evil.

The response that has been given to this objection from moral quietude has been addressed by Daniel Howard-Snyder, William P. Alston, and Michael Bergmann. They suggest that this conclusion doesn't follow, because in assessing what we will do we are limited by the goods that we can grasp, whereas the supposed greater goods that God allows are beyond our grasp. Thus, we should still act to prevent events that are, by our best lights, evil.[9]

However, this response overlooks the fact that we are not limited to what is within our cognitive grasp in making moral decisions when we have an authority with much greater knowledge than we possess whose conduct demonstrates that we should refrain from acting. Consider an example. A nurse intern has been working with a team of doctors who are very competent and appear to him to be very morally upright persons. He is tending a patient who goes into convulsions that threaten the patient's life. The hospital where he works has a drug that he learned in nursing school would certainly stop the convulsions. However, he noticed that when this particular patient went into convulsions on prior occasions, the other doctors did not administer the drug—even though they have given the drug to other patients in the hospital when they have had convulsions. The nurse has no idea why they haven't administered the drug in the past to this particular patient. The nurse cannot reach the other physicians and must act immediately. It certainly seems that the nurse has good moral reason not to administer the drug to the patient even though he has no idea why the drug was not given to this patient when it has been given to others under similar circumstances.

Consider now an analogous situation. Sue is a doctor who knows of numerous cases of suffering from prostrate cancer. She knows that millions of people have suffered horribly from prostate cancer. Sue has become a believer in the omni-god and believes that she is rationally justified in her belief. She has come to believe through reflection on the problem of evil that the omni-god must have reasons that she cannot begin to grasp to allow prostate cancer to ravage millions. She trusts that the omni-god is perfectly good and would not allow such cancers if they were not necessary to realize some greater good. She knows that, prior to the cure being developed, some people have had the cancer treated and have successfully prolonged their lives while others have not. She has no explanation for why some respond to the treatments and others do not, but she trusts that the omni-god has reasons. Now suppose that a drug is developed that cures prostrate cancer and is

---

9. William P. Alston, "Some (Temporary) Final Thoughts on Evidential Arguments from Evil," 311–32; Michael Bergmann, "Skeptical Theism and Rowe's New Evidential Argument from Evil," 278–96; Daniel Howard-Snyder, "The Argument from Inscrutable Evil," 292–93.

made available to Sue. Sue is confronted with the issue as to whether she will administer the new drug. It seems that Sue is in a relevantly similar situation to the nurse intern and thus would be morally justified in deciding that if she doesn't administer the drug, it is just as well, because if the omni-god in fact allows her not to administer it, she knows that He must have His reasons to not cure the cancer Himself. He must have had reasons to allow the treatment to be successful with some and not with others. Either way, if she does nothing, it must all be for the best, because otherwise the omni-god wouldn't allow it. Further, she believes that the omni-god knows more than any physician about curing cancer, and she also knows that the omni-god hasn't cured cancer before now. She concludes that the omni-god must have had a very good reason to allow the kind of suffering she has seen of those who experience prostate cancer. She also concludes that the evil of prostrate cancer is necessary to the realization of whatever very great good the omni-god had in mind. Thus, she concludes that administering the drug will prevent the greater good to which prostate cancer is a necessary condition. Because the omni-god allows prostate cancer to realize this greater good, whatever it could be, she concludes that she must not administer the drug because the omni-god is in a much better position than she is to assess the moral rectitude and interrelated considerations of preventing prostate cancer than she is. She can conclude that, whatever occurs, it is all for the best.

This thought experiment suggests that the problem of moral quietude is a real problem for the skeptic who claims that God must have sufficient reason that we cannot grasp to allow the particular evils that actually occur as a necessary condition to some greater good.[10] The person who believes that every instance of evil is necessary to the realization of some greater good also must believe that if the omni-god allows it to occur, then it is either not really evil or it is justified because it makes a greater good possible. Thus, there is no moral motivation to prevent any events that we take to be horrendous and radical evils. Even if it appears to us that, for all we can fathom, these events should be prevented, belief in the omni-god entails for us that our judgment cannot be trusted and that what appears to us to be unjustified evil cannot truly be so. Thus, it seems to me that this stance is fundamentally at odds with the injunctions of the gospel to feed the poor, care for the widows,

---

10. This thought experiment is inspired by comments by Derk Pereboom, "The Problem of Evil," 148–72.

and avoid evil. If we fail to do so, it is all for the best if the morally skeptical stance is adopted to defeat the argument from evil.

Moreover, such moral skepticism places everything we think we know about what is right and wrong in question. We cannot assess what is for the best; it is just beyond our grasp. How could we make moral judgments given such global moral skepticism?

Equally important, religious faith seeks to praise God for his moral goodness and beneficence. Yet if God's goodness is radically different than human goodness, then we have no basis in our experience for calling it goodness at all, and we have even less basis for praising and glorifying God as human faith is wont to do. A child who is totally ignorant of her parents' values has no reason to admire them and no ability to emulate them. If everything the child knows as "good" is different from how her parents treat her, and her parents insist that they are good and treating her for her best interests by starving and beating her, then the child must be mystified at what the word "good" could possibly mean to her parents. If the omni-god is good no matter what happens to us, then the terms "right and wrong," "good and evil," and "loving and hateful" lose all distinction and thus lose all meaning.

The Problem of Moral Quietude and Meticulous Providence

There is a very important distinction that must be made regarding whether Skeptical Theism can consistently be adopted. I believe that whether morality is undermined by consideration of our epistemic status depends on the notion of God that one entertains. Whereas an omni-god who exercises meticulous providence by either causing or ordaining every event that occurs undermines moral judgments, the view of open theists and process theists that God does not have foreknowledge (and can thus only exercise general providence) does not. A god who lacks foreknowledge must base judgments of what may justify particular events on general policies about allowing free choices. An omni-god who causes everything to occur (as asserted in Calvinism and Thomism) or specifically ordains every event by choosing a possible world to instantiate (such as in Molinism) must justify every event.[11] Following William Hasker, we may call the view that every event is the di-

---

11. I discuss these three theories of divine providence in Ostler, *The Problems of Theism*, ch. 11.

rect result of the omni-god's choices "meticulous providence."[12] However, for open theists and panentheists, God does not know what will result from any given circumstance and must wait on the free acts of agents to know what will be chosen and how others will freely choose to respond to those free choices.

To further this line of thought, I want to make a distinction between a particular free act that is an instance of justified evil and the concept of a *genuine evil*. To make this distinction, I will need one other distinction: the difference between the actual world and a "world-type." A world-type is a general kind of world that could serve to achieve particular purposes. However, the details of how those purposes are achieved are not solely up to God, because God leaves up to creatures many of the details of what the actual world's events will be. The actual world is brought about by both God and the creatures as co-creators. For Meticulous Providence, there is no distinction between the actual world and a world-type because every event occurs just as God wills it to occur. For open theists and process panentheists, however, God cannot ensure that everything that occurs conforms to God's will. Open theists believe that God does not know the future because it cannot be known, because it does not yet exist in any sense, or because God chooses not to know it. Process theists believe that God comes to know reality only as it becomes from moment to moment.

To grasp the distinction between a justified evil and a *genuine evil*, consider the possible world where all creatures freely choose to accept God and the possible world where almost none choose to accept God. For Arminians, open theists, and process panentheists, whether a person freely accepts God is not solely up to God. My acceptance of God, by its very nature, cannot be up to God but must be up to me to choose freely. There are two value judgments implicit in such a view: (a) love freely chosen is more valuable than any "love" that is not freely chosen; and (b) a world-type where persons can freely choose whether to have a loving relationships with God is more valuable than any world-type without the possibility for such freely chosen relationships. It seems fairly evident that any world where everyone freely accepts God is a "preferable world" compared to the possible world where none or only a few freely accept God. God is justified in allowing people to freely choose whether to have a relationship with Him because the most valuable kinds of relationship must be freely accepted.

---

12. William Hasker, *God, Time, and Knowledge*, 202–5.

Genuine relationships cannot be coerced, manipulated, or simply created by one person in the relationship. Thus, God must allow such freedom as a necessary condition to the possibility of genuine relationships.[13]

What follows is that God may be justified in creating a world-type where we are allowed to freely choose whether to return His love. In such a world-type, God cannot unilaterally guarantee either our salvation or what we will freely choose. However, the actual world is not, all things considered, better if I choose not to love. Within the world-types that God must allow to have the possibility of achieving his purposes, God must allow the possibility for events to occur that are not always for the best—even all things considered. In other words, a world-type where some can freely choose to accept God is better than any world-type where a lesser type of salvation could be obtained that doesn't require such freedom. A world-type where people *can* make evil choices is preferable to a world-type where they cannot; but that doesn't mean that a world where people *do* make evil choices is morally preferable to one where they make good choices. God must leave it up to us to choose. Thus, we can define a Genuine Evil (GE) within the context of a theistic "open future" world-view as follows:

> (GE) A Genuine Evil is any event or choice that God must allow in order to have the possibility of realizing the purposes for the world-type He created, but in which the actual world is not better, all things considered, that such particular choice or event occurs.

The point of a Genuine Evil is that not every particular event that occurs must be necessary for a greater good. What is necessary for a greater good is that the world-type makes achieving the greatest good a possibility. While allowing a person to freely choose to do a particular evil act may be justified by some greater good unknowable to us, it doesn't follow that the world is a better place, all things considered, merely because that particular evil choice was made—at least for open and process theists. A general policy of honoring free choices may very well be a necessary condition of soul-making and moral growth of individuals because they must be left free to make choices that have moral consequences in concrete situations of real danger. Given that honoring free choices is essential to soul-making, God must leave us free to make free choices that may have outcomes that make the

---

13. See Ostler, *The Problems of Theism*, 9–15.

world less desirable than it could have been. A world where free agents always make good choices is preferable to a world where free agents constantly make evil choices. Nevertheless, there can be genuine evils in such world-types.

The second point is that the problem of moral quietude does not plague the views of open theists and panentheists. God may be justified in leaving us free to make choices with real moral consequences, but that does not thereby logically imply that if we choose to do evil, we are always morally justified no matter which choice we make. If God doesn't know which choices we will freely choose, then He does not cause or ordain those choices. But if we believe that God does not cause or ordain our choices and must wait on us to make those choices before knowing exactly what we will do, then we are not justified in concluding that no matter what we do, it is all for the best. In this case, which possible world is actual is not solely up to God and is dependent on which choices we freely make. God can unilaterally create a world-type or kind of world that serves our needs for the possibilities of realizing soul-making and genuine relationship. However, the actual world is created also in part by our free choices. The actual world is co-created by both God and us. Thus, God may be justified in leaving us free to perform genuinely evil acts that make the world worse than the world would be had we not chosen to do evil.

Thus, such *genuine* moral evils that arise out of the evil choices freely made may nevertheless be Justified Evils because the possibility that they can be chosen is a necessary feature of any world-type that could lead to soul-making. If God has empowered us to have a significant say in the kind of world that exists because we participate in creating it through our free will, then it follows that God cannot unilaterally bring about every event that occurs. He can neither bring about every event that occurs nor ensure that every event is for the greatest good—precisely because He cannot bring about *our* free acts. God cannot cause our free acts if we are free in a non-determined or contra-causal sense. Thus, God may have a very good reason to allow free choices even if they leave open the possibility for us to choose genuine evils, or events that make the world more evil than it would have been otherwise had a person freely chosen to do something good rather than something evil. It follows also that we would have no reason to believe that the world always turns out for the best regardless of what we do.

For example, I want my children to grow to be responsible adults who deeply care about their own lives and love others. The only way for me to accomplish this goal is to allow my children increasing space as they grow to choose for themselves. There is an inherent risk in having children—they must choose for themselves at some point. I may want to make every decision for them because any individual decision would result in a better outcome if limited to consideration of what results from that particular decision. However, I must adopt a general policy of allowing my children to make free choices and learn from the consequences of such choices. Nevertheless, my children may make choices of which I disapprove. My son could be offered drugs, and I would like to control that particular decision if I knew he would choose to take drugs. However, I am justified in leaving him space to make choices, because it is the only way that he can develop into the person he chooses to be. Plus, I don't know for sure what he'll choose. I didn't give him life so that I could live his life for him or through him. I am thus justified in granting him space in which he can make choices. However, the world in which he freely chooses to refrain from taking drugs is morally preferable to the possible world in which he chooses to take them. My son could even choose, given that moral space, to commit very heinous crimes such as rape or murder. My choice to allow my son to have space to make choices so that he can grow to be a better person doesn't justify his action, but I am justified in my choice to grant him such space nevertheless.

It is the same for God if He is limited in knowledge about what we will freely choose. He is justified in the general policy of leaving us free to make responsible choices with real moral consequences. If He doesn't know how we will use our freedom, then He must wait on us to make choices. Genuine evil could result from such choices. Thus, even if we cannot discern God's reasons for allowing what appear to us to be unjustified evils, we are still morally obligated to bring about good acts as far as we can judge.

It is different for the Calvinist, Thomist, and Molinist views. The distinction between a world-type and the actual world collapses in such views. Thus, there are no genuine evils that would be consistent with the omni-god's existence. Consider the Calvinist view, which maintains that the omni-god ordains every particular event that occurs. With respect to human actions, John Calvin maintained that God works with us as individuals and not like He would with a rock or a stone.[14] For instance, Calvin defined free will as

---

14. Calvin states: "We allow that man has choice and that it is self-determined, so that if he does anything evil, it should be imputed to him and to his own voluntary

the absence of external coercion. A person is free as long as one can do as one desires.[15] However, God can cause the human will to directly will what is good by special grace.[16] Thus, God can directly form in us wants and desires,

---

choosing. We do away with coercion and force, because this contradicts the nature of the will and cannot coexist with it. *We deny that choice is free*, because through man's innate wickedness it is of necessity driven to what is evil and cannot seek anything but evil. And from this it is possible to deduce what a great difference there is between necessity and coercion. For we do not say that man is dragged unwillingly into sinning, but that because his will is corrupt he is held captive under the yoke of sin and therefore of necessity will in an evil way. For where there is bondage, there is necessity. But it makes a great difference whether the bondage is voluntary or coerced. We locate the necessity to sin precisely in corruption of the will, from which follows that it is self-determined." John Calvin, *Bondage and Liberation of the Will: A Defence of the Orthodox Doctrine of Human Choice Against Pighius*, 69–70; emphasis added.

15. Calvin asserts: "The will is [either] free, bound, self-determined, or coerced. People generally understand a free will to be one which has in its power to choose good or evil. . . . [But] There can be no such thing as a coerced will, since the two ideas are contradictory. But our responsibility as teachers is to say what it means, so that it may be understood what coercion is. Therefore we describe [as coerced] the will which does not incline this way or that of its own accord or by an internal movement of decision, but is forcibly driven by an external impulse. We say that it is self-determined when of itself it directs itself in the direction in which it is led, when it is not taken by force or dragged unwillingly. A bound will, finally, is one which because of its corruptness is held captive under the authority of its evil desires, so that it can choose nothing but evil, even if it does so of its own accord and gladly, without being driven by any external impulse. According to these definitions we allow that man has choice and that it is selfdetermined, so that if he does anything evil, it should be imputed to him and to his own voluntary choosing. We do away with coercion and force, because this contradicts the nature of the will and cannot coexist with it. *We deny that choice is free, because through man's innate wickedness it is of necessity driven to what is evil and cannot seek anything but evil.* And from this it is possible to deduce what a great difference there is between necessity and coercion. For we do not say that man is dragged unwillingly into sinning, but that because his will is corrupt he is held captive under the yoke of sin and *therefore of necessity will in an evil way.* For where there is bondage, there is necessity. But it makes a great difference whether the bondage is voluntary or coerced. We locate the necessity to sin precisely in corruption of the will, from which follows that it is selfdetermined." Calvin, 69–70; emphasis added.

16. Calvin asserts: "Not only is grace offered by the Lord, which by anyone's free choice may be accepted or rejected; but *it is this very grace which forms both choice and will in*

and based on these wants and desires we "choose" to act on our strongest desire. In this way, God can directly control what we do while supposedly leaving us free to do as we desire to do. In the Calvinist view, if we can do as we desire without external compulsion that forces us to do as we desire, then we act freely. It is irrelevant to this view of "free will" that there is a form of internal compulsion because we cannot resist God's will and God forms our wants and desires. God does not bring about our acts of will; He merely causes our desires and wants that inevitably lead to our acts of "willing." In this way, Calvinists claim that God acts through our personality structures to bring about His will.[17] Further, everything that occurs is decreed by God in the sense that he ordained it and ultimately causes it to occur.[18]

---

the heart, so that whatever good works then follow are the fruit and effect of grace" (Calvin, *Institutes*, 2.3.13; emphasis added). So any good work performed by a human is directly created in the person by special grace. Calvin also stated: "Whenever we are prompted to choose something to our advantage, whenever the will inclines to this, or conversely whenever our mind and heart shun anything that would otherwise be harmful, that is the Lord's special grace" (2.4.6). Here even the individual's will for well-being and self-preservation are attributed to that same special grace which account for all unregenerate good deeds. In a quotation of Augustine, Calvin affirms, "The human will does not obtain grace by freedom, but obtains freedom by grace; . . . Controlled by grace, it will never perish, but if grace forsake it, it will straightway fall; . . . The direction of the human will toward good, and after direction its continuation in good, depend solely upon God's will, not upon any merit in man; . . . and *whatever it can do it is able to do only through grace*." (2.4.14; emphasis added).

17. See my discussion of these claims in Ostler, *The Problems of Theism*, ch. 2.

18. Calvin asserts: "When we attribute foreknowledge to God, we mean that all things have ever been, and perpetually remain, before His eyes, so that to His knowledge nothing is future or past, but all things are present: and present in such a manner that He does not merely conceive of them from ideas formed in His mind, as things remembered by us appear present to our minds, but really beholds and sees them as if actually placed before Him. And this foreknowledge extends to the whole world and to all the creatures. Predestination we call the eternal decree of God, by which He hath determined in Himself what He would have to become of every individual of mankind. For they are not all created with a similar destiny; but eternal life is foreordained for some, and eternal damnation for others." *Institutes*, III: xxi. Calvin also stated that God "foresees future events only by reason of the fact that he decreed that they take place, they vainly raise a

Given this view, there can be no genuine evils. The omni-god does not merely have a general policy to guard the efficacy of free will as a moral strategy; rather, the omni-god brings about every individual act or event and thus must have a justification for each event or human "act" considered separately. That is, every evil event must be such that it is necessary to the realization of some greater good. Otherwise, God would be evil to decree that it occur and bring it about through his causal efficacy. However, the believer in such an omni-god can still maintain that the omni-god has justifying reasons for decreeing and bringing about what we regard as evil. Somehow every event, from the kidnapping, murder, and rape of little girls to atrocities of the Holocaust, are all necessary for a greater good that we cannot begin to fathom.

Does Molinism, the view that the omni-god knows what a free person would do in any given circumstances if actualized, change the result? I don't see how. Given Molinism, the omni-god chooses which possible world to actualize given the optimal complete set of counterfactuals that describe a possible world. It is true that God doesn't bring about or decide which of these counterfactuals is true. But it is also true that the truth of these counterfactuals is not up to the possible persons whose acts they purport to describe either. "Personal essences" are merely logical indexicals that describe what a merely possible person or "individual essence" would freely do if located in any given particular circumstance. However, what isn't actual (i.e., doesn't exist because it was never created by omni-god) cannot cause anything at all—not even the truth value of the counterfactuals that supposedly describe how a possible person would freely act if actualized by God. It follows that the truth-value of the counterfactuals of freedom is neither up to the omni-god nor up to the possible persons whose free acts they supposedly describe; their truth values are a mere surd given (totally unexplained and a-rational) fact about the universe.

If the omni-god actualizes the optimal set of counterfactuals, then it follows that anything we do is a part of the best complete set of counterfactuals describing a possible world that the omni-god could actualize. We can be assured that, no matter what we do, there was not a more optimal set of counterfactuals open to the omni-god to actualize and that the truth of our actions was ordained by the omni-god's choice of which possible world to actualize before we even existed. For all we know, every act is part of that

---

quarrel over foreknowledge, when it is clear that all things take place rather by his determination and bidding." *Institutes*, 3.23.6.

optimal possible world the omni-god could actualize. Every particular event is necessary to the optimal world because no better world was open to the omni-god to actualize. Given such meticulous providence, Molinism must justify every single event that occurs as part of the optimal set of counterfactuals—as part of the greater good that the omni-god sought to achieve in actualizing the actual world we live in. If I commit an evil act, then it follows that the omni-god chose this particular act as part of his optimal world. If I had done a different act, perhaps the world would be worse in some way, all things considered. I cannot fathom how my evil acts are necessary to the overall optimal set of counterfactuals, but the omni-god can. No matter what I do, it is part of the best (or one of the best, if worlds can be equally good) worlds open to the omni-god to actualize.

Given these views of meticulous providence, we can be sure that every event that actually occurs is essential to a better world. The distinction between a preferable world and a general policy for the kind of world that is best collapses if the omni-god either brings about or ordains every event that occurs. There are no genuine evils, given meticulous providence. There are only apparent evils that are each necessary to the realization of a greater good—and thus there are only good events in reality regardless of how we judge them. If the believer in meticulous providence fails to stop a rapist in the very act of raping a young girl, they can be confident that this act is essential to the realization of a greater good that cannot be fathomed by humans. Thus, the believer in Meticulous Providence is morally justified in never acting—for every individual event reflects the omni-god's will. The believer in meticulous providence is thus constrained to reason as follows:

(Ca) Every event that occurs is necessary to the realization of a greater good even if what the good is or how it is necessary is beyond our cognitive grasp. (Assumption Skeptical Theism)

(Cb) It is always morally permissible for us (human beings) to bring about the greater good whenever it is in our power to do so (even if we don't know what the greater good is).

(Cc) Any act that we actually do is necessary to realization of a greater good. (From Ca)

(Cd) Therefore, any act that we actually do is morally permissible. (From Cb and Cc)

WHAT WE LEARN FROM THE PROBLEM OF EVIL

Given this view, virtually every evil event is brought about by the omni-god because it is necessary to some greater good. It follows that whatever we do is morally justified by the rationale that it is necessary to realize the greater good, even if our moral intuitions may otherwise suggest. We are in no position to judge what is ultimately for the greater good. Such a view, however, surely leads to an absurd conclusion. The view that we are morally obligated to resist evil and stop it wherever we can is essential to Christian theism. Thus, Skeptical Theism leads to unacceptable conclusions.

It will do no good to argue that the moral judgments made to support the argument from moral quietude assumes a consequentialist flavor. The Skeptical Theist has already raised the "greater goods we cannot fathom" defense to the argument from evil. The greater goods defense itself assumes a kind of consequentialist weighing of goods and evils against one another. It is the Skeptical Theist who needs the consequentialist framework to argue that the existence of what appear to us to be radical evils don't count against the existence of the omni-god. Such consequentialist ethics are highly debatable, but such a framework seems to be a moral assumption essential to the Skeptical Theist's position. If such a framework is mistaken, then so is Skeptical Theism.

The argument for moral quietude is logically valid. The only premise that could be rejected by the Skeptical Theist is premise (Cb). Perhaps it could be rejected by claiming that only those goods which we know of can justify inaction in the face of what seems to us to be a duty to intervene based on everything we know.[19] However, the premise doesn't claim that we have a moral duty to always try to bring about some greater good that we cannot grasp; rather, it is that we are morally justified no matter what we do. We lack sufficient knowledge of moral facts to judge accurately. However, the omni-god supposedly does have perfect grasp of such moral facts. If the omni-god allows me to steal candy from a baby, then that must have been for the best. If I don't steal, then that must also be for the best, because whatever *actually* occurs is always all for the best. Thus, we can be assured that no matter what we do, it will result in some greater good even though we cannot begin to grasp how.

---

19. Michael Bergmann and Michael Rea, "In Defence of Skeptical Theism: A Reply to Almeida and Oppy," 241–51; Howard-Snyder, "The Argument from Inscrutable Evil," 286–310.

Consider an analogy. A tribesman walks into a field hospital and sees someone (that we know as a surgeon) who has a knife and saw and is about to cut into the abdomen of the tribesman's wife who lays unconscious on a table. For all he can tell, it appears that his wife is under a deadly assault. He has very good reason to attack the doctor and no reason is known to him not to. But suppose that he has also heard that the doctors in the hospital have powerful medicine to cure others, and he believes that if cutting his wife were necessary to save her life, he would be completely unable to grasp why. The incision is about to be made, and he has no time to make any further inquiry before acting. Given his beliefs and lack of ability to grasp what surgeons do, does it follow that he is obligated to stop the surgeon (and thereby prevent the doctor from performing a life-saving appendectomy)? I don't see how. What follows is that he would be justified if he attacked the surgeon and justified if he refrained from doing so. He just doesn't know enough to judge right or wrong regarding what he sees happening. No matter how he responds, his lack of ability to grasp the moral facts necessary to assess what is right and what is wrong justifies his response.

Thus, Skeptical Theism conjoined with meticulous providence undermines morality. It is morally absurd to believe that we are morally justified no matter what we do—unless there just are no moral facts to assess. Yet no theist could accept that. The belief in meticulous providence ensures moral impotence and destroys any confidence that we can make appropriate moral judgments. As such, it doesn't appear to be a position that is open to a theist. The skeptical defense is thus self-defeating for those who accept meticulous providence.

2

THE NO MINIMUM EVIL DEFENSE

Peter van Inwagen has argued that there is no minimum amount of evil necessary for divine purposes. He argues that God can therefore permit more than the minimum necessary (because there is no such minimum). He concludes that the view that an omni-god must prevent all Unjustified Evils is therefore mistaken:

> But what of the hundreds of millions (at least) of instances of [horrendous suffering] that have occurred during the long history of life? Well, I concede, God could have prevented any one of them, or any two of them, or any three of them . . . without thwarting any significant good or permitting any significant evil. But could He have prevented all of them? No, not without causing the world to be massively irregular. And of course there is no sharp cutoff point between a world that is massively irregular and a world that is not. . . . There is, therefore, no minimum number of cases of intense suffering that God could allow without forfeiting the good of a world that is not massively irregular.[1]

Thus, Van Inwagen provides an independent basis for rejecting both premises 7* and 9* from the previous chapter. This is a truly revolutionary move because Van Inwagen rejects what has been accepted as an unimpeachable moral principle in the debate regarding the problem of evil: God cannot allow Unjustified Evils and also be perfectly good. Van Inwagen claims that this principle is not universally valid as a moral principle where it is the

---

[1]. Peter van Inwagen, *God, Knowledge and Mystery: Essays in Philosophical Theology*, 15–19. A "massively irregular" world is one where the natural laws are constantly suspended so that they don't operate with uniformity or regularity.

case that (1) a person is morally justified in *allowing some evil* to accomplish a greater good, and (2) there is no minimum that is necessary to accomplish that greater good. In effect, he claims that it is conceptually incoherent to claim that there is some level of evil that is unjustifiable if any evil at all can be justified, because then there is no minimum amount to provide a cut-off where evil is no longer justified. The notion is that if it is conceded that God is justified in allowing some evils, then we cannot judge whether the maximum amount allowable is three deaths or six million. He argues that God is justified in allowing some evil because some evil is necessary for God's purpose of effectuating atoning reconciliation. According to Van Inwagen, evil is necessary to motivate us to seek such reconciliation. Moreover, allowing some evil is necessary to provide an environment for moral challenge. If there is to be morally significant free will to choose between good and evil, then we must be allowed to actually choose evil at least on some occasions. But what is the lower limit of the number of evil free choices that it is morally permissible for God to allow, given His purposes?

As Van Inwagen puts it, "[T]o ask what the minimum number of horrors consistent with [God's] plan is, is like asking, What is the minimum number of raindrops that could have fallen on England in the nineteenth century that is consistent with England's having been a fertile country in the nineteenth century?"[2] But if there is no minimum number of evils, it is logically impossible for God or anyone else to determine what is unjustified and hence unreasonable for anyone to expect that He do so.[3] Van Inwagen argues:

> [God] cannot remove all the horrors from the world, for that would frustrate his plan for reuniting human beings with himself. And if he prevents only some horrors, how shall he decide which ones to prevent? Where shall he draw the line?—the line between threatened horrors that are prevented and threatened horrors that are allowed to occur? I suggest that wherever he draws the line, it will be an arbitrary line.[4]

Van Inwagen's response to particular radical evils is that they are morally justified because God must allow some evils, and the cut-off line between what is permissible and what isn't is vague *even for God*. There is no fact of the matter about the precise boundaries between the terms "evils necessary for

---

2. Van Inwagen, 76
3. Van Inwagen, 78–79.
4. Peter van Inwagen, *The Problem of Evil*, 105.

success of Atonement" and "evils unnecessary for success of Atonement." Since there is no precise boundary as to whether allowing the three-year-old girl's murderer to exercise his free will is among the justified instances that must be allowed to preserve the possibility of morally significant free will, God is not morally obligated to prevent this particular instance of misuse of free will. There is no special reason for this exact placement of the boundary of what God will permit and what He will allow. God could have stopped the murder. This particular instance of allowing misuse of freedom isn't necessary to the accomplishment of His plan for Atonement. It isn't necessary to preserve the value of free will because, even if it were allowed, there would still be morally significant free will. However, God must allow at least some instances of morally evil choices, like this murder, to preserve the possibility for free will. Thus, Van Inwagen concludes that God is not morally obligated to stop it because the boundary as to what is and what isn't permissible is vague. The no-minimum-evil thesis thus appears to justify virtually any amounts and kinds of moral evils whatsoever.

It should also be kept in mind that Van Inwagen is approaching the issue from the perspective of the open theist. He adopts the view that God does not have foreknowledge of free acts, and so God does not know in advance just how much evil will be freely chosen beforehand. God doesn't specifically plan and ordain each evil to accomplish His plan. The best that God can do is to determine general strategies about the kinds of evils He will permit. Given that He must allow some genuinely evil choices to be carried out to preserve freedom, God doesn't know beforehand what may be excessive because the total plan of the world does not entail an exact amount of evil. Nor is any evil choice permitted knowing what effect it will have on those who must freely respond to the evil. The no-minimum thesis couldn't function as an explanation for those who adopt meticulous or all-controlling providence.

But does it follow from the fact that there is no sharp cut-off point that the omni-god would be justified in allowing any kinds and amounts of evil? I don't see how. As a parent, I must judge every day whether to allow my children to confront dangers like playing in the street, riding a bike, participating in football, rock climbing, riding motorcycles, going on dates, driving cars, and so forth. I allow all of these at age eighteen; I don't allow any of them at age three. I don't want to hover or be overprotective, but I am committed to protecting them against dangers that they cannot or do not yet grasp. I don't allow my three-year-old to cross the street alone, but I do let my ten-year-old. At some point I have to let go and let them choose so that they can grow into adults and make decisions for themselves. I'm never sure just when the right hour and day is to let them decide, nor am I sure about what level of danger is just the right amount for their growth. It is clear to me that allowing my three-year-old to drive a car is too dangerous. I'm also sure that allowing my ten-year-old daughter to date a twenty-year-old guy is way beyond responsible parenting. While I'm not sure where to draw the line on dating twenty-year-olds, I am not thereby logically precluded from making these kinds of judgments. If I were, then I would be precluded from making any moral judgments about what is appropriate for my children. Indeed, if I failed to make such judgments, I would be a negligent and unfit parent. There are cases that are clearly excessive even if the exact cut-off in age isn't clear.

The theist can't have it both ways—that the omni-god's goods are so far beyond our grasp that we cannot begin to fathom what they may be, and also that the omni-god cannot figure when enough is enough. If I can make judgments as a father regarding the level of risk that is appropriate for my children, with some judgment calls being more sound than others, then the omni-god would have to be infinitely more capable than I am at such judgments.

Ironically, Van Inwagen himself provides a compelling *reductio* of his view. Consider a jail warden who considers whether shortening a ten-year prison sentence is justified based on the principle that the prisoner should be left with at least the minimum number of days necessary to achieve the good purpose of deterring him from committing another felony.[5] Will letting a prisoner out one day early reduce the deterrence value of the ten-year sentence? The warden concludes that it won't. How about two days early? The warden concludes that ten years minus two days won't serve any greater deterrence than ten years. The same is true of ten years minus three days and so forth. Then the warden considers the reduction to one day in prison. Would one day in prison have greater deterrence value than no days in prison? The warden concludes that one day in prison would have no greater deterrence value than no prison at all. Thus, the criminal never goes to prison if the criterion is the minimum number of days *necessary* to deter from another crime because the minimum is inherently vague. Similarly, Van

---

5. Van Inwagen, 101.

THE NO MINIMUM EVIL DEFENSE

Inwagen claims that the minimum amount of evil necessary to accomplish atonement and permit significantly free choices has no minimum as well.

But this result is absurd. It just isn't true that one day in prison has no deterrence value. It isn't true that five years in prison has no more deterrence value than one day. It isn't true that ten years has no greater deterrence value than no prison at all. While it is true that the decision to put the felon in prison for 3,000 days instead of 2,999 is somewhat arbitrary, it just doesn't follow that no prison time has no more deterrence than ten years in prison. It seems that Van Inwagen's thought experiment exposes the problem with his no-minimum argument.

Thus, Van Inwagen's argument isn't going to work. Even though there in no clear cut-off to the amount of evil that is essential to achieve God's purposes for atonement and free will, there are evils that are clearly excessive both in kind and amount. Where the proper line is for the number of deaths from smallpox cases is difficult to say, but can the theist really claim that God drew the line appropriately at several billion cases with a straight face? Van Inwagen's no-minimum thesis proves way too much because it justifies any amount and kind of evil even when it is clearly excessive. Even if the world were characterized by no good whatsoever and a constant refrain of radically evil actions where every person's entire life is wasted in unredeemed agony and pain, Van Inwagen's no-minimum thesis entails that God is clueless to the fact that such excessive and pointless evils are way too much to justify the divine purpose. God could have prevented the brutal murder of a three-year-old girl and it wasn't necessary to some greater good; God just couldn't see that it was clearly beyond the line. Would anyone accept that as a defense were it offered by an armed police officer who just stood by watching as the murderer bludgeoned this little girl to death? What does it take to see that such a brutal crime is excessive? Would anyone accept it as a defense to the scientist who introduced a mutated smallpox virus because we can't be sure if the minimum number of permissible deaths from smallpox was several billion? Heaven keep us from ever encountering those who answer this affirmatively.

However, there is something right about Van Inwagen's no-minimum argument. While, it doesn't work as a defense based on the supposed *ontological fact* that there is no minimum, it seems to me to be an essential part of any viable theodicy in a modified form. The no-minimum-evil thesis doesn't work as a defeater of the problem of evil, because there are clear instances of evils that should be prevented even if not all are clear. But in context of a theodicy, it does seem to work as *an epistemological limitation* to our judgments about what amount of evils is necessary to accomplish God's purposes. John Hick points out in his soul-building theodicy that a world without any evil at all cannot function as a world where soul-building is possible. A world where soul-building is possible cannot be a "hedonic paradise" with no real challenges. For the world to function as an arena for personal growth into mature personhood, it must appear that, for all we can see, there are evils that should be eliminated. It must appear that there are unjustified evils that can function to elicit compassion when they occur and to motivate us to prevent evils and to confront them head-on as a means of developing character traits such as courage, compassion, virtue, and so forth. It seems unassailable to me that God must leave us free to choose evil on at least some occasions if we are to have morally significant free will. A choice between good and evil means sometimes being able to choose evil. In this sense, the no-minimum-evil thesis works, for any amount of evil that can so motivate us must appear, and could actually be, for all we know, unjustified. Such an environment is necessary to a very valuable good that cannot be accomplished in any other way—the ability to be challenged to develop moral mettle. Further, no matter what kinds or magnitudes and distribution of evils existed, they would be intolerable for us. In other words, whatever lesser degree of evil actually existed, that amount of evil would still be unacceptable to us.

That said, I don't see any reason why the omni-god must create immature creatures who require such challenges to grow to become morally response-able agents when it had the choice of creating virtually omniscient agents who would go wrong much less than we do. It is necessary to allow my children to confront these challenges because of their nature as immature humans who are unformed and not yet capable of fully responsible decisions. Their brains must undergo a process of development before they can engage in critical reasoning and sound judgment. However, the same limitations don't confront the omni-god. There is no reason that the omni-god could not have created only persons with capacity for adept moral reasoning and virtual omniscience to assess the best interests.

Further, the soul-building theodicy cannot be the total story. First, the instances of radical evil that I have identified make it impossible for the victim of the evils to be benefitted precisely because their very personalities are overwhelmed and snuffed out by the evils in question. It is true that observers may be motivated to be more compassionate, caring, and courageous as a result of confronting these types of evils. The fact that bystanders and friends may be benefitted, however, doesn't justify these evils. As noted previously, the suggestion that these innocents should be allowed to suffer so that we can benefit from their suffering violates Kant's second formulation of the categorical imperative that every person ought to be treated as an end in themselves and never as a means only. Thus, the notion that some evil may be necessary for soul-making doesn't entail that all evils of any type and magnitude are justified by the soul-making rationale. Other considerations, such as consent and provision for an afterlife, would also have to be part of the story to constitute a viable theodicy.

3

THE FREE WILL DEFENSE

A defense is different than a theodicy. A theodicy attempts to give possible reasons why God might allow certain types of evils to occur. A defense, on the other hand, attempts to demonstrate that the arguments showing that God does not exist are logically or empirically unsound. The most prominent defense against arguments from evil is the free will defense. However, it is a defense of a limited nature. All that the believer needs to disarm the logical argument from evil is the observation that God may just have His reasons for allowing evil. The argument from evil is thus no longer merely about logic but a matter of evidence and the likelihood that all evils are merely apparent and are in fact justified by a greater good (regardless of whether we can see how that is). However, if it could be shown that the theist is committed to the belief that there are unjustified evils, then a logical argument is possible. Thus, the logical argument is presented by means of an inconsistent triad:

(I) The omni-god exists.

(II) Unjustified evil exists.

(III) If unjustified evils exist, then (I) is not true.

Before the philosopher Alvin Plantinga, many had argued that (III) is a necessary truth. It follows that if (III) and (II) are true that (I) is false. However, it could be denied that (III) is a necessary truth, and instead, by way of what is called "Moore's Shift"[1] in logic, the following is true:

---

1. G. E. Moore's Shift is a term coined by William Rowe to note how Moore's argument against skepticism arises from merely rearranging the major and minor premises of two valid arguments with identical premises. For any two valid forms

(I) The omni-god exists.

(III) If there are any unjustified evil events, then the omni-god does not exist.

(II) Therefore, there are no unjustified evils.

Thus, it must be shown that there is some unjustified evil—where "unjustified evil" just means that theists are bound by their own beliefs to affirm that there exists evils that the omni-god need not have permitted because he had a less evil option available to him in creating. J. L. Mackie proposed an instance of unjustified evil to which he believed that the theist is theologically committed and a rule about an omnipotent being's power to which he also believed the theist was committed:[2]

(IV) An omni-god could create persons who always freely choose what is good.

(V) An omni-god would create persons who always freely refrain from choosing evil if it could.

(VI) God created persons who sometimes freely choose to do evil.

These premises present an inconsistent triad. The Christian is committed to (VI) because Christ atoned for the morally evil acts freely done by us—and if the evils were not really evil, then no atonement would be necessary. Moreover, the evil choices must be truly and not merely apparently evil to justify God's damnation of some persons for making evil choices. Mackie believed that the theist is also committed to (IV), because the existence of persons who never do evil is a logically possible state of affairs. Indeed, Christians maintain that Jesus was in fact one such sinless person. Further, Mackie argued that the theist is committed to the view that the omni-god is omnipotent in the sense that God can bring about any logically possible state of affairs. However, (IV) and (V) together entail that (VI), the creation of persons who sometimes do evil, is an unjustified evil. Mackie argued that the theist is also committed to (V) because the omni-

---

of an argument with a major and a minor premise, an argument can be created merely by rearranging the major and minor premises of the argument to arrive at opposite conclusions. G. E. Moore, *Some Main Problems of Philosophy*. See also, William L. Rowe, "The Evidential Argument from Evil: A Second Look," 262–85.

2. J. L. Mackie, "Evil and Omnipotence," 200–212.

THE FREE WILL DEFENSE

god is necessarily a perfectly good being, and any perfectly good being who creates persons who choose evil when it could have perfect persons is not really perfectly good. Thus, Mackie argued that the theist—and the Christian theist in particular—is stuck with an incoherent view.

It was intended to be a logical argument with premises that the theist could not deny. Further, Mackie assumed a particular view of free will—that is, the compatibilist view that has been the majority view among Christians since at least Augustine and also among Muslims. Compatibilism is the view that causal determinism and morally significant free will are compatible. Given the compatibilist view, a person's acts are determined by the past chain of causal events and natural laws that obtain. An omnipotent being could bring about a person's acts that are still free in a compatibilist sense by causing them—or by causing a person's desires and then allowing the person choosing to act in accordance with his or her strongest desire. God could cause persons to always do what is right or, at the very least, give them a strongest desire to always do what is right. It follows that the omni-god could create creatures and bring it about that they always freely do what is right (in a compatibilist sense of "free"). Thus, if there are ever evil choices, then there is an Unjustified Evil that God could have prevented consistent with that person's free will.

Plantinga developed a defense to this argument by rejecting Mackie's assumptions about what Christians must accept. Plantinga denies both the implicit notion of compatibilist free will and the notion that an omnipotent God could bring about the morally significant free acts of humans. Instead, Plantinga argues that free will and causal determinism are not compatible—what he called *contra-causal freedom*.[3] Thus, not even an omnipotent being could create a person and also ensure that the person always freely chooses to do what is only good. An omnipotent being cannot bring about another person's free acts at all, because such free acts can only be brought about by the person whose acts they are. Plantinga called the view that an omnipotent being could bring about the free acts of another "Leibniz's Lapse," named after the great philosopher and mathematician Gottfried Leibniz, whom Plantinga claims made the same mistake as Mackie.[4] Thus, Mackie's argument is unsound because premise (IV) is false given incompatibilist

---

3. Alvin Plantinga, *The Nature of Necessity*, 180–84.
4. Mackie, "Evil and Omnipotence," 200–212.

freedom. However, it should be noted that Plantinga's observations about Leibniz's Lapse is no mistake for those in the Calvinist and Banezian traditions that adopt the compatiblist view of free will. Mackie's argument is sound with respect to those traditions.

In fact, it is even worse for these traditions of deterministic meticulous providence, because they hold that God Himself, in His meticulous providence, chooses to save some and to leave others to damnation when He could save all. God's act of predestination, which only chooses to save some and leaves others to damnation, is itself an instance of Unjustified Evil, because failing to save some is not necessary to any greater good. The omni-god could save everyone just by willing it, and eternal damnation is an intrinsic evil if ever there was one. We do not need to ask if there is some greater good known only to God that could justify this evil, because Calvinists are committed also to the view that eternal union with God is the greatest good possible for humans. Yet God himself supposedly precludes those He does not predestine to be saved from realizing this good by His own choice. It is His free choice itself that is the instance of unjustified evil, given predestination. It follows that this God does not exist, because any being that can count as God is good. We should never worship such a malevolent being.[5]

If Plantinga had merely stopped at pointing out Leibniz's Lapse, it would have been enough to defuse Mackie's argument—at least for those who accept libertarian free will. However, Plantinga's program was more ambitious than merely pointing out the problems with Mackie's argument. He also sought to show that it could be demonstrated that evil and the omni-god's existence are logically compatible. What is remarkable is that the vast majority of philosophers agree that Plantinga was successful—and such agreement among philosophers is a rare thing indeed.

To begin, Plantinga adopted the logical rule that two premises are logically consistent if there is a third premise that is itself logically possible

---

5. I could almost believe that the omni-god could have his mysterious reasons for leaving some to damnation when God could save all by grace just by willing it—I could, that is, if I ever met a Calvinist who believed that he or she wasn't one of the saved elect. I've never met a Calvinist who didn't believe that God had elected him or her. Somehow, it's alright if everyone else is damned, but heaven forbid that one entertain the thought that one's self has been damned for God's mysterious reasons. How could such a person ever entertain the idea that God loves him or her even though God refused to save them when God could as easily save everyone?

and is logically compossible with the first premise, and they together entail the third premise. Thus, Plantinga set out to show that (I) and (II) are logically consistent by showing that there is such a third premise. To show this third premise, Plantinga engaged possible worlds logic and essentially recreated the Molinist view.

He argues that there are some logically possible worlds that God cannot actualize.[6] The reason that God cannot actualize some possible worlds is that for every possible world (W1) in which a free creature (we'll call him Rock) who would choose to refrain from doing an evil act of stealing at a time (t1), there is another possible world (W2) with exactly the same natural laws and historical events up to t1 in which Rock would instead choose to steal. Due to Leibniz's Lapse, whether the possible world W1 or W2 is brought about is not solely up to God. God can only actualize the circumstances in which people choose. He cannot unilaterally bring about another's free choice. I'll call the circumstances including the entire history of the world and the laws of nature up to time t1 "circumstances C." Whether Rock steals in circumstances C is not up to God. Nor is it up to Rock! The "counterfactuals of freedom" that describe what Rock would do if he were created by God are supposed to be true not only prior to and independently of the *actual* existence and *actual* choices of Rock or any creature free in an incompatibilist sense, but also prior to the divine choice as to which possible world to actualize. As such, they are fates or "surd truths" that God has to work with and that restrict His creative options. (I'm sure Plantinga would never call them "fates"—though he does say that the truth of counterfactuals of freedom just "falls out" of the given facts the omni-god has to deal with).[7] When God decides which among the infinite number of possible worlds to create, God consults which choice-patterns the fates make available to him in the circumstances he can strongly actualize. God then chooses to actualize free persons in circumstances that will result in the optimal scenario congruent with divine purposes. Thus, which possible world becomes the actual world is a function of (I) the circumstances God actualizes, which includes all the circumstances in the

---

6. Alvin Plantinga, *God, Freedom, and Evil*, 48.

7. Alvin Plantinga, "Transworld Depravity, Transworld Sanctity & Uncooperative Essences," 190. I take the term "fates" from Marilyn McCord Adams, "'Plantinga on 'Felix Culpa': Analysis and Critique," 124.

history of that possible world up to the time of the free act (Plantinga says that God "strongly actualizes" these because He brings them about directly through His causal power); and (2) the fates, which God cannot control. Coming up with the optimal world—that is, actualizing the world that displays the most favorable balance of moral good over moral evil that God can get given the fates—is like a mathematical formula that dictates God's decision as to which possible world to create.

Next, Plantinga argues that it is logically possible that the fates deliver to God only possible persons who are "transworld depraved"—meaning only possible persons who would go wrong at least once in any possible world that He could strongly actualize them in. Thus, if the truth is that "Rock steals at tI in circumstances C" is part of the optimal world God could strongly actualize, then Rock steals, and it isn't up to God that such a scenario is the best that God can do. But it is also logically possible that every possible person God could actualize would also go wrong at least once in the optimal circumstances God could strongly actualize. Thus, Plantinga has his candidate for the elusive premise that is logically possible, and that entails that "God creates persons who sometimes freely choose to do evil" and is consistent with "God exists." That premise is something like the premise of transworld depravity (TD):

> TD: The optimal possible world that omni-god can actualize includes persons with incompatiblist freedom who each go wrong at least once (and maybe often).[8]

Thus, Plantinga claims to have shown that "the omni-god creates persons all of whom freely choose to do at least some evils" is logically consistent with "the omni-god exists." What is interesting is that while almost everyone agrees that Plantinga has solved the "logical problem of evil," very few are satisfied that the notion of possible persons who suffer from transworld depravity is intelligible.[9] It is easy to see why. In responding to

---

8. Plantinga has reformulated transworld depravity and admits that it may not "do the trick" to show that (I) and (II) are compatible. He also introduces a new notion, that of individual essences that just will not cooperate. See Plantinga, "Transworld Depravity," 178–90.

9. Bruce Langtry, "The Prospects for the Free Will Defence," 142–152; Richard Swinburne, *Providence and the Problem of Evil*, 127–31; Robert M. Adams, "Middle Knowledge and the Problem of Evil," 109–17; William Hasker, *God, Time and*

Leibniz's Lapse, Plantinga points out that a person's free acts must be up to the persons whose free acts they are. But given his possible worlds analysis, the truth value of the counterfactuals of freedom given by the fates is not up to the possible persons who haven't even been actualized—and may never be actual. Thus, the counterfactuals don't describe free acts.[10] Whether it is true that Rock will steal in circumstances C is not up to him, and therefore Rock is not free with respect to whether he steals in circumstances C.[11] Moreover, it is very doubtful that these so-called counterfactuals of freedom could even have a truth value. But if they don't have a truth value, they cannot guide the omni-god's decisions with respect to which possible world is optimal to actualize.[12]

Moreover, the existence of such fates that exist prior to and independently of the omni-god's will seems to deny the existence of the omni-god because it is inconsistent with omnipotence of the type entailed by the doctrine of creation out of nothing. It seems that if the omni-god creates *ex nihilo*, then these kinds of potentialities must be a result of the omni-god's creative activity and not something that limits god's creative choices.[13]

Knowledge, 39–52. See especially the essays in Kenneth Perszyk, ed., *Molinism: The Contemporary Debate*, which provide both pros and cons regarding the middle knowledge assumptions in Plantinga's free will defense.

10. See my discussion in Blake T. Ostler, *Exploring Mormon Thought: The Attributes of God*, 171–81.

11. Richard Gale, "Freedom and the Free Will Defense," 397–423.

12. Robert M. Adams, "An Anti-Molinist Argument," 343–53; Robert Gaskin, "Conditionals of Freedom and Middle Knowledge," 412–43; William Hasker, "A New Anti-Molinist Argument," 291–97; Timothy O'Connor, "The Impossibility of Middle Knowledge," 139–66; Peter van Inwagen, "What Does an Omniscient Being Know About the Future?" 216–30; David Hunt, "Middle Knowledge: The 'Foreknowledge Defense,'" 1–24; Dean Zimmerman, "Yet Another AntiMolinist Argument," 33–94; Joseph Shieber, "Personal Responsibility and Middle Knowledge: A Challenge for the Molinist," 61–70; Steven B. Cowan, "The Grounding Objection to Middle Knowledge Revisited," 93–102.

13. This point is argued effectively by Mark Thomas Ian Robson, *Ontology and Providence in Creation: Taking ex nihilo Seriously*. See Wes Morriston, "Is Plantinga's God Omnipotent?" 45–57; William J. Wainwright, *Philosophy of Religion*, 86–88; Gabriel Horner, "Impaled by the Two Horns of Logic: The Paradox of Omnipotence and Free Will," 1–5; Benjamin Huff, "Contingency in Classical Creation: Problems

For these reasons, Plantinga's response to Mackie is decisive, but it is so only for those who affirm libertarian free will. Mackie's argument commits Leibniz's Lapse. However, Mackie's argument provides a very good reason to believe that the omni-god cannot exist if taken to also exercise meticulous providence of the type found in the majority of Christian theology historically, including Augustine, Luther, Calvin, Aquinas, Banez, Leibniz, de Molina, and Suarez, as well as their modern-day successors.[14]

What of natural evils that are not a result of free choices, like cancer, viruses, earthquakes, tsunamis, tornadoes, and so forth? Since these don't result from acts of free will, it seems that Plantinga's defense just won't work to make them consistent with the omni-god's existence. To remedy this problem, Plantinga argues that it is just logically possible (though wildly improbable) that these natural events are brought about by the free acts of non-human persons, such as spirits or angels.[15] While it may seem obvious to us that these things are brought about by natural forces, Plantinga's defense against an argument that attempts to logically exclude the possibility of God's existence need only show what is logically possible. Is this logically possible? Of course it is. It is likewise logically possible that we are all brains in a vat sitting safely in the divinely protected Matrix and that God is just feeding us the experiences we think we have as data to our brains. There would be no evils on that view because we could be safe and sound in our little divine cubicles where God is just giving us simulated experiences that are not real. It is possible that there is no death, no real danger, and that the pain we experience is merely a phenomena of our dreams. But is such a thing really a defense to a logical problem of evil? Could be every bit as much as Plantinga's free will defense. It is wildly implausible, but it is just logically possible.

---

with Alvin Plantinga's Free Will Defense"; Heimir Geirsson and Michael Losonsky, "What God Could Have Made," 355–76.

14. James Cain, "Free Will and the Problem of Evil," 437–56. See the discussion in David Ray Griffin, *God, Power, and Evil: A Process Theology*, chs. 6, 7, 9, 10, and 11; James F. Sennett, "The Free Will Defense and Determinism," 340–53. A. A. Howsepian argues that the free will defense does not require libertarian free will; however, it does require a new notion which he calls "middle freedom." The problem is that his theory is both unintelligible and still leaves the will unfree. "Compatiblism, Evil, and the Free-Will Defense," 217–36.

15. Plantinga, *Nature of Necessity*, 191–93.

Nevertheless, I do not accept Plantinga's defense of natural evils based on the free will defense. While it is logically possible that non-human persons have these powers, it is not possible that God is nevertheless also good while creating beings with sufficient power to bring about things like tornadoes, viruses, tsunamis, and cancer. If God did such a thing, what possible reason could God have for granting sufficient power to such irrelevant agencies to meddle in earthly affairs to wreak havoc on humans? I cannot see any, and it appears to me to be analogous to the problem of predestination in implicating God in evil. If God creates these non-human persons with sufficient power to cause such natural evils that we ourselves cannot control or cure, knowing beforehand that they will in fact exercise their agency to bring about such natural evils in the possible world that God chooses to create, then Plantinga has only succeeded in giving us a logical scenario of God's culpability for natural evils as their indirect cause and accomplice before the fact. Surely God can stop a tornado or virus without eliminating the value of free will that has any value sufficient to justify such natural evils. The suggestion that God would allow such natural evils to guard the contra-causal freedom of these creatures is not logically consistent with God's goodness. The value of whatever freedom such beings may have to bring about natural evils is rather clearly outweighed by the pain and suffering caused by natural evils. Thus, such natural evils cannot be Justified Evils, even were they to be freely brought about by these non-human persons.

Such a view highlights another assumption of the free will defense that is extremely problematic. Is leaving creatures free to act of sufficient value to justify the kinds of evils that occur? Is free will *per se* worth it? The free will defense does not answer this question; it assumes that the answer is affirmative. Such a query shows why a theodicy is essential. It is necessary to show why allowing freedom to creatures is valuable and worth the evils that actually occur to justify this basic value judgment essential to the free will defense. The defense remains incomplete because, even if we grant that Plantinga's free will defense shows that an omnipotent being cannot bring about the free acts of others (as we should), it doesn't follow that the value judgment underlying the defense is also logically defensible.

The free will defense assumes that free will, by itself, is of such great value that God is always justified in not overriding that free will with coercive force. But that assumption is surely open to question. When I save my child's life by preventing her from being run over by a car by stopping her from running into the street by picking her up and physically restraining her, I am taking away her free choice to run into the street. However, I am hardly doing something wrong by truncating her free will. If I were present, I would have done everything in my power to stop a three-year old girl's murder—by force and physical coercion if necessary. My use of coercion would be seen as good, even heroic. Nobody would consider it wrong to have taken away the freedom of this man to murder the helpless little girl. His freedom to murder just isn't worth the cost. We all make this value judgment.

4

THE LESS EVIL OPTIONS ARGUMENT

The omni-god had other options open to it in creation that neither take away free will nor require as much evil as exists in this world. We will call this the "less evil moral option" argument. What it shows is that the omni-god did not need to allow as many evils that actually occur in order to protect free will. Such evils are therefore not necessary to some greater good. Thus, they are Unjustified Evils. The existence of the omni-god is logically inconsistent with at least the range of natural evils that He could have empowered us to freely eradicate. The omni-god had less evil options open to Him than creating creatures like us who are so limited in ability to deal with natural evils. He could have created more knowledgeable and morally sensitive and astute creatures than we are. Indeed, there is no logical barrier to having created virtually omniscient creatures who make free choices. God didn't need to create us morally perfect—indeed, he couldn't do so even though omnipotent. However, an omnipotent being could have created us cognitively perfect and virtually omniscient.

A creature that has "virtual omniscience" is one that has all the knowledge and perfection of cognitive faculties that a being created from nothing could have. I cannot see any reason that the scope of knowledge of a virtually omniscient creature isn't the same as that of the omni-god or omniscient being *simpliciter*. However, the omni-god is supposedly both uncreated and the creator of all things, and thus perhaps has knowledge in a different way than creatures created out of nothing could possess. Nevertheless, I cannot see anything that would prevent an omniscient and omnipotent creator that creates all things *ex nihilo* from creating creatures with capacity to know all that any being could know and imparting to them all that it knows. The omni-god's power is not limited by any non-logical considerations. Moreover, we can point out that Christ was a physical being who was supposedly omniscient; if physical and temporal beings cannot be omniscient, then the incarnate Son couldn't be either. I just cannot think of any argument that God is somehow logically limited in creating creatures with perfect cognitive faculties.

Consider what creation of such virtually omniscient creatures means. If the omni-god had done so, we would have avoided all-natural diseases that could be cured or prevented by medicine. As soon as they made their appearance, we could eradicate smallpox, bubonic plague, AIDS, cancers, and so forth. The omni-god could have thus had creatures capable of eliminating more natural evils—many of which we are not capable of removing at present. Moreover, the omni-god could have had this option without truncating free will in the least. Indeed, it appears that our free will would be greatly enhanced, because we would be aware of a greater set of options over which our freedom would range. In addition, we would not be stupid enough to take substances that are addictive and limit our freedom. We would avoid dangers that arise from sheer stupidity, like driving drunk or just failing to pay sufficient attention. The free will defense doesn't provide a defense to these kinds of less-evil options available to the omni-god. Instead, it only attempts to show that it is logically possible that it was not within the scope of power of the omni-god to create *morally* perfect beings. The free-will defense, however, fails to recognize that it is logically possible for the omni-god to create *cognitively* perfect beings. The omni-god thus was not stuck by the fates with creating cognitively limited creatures like us at all if he creates what we are out of nothing and is limited only by what is logically feasible to create.

The "less evil options" argument is essentially Mackie's original strategy. He looked for a state of affairs that exists and argued that the omni-god had a better option. It follows that these evils that actually obtain are not necessary to a greater good because the omni-god had better options available that entail less evil. They are thus Unjustified Evils. God created creatures who go wrong with distressing frequency. J. L. Mackie argued that the omni-god could have created creatures who never went wrong if He were truly omnipotent. Due to Leibniz's Lapse, Mackie was wrong with respect to morally significant actions that must be free in a libertarian sense. However,

THE LESS EVIL OPTIONS ARGUMENT

God could have created cognitively perfect creatures instead of us, and such creation is not incompatible with libertarian free will in the most robust sense.

What could a believer in the omni-god respond? Is it possible that the omni-god was stuck by the Molinist's fates with creatures as limited in knowledge as we are? No. Virtually omniscient persons with perfect cognitive faculties are logically possible. How perfect our cognitive faculties are is not a result of our free will. Rather, our free will is a result of having sufficiently developed cognitive faculties. There is an infinite number of possible persons with virtual omniscience that God could have created. Moreover, the possible worlds in which they are located are not inaccessible to the omni-god, because our cognitive capacities are not up to us. They are a part of what we are, not what we freely choose. How we develop our inherent capacities may be up to us, but in this actual world our innate intelligence is a matter of genetics that is not a matter of free will. According to the Biblical account, God created the entire range of animal intelligence. Why was God limited to creatures with our cognitive limitations? I cannot see any valid argument that the omni-god didn't have these options open to Him. Thus, the omni-god, if He exists, is morally indictable for not having created creatures who could eradicate many natural evils that we cannot, and who would have eradicated evils such as smallpox virus and bubonic plague bacteria long before these devastating fatal diseases were in fact eradicated.

We can define "virtual omniscience" as knowing all that can be known by any creature. For purposes of this argument, a "creature" is one that is created in whatever sense is entailed by creation out of nothing. One thing is certain, since beings having only our imperfect cognitive faculties eventually came up with a smallpox vaccine and antibiotics for bubonic plague: it is certainly within the scope of a virtually omniscient being's cognitive capacities to know such things. Thus, we can restate the logical argument from evil using this "less evil available options" argument:

(A) The omni-god exists.

(B*) An omni-god could create creatures who are virtually omniscient and who would be capable of freely eradicating many natural evils that occur.

(C*) An omni-god would create creatures who are virtually omniscient if it could to empower them to freely eradicate these natural evils.

(D*) Humans are not virtually omniscient.

(F*) If (B*), (C*), and (D*), then not (A).

Objection #1

The believer in the omni-god may reject (B*) by arguing that even the omni-god cannot impart properties of near divinity to creatures. Not even the omni-god can create creatures with properties that only an uncreated being could possess. For example, humans are limited by physical constraints. So limitations in knowledge are inherent in the creation of humans with physical bodies like ours.

The objection misses the point of creation out of nothing by an omni-god. I defined a virtually omniscient being as one that has the maximum knowledge that a created being could have. So whatever the maximal knowledge that a created being can have, that is what such virtually omniscient beings would have. Since we know that beings with limited cognitive faculties like us actually came up with the vaccine to the smallpox virus and the antibiotic to the bubonic plague, we know that it is possible for beings at least as knowledgeable as us to come up with these things. I don't know what the upper limit of intelligence is for created beings, if there is one, but it is vastly more than we know or can cognitively grasp. If all of the matter and physical information in the universe can be compacted into a dimension that is less than the size of an atom at the time of the Big Bang, then surely it is physically possible to pack a lot of information into an organ the size of the human brain.

I cannot see any reason why the omni-god couldn't create us with the same range of omniscience that the omni-god has since it is logically possible that He do so. If the omni-god were limited to creating what is physically possible, then this argument could suggest some limitations to what could be created. This is a defense that a process theologian or Latter-day Saint could offer, but it isn't available to the believer in the omni-god. The omni-god isn't limited by what is physically possible—since creation out of nothing isn't physically possible either. The omni-god is limited only by logic, and there are no non-logical limitations on what a created person can know or how rational a created being can be that wouldn't also apply to an omniscient being *simpliciter*. Perfect cognitive faculties include both perfect knowledge and perfect rationality—and there are no logical limitations on either that don't also apply to the omni-god.

Objection #2

A person may reject (B*) by arguing that the omni-god cannot create virtually omniscient beings and guarantee that they would freely derive the relevant vaccines or cures even though they can do so very easily. Whether any given person develops a cure to smallpox or bubonic plague is a matter of free will. God cannot create creatures, even very smart creatures, and bring it about that they freely choose to develop cures to such diseases. Perhaps the omni-god viewed all of the possible worlds that He could create and saw that creatures with just our level of knowledge were optimal for the world available in terms of its goodness. It is logically possible that every possible person with perfect cognitive faculties that the omni-god could create would freely choose to refrain from developing these vaccines and antibiotics. The fact that we have done it doesn't entail that we *would* freely develop such cures if we had been created with perfect cognitive faculties. It only entails that we *could* develop such cures. Thus, Plantinga's free will defense works against this argument if it works against Mackie's, and it does so for the same reasons.

My inclination is to accept the premises of the criticism but reject its conclusion. It is true that the omni-god couldn't *causally bring about* (or strongly actualize) what virtually omniscient creatures would freely choose if created—but he could be certain what perfectly rational creatures would freely choose. It is virtually certain that creatures with perfect faculties of reason would easily see the solution to the problem presented by such diseases and eradicate them. It would be entirely irrational not to do so. Persons with perfect cognitive faculties would also be perfectly rational; they wouldn't engage in the foolish conduct of allowing dangerous diseases to run rampant when they could have easily devised a cure. That is just part of what it means to have perfect cognitive faculties.

What the omni-god could do is ensure that we were intelligent enough to know or easily intuit how to generate the relevant vaccines and antibiotics. Assuming that He created virtually omniscient persons who already knew or could easily intuit the cure to any such diseases, there is no rational basis for asserting that they wouldn't help themselves to the cure.

Such advanced beings would not have to go through the same painstaking research and development as creatures like us with limited cognitive faculties. This objection is logically equivalent to asserting that the omni-god creates people who need water to live, know where water is, and can access it, but they rationally choose to die rather than drink the water because they are free to not do so. The problem is that such stupidity of the first order is precisely what persons with perfect cognitive faculties would never do. There is no feasible world in which persons having at least our survival instinct and perfect cognitive faculties will just sit around wondering if they and their loved ones will die from diseases that they could prevent. That is irrational and exactly the kind of decision that having perfect cognitive faculties of rationality rules out. Thus, there is no feasible world in which creatures would freely and rationally choose to confront smallpox rather than develop a vaccine.

Nevertheless, the objector is correct that God couldn't strongly actualize such persons with the essential property that, if actualized, they would be guaranteed to freely develop such cures. For then the acts would not be free because they would be essential to the nature of such possible persons. That is, they would develop the vaccine as a result of their nature—just like I am human by nature. I am not free to not be a human. What the omni-god could do, however, is actualize them with the essential property of being perfectly rational so that they will freely choose on their own to protect their loved ones from the ravages of such deadly diseases.

Let me make clear: If the omni-god merely gave us the cognitive *capacity* to intuit cures to diseases that we cannot presently cure so that we could cure them if we were to choose to do so (and who wouldn't?), then that would solve the problem of evil, because then God is not culpable for failure to develop such cures; we would be. God's culpability isn't in the fact that we don't freely cure these diseases when we could; it is in the fact that we are unable to do so given our knowledge and capacities to generate cures. The pandemics that have in the past and that presently ravage humankind, like AIDS, are not natural evils because we choose not to cure them; they are evils because we can't despite our best efforts to do so. The argument that the omni-god couldn't cause us to freely create cures is not the problem. That we cannot find such cures despite our best efforts is due to our cognitive limitations that the omni-god supposedly created us with.

Further, I don't believe that the possible worlds framework of logic works when it comes to what free persons would freely do. There are compelling arguments that all of the so-called counterfactuals of freedom that describe what a person *would* freely do lack truth value. There is nothing in reality to ground such "possible person S would freely do X if in circumstances C" kinds of propositions. Similarly, such possible world semantics don't work well when assessing what is within our power to freely do. There is a possible world in which I freely walk out of my house even though I am chained to the water heater in my basement. However, it simply isn't physically possible that I do so. Thus, such a world is a possible world but not a physically feasible one. What is within my power to do is not merely a function of what is logically possible; it also depends on what is physically feasible. I am inclined to think that causal determinism is a form of what is physically feasible. It isn't physically feasible for us to change the past events and natural laws—though it is logically possible that we do so. There is a distinction between what is logically possible, what is physically possible for an agent S to do in given circumstances, and what is rationally possible for agent S to do in any given circumstances. It is logically possible that I pick up my car and throw it over the cliff; however, it isn't physically possible for me to do that. It is physically possible that I intentionally drive my car off of a cliff; but it isn't rationally possible for me to do that.

If rational possibility were like physical possibility, so that it wouldn't really be within my power to act freely if I were perfectly rational, then this objection shows that rational perfection is incompatible with morally significant free will. It would also show that the omni-god isn't free to do morally significant acts. However, I believe that our rational faculties don't constrain what is physically possible for us to perform. Rather, the intellect is a prior condition to the process of deliberation and assists in the process of assessing what options are available and weighing which among those options is most valuable. The intellect does not make possibilities of choice impossible to actually choose; rather, it suggests which among the possibilities it isn't wise or prudent to choose. "Ought" doesn't imply "is." Thus, rational perfection is quite different than the constraints of causal determinism that physically forecloses which options are open to us to choose.

There is a possible world in which the adult Einstein freely chooses to fail a third grade math test even though he knows that failing will lead criminals to torture and kill everyone in his family that he dearly loves.

However, there is no such feasible world in which Einstein would make that same choice *rationally*—because such an act would be irrational insanity. The distinction between a feasible world and a logically possible world is not easy to detail without a full-blown assessment of possible world semantics. That is another book. However, roughly the distinction is between what is a logically consistent description of the way things could possibly be and what is a consistent description of the way things could be grounded in our actual physical limitations, mental capacities, values, character, and personality. What a person with perfect cognitive faculties could freely do rationally is different than what a person could freely do *simpliciter*. A person with defective or deceptive cognitive faculties can freely choose to act irrationally; a person with perfect cognitive faculties will see that irrational acts are not in our best interest and therefore stupid and will always freely choose to not act irrationally. Einstein could not *rationally* choose to fail the third grade math test if his family's well-being depended on it. Thus, the possible world in which Einstein freely chooses to rationally fail the third grade math test even though it leads to the death of his family isn't a feasible world. However, it is logically possible that Einstein freely fails the test even in those circumstances. Thus, there is a logically possible world where all virtually omniscient persons freely refrain from developing vaccines; it just isn't a feasible world that the omni-god could actualize. Given that there is some actual world, it is not one of the possible worlds where all virtually omniscient persons freely choose to refrain from creating vaccines. Thus, a Plantinga-like defense is defeated.

This objection brings up a big problem with the entire project of possible world semantics. Would we be the same persons that we are if we had perfect cognitive faculties? How do we compare persons having all the same essential properties as us across possible worlds? There is a possible world (W2) having exactly the same possible persons (i.e., having all of the same person-identity-indexed essential properties) that exist in this world, except in W2 they have perfect cognitive faculties. Are we still the same persons in W2? Certainly I could be smarter than I am and still be me. In fact, I am smarter than when I was five years old, and I am still me. However, I am a very different person that when I was five years of age. Answering this question would take me far afield of the issues addressed here, but I am inclined to say that the persons in W2 are still us, just smarter. What if they weren't us? The omni-god would prefer a possible world W2 with "them"

THE LESS EVIL OPTIONS ARGUMENT

rather than this world with us because it contains less evil. However, I would be very put out if I didn't exist!

Nevertheless, let's assume, just for the sake of argument, that the objection works to show that it is just logically possible that the omni-god could not find among the infinite number of possible cognitively perfect persons even one who would freely choose to save their own family from the threats of smallpox and bubonic plague. The argument still works as a knock-down evidential argument. It is so unlikely that the omni-god couldn't find any possible persons with such cognitive faculties who would freely make vaccines when faced with deadly diseases that it just isn't really practically possible. Thus, it is something on the order of 99.99 percent likely that the omni-god could have created such virtually omniscient persons who create vaccines. Thus, it is 99.99 percent unlikely that the omni-god exists.

Objection #3

Premise (B*) could also be objected to on the grounds that there are some goods that the omni-god cannot create out of nothing in persons, because they can be developed only by creatures who endure challenges over a period of time. For example, even the omni-god cannot create virtue in creatures that arises only by confronting real-life challenges such as courage, which requires confronting danger, fear, and the risk of personal harm. Courage untested isn't real courage. Moral virtue requires such real-life challenges to develop, and thus such virtue cannot be created *ab initio* (at the origin of a person's existence). Further, there are types of knowledge that require time and real-life experience to possess. A person cannot know what the experience of feeling fear is unless in a situation that presents a reason to feel fear. Experiential knowledge can only be gained over a period of time by real-life experience. Thus, if the omni-god actualized virtually omniscient persons, He would have to forego these greater goods.[1]

---

1. This is the argument given by Carl Mosser, "Evil, Mormonism, and the Impossibility of Perfection *Ab Initio*: An Irenean Defense," 56–68. See my response, Blake T. Ostler, "A God Who is Morally Praiseworthy," 65–70. Mosser asserts: "For example, God could not create an elderly man *ab initio*. Clearly, the existence of elderly men is metaphysically possible, but that does not mean that an elderly man can be created *ex nihilo*. God could create a man with grey hair, frail bones and even apparent memories, but this would not truly be an elderly man. Nor could

I am also inclined to agree with everything asserted in this objection but reject its conclusion. A person being virtually omniscient does not change the fact that they could eliminate virulent and bacteriological diseases that we cannot while still having a developmental process of gaining experiential knowledge from real-life experience. (In fact, that is precisely what I believe God does.) They could still have eliminated smallpox and AIDS before they became pandemic even if they faced other challenges in which they could develop courage. There is no reason that a virtually omniscient creature couldn't develop courage and experiential knowledge through a developmental process. They could be challenged to learn what it is like to love others in ways requiring patience. They could develop courage by facing natural evils that cannot be cured by vaccines because they lack the kind of power necessary to avoid them, like earthquakes, tsunamis, and tornadoes. Thus, this objection is irrelevant. The omni-god still had the option of creatures who could eliminate and totally avoid the evil of the most deadly viral contagions known to humankind even if they faced other kinds of challenges from which they could learn to develop compassion, courage, and love. I would also point out that the implication of this objection is that the omni-god lacks courage, virtue, and experiential knowledge.

Objection #4

If rejecting (B*) won't work, perhaps the theist could reject (C*). It isn't necessary that the omni-good would create only virtually omniscient

---

God create a woman who *ab initio* knows what it is like to raise three children. At best God could create creatures that mimic these realities. . . . God cannot create human beings who *ab initio* have a knowledge of good and evil of such a kind that they will, in the likeness of God, always love good and hate evil. It is simply not possible for recently created beings to be anything other than 'unaccustomed to, and unexercised in, perfect discipline.' While God can possess this property eternally by virtue of his divine being, contingent creatures must come to this knowledge by experience. . . . Even though God has the power to create *ex nihilo*, it does not follow that he could have created humanity with an already-developed moral fortitude that would guarantee that they always choose the right. This could be created only through experience. Humanity could repeatedly exercise the will to choose the right in obedience to God's commandment and thereby develop an immutably good moral character." Mosser, 62–63.

beings. It is good that the omni-god creates the fullest chain of being that it can consistent with what is good. The omni-god has created a full continuum of beings having a full range of intelligence, from viruses and bacteria on the lower level of sentience to near-omniscient angels on the upper end of sentience. It is good that the full range of intelligence is manifest. It is just possible that God has created an infinite number of multiverses with the full array of every logical possibility of kinds of beings to display the fulness of his creative powers and the beauty of his glory. We just happen to fall within the range of beings having just our capacities for knowledge and cognitive rationality. Thus, the omni-god wouldn't create merely virtually omniscient beings even though it can.

My response to this objection is that it goes way too far. First, it suggests that God's primary concern is simply variety without regard to the goodness of what he creates. Is it good that the possible world in which all creatures suffer in agonizing pain for their eternal existence can also be created? There is some limit on the kinds of worlds that a perfectly good being would be willing to create consistent with its goodness. At the very least, it seems that a loving God would ensure that each creature's existence and life were a good on the whole for that creature. So perhaps the proponent of a multiverse theodicy would suggest that God creates all and only those worlds that have a net positive of good over evil and where the life of each is an overall good to the sentient creatures so created.

Our world, however, is plagued with evils that destroy the very humanity of the sufferer and obliterates their personalities and ability to personally benefit from their painful experiences. The world is rife with suicide and such pain that life has lost its value from the point of view of those suffering. It is just a tragic fact that many have made their own choice to give back to God the ticket to their lives. The upshot of the multiverse theodicy is that the desire for variety overrides such concerns. Further, it suggests that the fact that such evils exist is merely an arbitrary feature of creating the fullest array of possible creature-types. Yet, if suffering is arbitrary in this way, then it is unjustified as well. It may be necessary to the realization of the most complete continuum or array of possible varieties of creatures, but the goodness of mere variety seems much less valuable than avoiding radical evils. As such, it is very questionable whether the suggested good of variety could qualify as a Justifying Good.

It seems to me that the value judgment that the great chain of being justifies particular radical evils is mistaken. First, it isn't true that having every type of evil, pain, and every kind of malevolent agent is a good thing merely because it increases the various kinds of things that exist. Further, God could have that full range of types of sentient life without the particular events of radical evil that I discussed. We know enough to see that in order to have the full range of intelligence among sentient beings, God need not allow little girls to be bludgeoned or run over by cars, or smallpox virus and bubonic plague ravaging millions. Is it good that the smallpox virus and bubonic bacteria exist to manifest God's glory? If so, then we damaged God's goodness and glory by wiping them out. The implication of this view is absurd: if we are successful in eradicating AIDS, then we reduce the overall value of the world, because then the variety of types of creatures is reduced.

Objection #5

The believer would undoubtedly retort that the omni-god may have His reasons for making us as cognitively limited as we are, even if it means that many natural evils continue that we could eradicate if we had better cognitive faculties than we actually do. After all, the omni-god Himself could have eradicated these same evils because it is omniscient and able to eradicate them, but He apparently chose to not do so. We have no clue why the omni-god would subject us to such devastating natural evils. We admit that preserving free will is not among the reasons that the omni-god didn't create virtually omniscient beings instead of us. The evils that occur must be a necessary condition to the realization of some greater good that we cannot fathom.

To that, my response is twofold. First, why should we try to eradicate any diseases or cancers if they are all necessary to some unknown greater good? It follows that we are morally impotent if you are right. Such a response isn't consistent with the numerous scriptural injunctions to bring about good. It just isn't a position consistently available to the believer in the omni-god.

The second reason is even more decisive. This is an alternative with much less natural evil that the omni-god could have chosen. We know that it is within the scope of power of an omni-god to create much more intelligent creatures than we are—and there is no reason the omni-god could not have created us (or others like us in every other relevant sense) virtually omniscient. We also know that beings having only such limited power as we have are capable of eradicating these diseases. We know that smallpox and bubonic plague in fact are not now necessary to the realization of some greater good because we have eradicated them. It is unlikely *in extremis* that the nature of whatever goods could be obtained has now changed since before we eradicated these natural evils. We also know that humanity could have eradicated them earlier if they just knew earlier what we know now. Such evils as smallpox and AIDS are intransigent evils. We also know that they are horrific natural evils that killed untold millions and caused incredible suffering and the virtual annihilation of some tribes of Native Americans. What more do we need to know to show that the omni-god had an alternative that it could have chosen that entailed much less evil and did not interfere with free will in the least? I suggest: not a thing.

Moreover, we could have avoided the three instances of radical evil if the omni-god would have created us (or others relevantly similar in all other respects) cognitively perfect. We would have known where the three-year-old girl's murderer was in time to prevent her murder. Further, if we were virtually omniscient, then the pain and suffering that results from negligent acts, like the death of my friend's daughter, would have been avoided. The driver would have known immediately that the parking brake wasn't set and would have avoided my friend's daughter's death. We would have known how to cure smallpox before it killed millions. In so creating us, God would have empowered us to take care of these moral and natural evils ourselves—of our own free will.

Indeed, it is difficult to see how a being with perfect cognitive faculties wouldn't see that morally evil choices are not in our best interests individually or collectively and refrain from such evils. For it is quite plausible that only creatures with defective cognitive faculties fail to see the desirability of morally virtuous and good acts. At the very least, it seems incredibly likely that we would go wrong with much less frequency than we do if we had cognitive faculties far superior to those we actually possess. We would be better able to see what God's purposes are and how they serve our best interests—and how we could best further them. We wouldn't be morally paralyzed by our inability to detect what must be allowed to achieve a greater good. The omni-god had these alternative options open to it in creation and yet supposedly chose to create us with limited and defective cognitive faculties instead.

I believe that this argument from available lesser evils shows that the omni-god of classical theism does not exist. That is what we learn from the problem of evil. But we can only see it when we get up close and personal with actual instances of evil that rip the hearts from our chests.

5

NATURAL LAW THEODICIES

Prior to discussing live options of theodicy in Mormon thought, I want to lay a bit of groundwork regarding God's relation to natural law and the eternal realities that are posited in Mormon scripture. Such a discussion is essential to grasp the nature of God's providential action in the world. After considering the nature of providence and of God's relation to natural laws given the various views of divine providence, I propose three divergent theodicies that are open options in Mormon thought: (1) a finite God theodicy; (2) a process philosophy theodicy; and (3) an Agape theodicy.

It seems to me that despite their potential problems, the effort to produce a theodicy is an important endeavor. Theodicies have been criticized as being presumptuous for attempting to give possible or actual reasons that God could have in bringing about a world where evils are not only not prevented but even allowed to occur. We obviously do not know God's actual reasons. Further, it is often argued that if we were to provide a successful theodicy, we would of necessity be justifying evil. I agree with this latter criticism as far as traditional theology goes. As I have argued, the skeptical response to the problem of evil by those who adopt an all-controlling or meticulous view of providence entails that we are morally impotent. However, the theodicies that I present do not have this effect. To the contrary, they explain why God cannot have a world that serves His purposes without our assistance in bringing about a world in which God jointly works with us against evil, pain, and suffering. God requires our assistance to accomplish His purposes—not least for the reason that His purposes include us and our free response to His love. These theodicies are maximally morally motivating.

A religious tradition is most satisfying and valuable when it provides a revelatory framework for making sense of and giving meaning to our experiences of the various types of evils that confront us. Any religion that leaves us clueless as to God's goodness in light of our actual experience of the world or that fails to provide an optic to see God's loving hand in the world's events fails in its task as religion. I believe that the revelations given to Joseph Smith are an incredible divine gift because they cast considerable light on God's purposes and our experiences of evils. A religious tradition is entitled to, and ought to, draw on all of the resources of its revelations to give meaning to our experience of evil and provide a basis for faith and trust in God. A religion is not limited to minimal theistic commitments that usually form the basis for discussion of the problem of evil in philosophy classes. The revelatory tradition provides not merely a logical possibility that just barely might exist; it reveals its relationship to God. It is also a pastoral response that responds to the yearning for a way to continue to trust God and get beyond a feeling of betrayal in light of our concrete experiences of radical, horrendous, and gut-wrenching evils that rip our hearts from our chests.

Finally, it seems to me that necessarily a theodicy that relies on basic beliefs accepted in a tradition on the basis of revelation cannot function as a theodicy for those who do not accept the basic faith commitments of that tradition. The basic belief structure used in a theodicy will only be accepted as true from within a religious tradition and as established by revelation. Such a theodicy will thus function only as a defense to the argument from evil for those who do not accept the beliefs used to place evil in context of a religious tradition. For the non-believer, the beliefs in question can be merely "true for all we know" or "true as far as we can see" types of truth. The argument may be sound for those who accept the premises as true, but at most it would be merely logically valid for those who do not. Nevertheless, an argument ought to attempt to engage beliefs that are at least plausibly true in the sense that, for all we know, they could be true. At any rate, a theodicy that isn't true "for all we know" will fail in its purpose as a means of placing our experience of evil into a context where faith in God can be maintained by those of the faith and seen as rationally possible for those who do not accept the faith commitments that underlie the explanations.

NATURAL LAW THEODICIES

God's Relation to Natural Regularities in the Tradition of Creation Out of Nothing

The nature of God's providential action in the world is essential to what we may call the "world formation" issues related to theodicy. That is, a theodicy usually notes both what God can do unilaterally to eradicate evils and what God must allow the creatures to do in order to achieve God's purposes in creating the world. For all in the tradition (i.e., the Judeo-Christian-Muslim theistic view that accepts creation out of nothing), God strongly transcends the material universe. Because the material universe was created out of nothing on such a view, God has unfettered discretion as to how it will be fashioned, how it will function, and the purposes it will serve. God created space and time along with creation of matter. In creating, He also ordained the natural laws that would govern it. By "natural law," I am referring to a constant regularity, of the type *water always freezes when it is 32 degrees F* or *the speed of light is C*. Natural laws can be descriptions of these regularities or explanations for why they obtain. There are numerous theories of what natural laws are and how they are best conceived. For now, to avoid going too far afield into such important issues, I will leave the discussion with the simple notion of consistent regularities that in fact obtain in the world about us. It is indisputable that there are such natural regularities. For all in the tradition, God establishes and sustains these regularities, and He can suspend them at any time.

For those in the "total divine control" traditions, God controls both what the natural regularities shall be and also what every human "freely" chooses and does. For Calvinists and Lutherans, everything that happens is within God's direct control because God brings it about through his efficacious power; for Thomists (i.e, those who accept the theological system developed by Thomas Aquinas (1275–1274)), God infallibly brings about everything through creation-constitutive concurring power. God chooses who is saved and who is damned, who is ordained to do evil and who is not, and who is subjected to pain and suffering and who escapes such challenges. I think it must be admitted that it is incomprehensible why a loving God would not predestine all to salvation and glory when it is God's own choice that is manifest in the decision. God's purpose in creating a world is to enhance His own glory. After all, nothing else exists that has any value when (in a logical sense of time) God sets out to create on such a view. God is already the apex of all value, and creation adds nothing to God's glory—yet, in creating, God supposedly enhances His glory by the variety of creation. Creation expresses the abundance of God that overflows into creation, so to speak. God unilaterally brings about every event that occurs.[1] God is in complete control of the natural universe because God institutes or authors the laws of nature that govern the universe and He brings about the supposedly "free" actions of all creatures.

The "meticulous providence" views of Jacobus Arminius (1560–1609) and Luis de Molina (1535–1600) maintain that what creatures would do freely cannot be brought about by God.[2] Because of this, God may be stuck with a world that is different than that which He would have unilaterally created if He could control the fates. Nevertheless, God still has unfettered control over the natural regularities that obtain and that God can suspend or revoke at any time. God may not be able to achieve exactly the world He would choose depending on how the counterfactuals of freedom "fall out" given the fates. However, God uses His omniscient knowledge of what "free" persons would choose if created in a particular circumstance, and God creates out of nothing a world wherein every event that occurs is an essential part of bringing about the best (or one of the best) results that are open to God. If God foresees that a possible person (let's call him Paul) in a particular possible world (W1) would "freely" reject the grace of salvation were it offered, then God withholds His efficacious grace to save Paul (since it would be rejected anyway), and Paul is fated to be reprobated given God's choice of which possible world to create. It is possible that Paul would be saved in another possible world (W2) so that Paul's interest in salvation is sacrificed to the interests of the world-as-a-whole on such a view—even before Paul is created. It seems that Paul is truly treated unfairly

---

1. I am aware that some Thomist scholars would reject this characterization of Thomistic thought. However, I believe that it is both a defensible reading and the better reading of Aquinas on issues such as reprobation and predestination. I also believe that Thomas was inconsistent in his acceptance of libertarian free will and the notion of providence that he adopts.

2. The complete works of Jacobus Arminius have been published in Jacobus Arminius, *The Works of James Arminius*. Luis de Molina's most famous work was the *Liberi arbitrii cum gratiae donis, divina praescientia, providentia, praedestinatione et reprobatione concordia* ("A Reconciliation of Free Choice with the Gifts of Grace, Divine Foreknowledge, Providence, Predestination and Reprobation").

by God if he is not saved in W1 when he would have been saved had God created W2 instead. However, if Paul would "freely" accept the grace when offered in W1, then God gives concurring efficacious grace to bring about Paul's salvation, and Paul is saved because that is the way the fates fall out for possible world W1. It must be admitted, I think, that there is a certain injustice and arbitrariness about efficacious grace and salvation on such a view. Further, on such a view, individuals are treated as cogs—mere things whose personal interest can be sacrificed to the harmony of the whole.

In contrast to this view, open theists maintain that God does not foreknow the free choices that will be made. God instead offers sufficient saving grace to all, and whether that grace is accepted is up to the persons who remain free to reject it. God governs by knowing all that presently obtains and any probabilities of natural regularities. God could have a world that He unilaterally determines with His sheer power; however, He has determined that a world with free creatures is more valuable than a world without such free will. His purpose in creation is to bring creatures into relationship of fellowship for all those who freely choose to enter such a relationship. God's power is thus self-limiting. Nevertheless, this also means that God can un-self-limit at any time. God could override the free decisions of evil humans any time He determined it would be best to do so.

Given that God *could* intercede more in open theism but chooses not to, I think that we have to admit that it looks like God exercises such coercive power a lot less than He should, given the kinds and amounts of moral evils that obtain. Further, it appears that God literally took one hell of a risk in creating a world where the vast majority of people might be lost and even damned to hell. Moreover, because God remains the sovereign of natural regularities, He determines what they shall be and has open to him the entire range of regularities that are logically possible and that He can suspend and revoke at any time. Thus, the God of open theism could have a world devoid of killing cancers and viral plagues as much as the all-controlling god or the god of meticulous providence.

Differing significantly from these views, in process thought God does not and cannot bring about any state of affairs unilaterally. God does not create *ex nihilo*. The world is instead eternally populated by bits of creativity that are the most basic constituents of matter (modeled on quantum events). Every bit of reality expresses its creativity in the act of becoming by incorporating data from its prior moment to be synthesized into a new moment of reality. Each bit of reality incorporates into its momentary existence data from its own past, from surrounding realities, and from God. The bits of reality, known as "actual occasions," "prehend" or "feel" the influence of other realities. God lends His "initial aim" to be incorporated into a new synthesis of data included in each momentary actual occasion. God governs the world by giving this "initial aim" to actual occasions. However, God does not unilaterally control the extent to which such influence will be incorporated into the new momentary reality. God can only exercise persuasive power as a matter of metaphysical necessity. A thing is "metaphysically necessary" if it is a law of absolute generality that governs all events but is not logically necessary. Thus, God lures the universe to evolve its natural laws without being able to control what they shall be. When the natural laws are molded into the fabric of the universe as its governing structure, complexity begins to evolve in stars and galaxies as they form. Over time, life evolves and moves toward greater complexity. This complexity of matter and of biological life is the result of the bits of reality incorporating God's initial aim into their structure and over time reflecting God's organizing influence. God's goal is aesthetic beauty in the creation that God lures into being through persuasive power over eons of time.

Prospects of a Natural Law Theodicy in the Tradition of *Ex Nihilo* Creation

Natural law-like regularities are important to the ability of persons to make choices with predictable outcomes and consequences for their actions. Such regularities seem to be an essential feature of any world that could support beings who are morally responsible for what they do. We have to have a stable environment in which our acts have consequences that are under our control to function as agents. If my arm flew out at random every now and then regardless of my intentions, then I could not be responsible for such bodily actions. If I pulled the trigger on a gun and a flower sprouted instead of a bullet firing, such unpredictability would make ordering our intentions to act impossible, and our lives would be chaos. A stable environment characterized by predictable regularities is essential to biological life as we know it. Our cells could not reproduce or our bodies sustain the functions necessary to survive. However, the same laws of momentum that enable us to create amazing machines like cars that function with reliability also cause a falling boulder to crush us if we happen to be under it. The laws of thermodynamics and fluid dynamics that allow us to talk by pushing air through our vocal chords also enable hurricanes and tornadoes. In general, the sources of natural evil that afflict us and animals—disease, sickness, disasters, birth defects, and the like—"are all the outworking of the natural system of which we are a part. They are the byproducts made possible by that which is necessary for the greater good."[3]

But are the very natural laws that obtain really necessary for the goods of consistent regularity, free will, and so forth? Why didn't the omni-god arrange the world with more congenial natural laws that do not naturally create viruses, earthquakes, tornadoes, tsunamis—and house flies? It is often argued by those in the tradition that in creation God had a very narrow range of natural constants that are "balanced on a knife's edge, within an extremely narrow range that is essential for the existence of life as we know it."[4] Those constants are (a) the ratio of the strength of the electrical forces to the force of gravity; (b) the fraction of the mass of hydrogen that is converted to energy in the process of hydrogen fusion; (c) the ratio of the density of matter in the universe and the density that would lead to a flat universe; (d) the "cosmological constant," which balances gravity and caused the expansion of the universe to accelerate for an inflationary period; (e) a measure of irregularities of the otherwise uniform early universe; and (f) the number of spatial dimensions of our universe.[5]

However, such a view adopts a more constricted view of what was open to the omni-god than is entailed by the notion of omnipotence implicit in creation *ex nihilo*. The problem is that these theistic defenders respond only on the basis of what is physically possible given the actual laws of the natural world that obtain; rather, they need to show that such adjustments are not *logically* possible. The omni-god could have had water that freezes at thirty degrees instead of thirty-two—or that doesn't freeze at all. It turns

---

3. Peter van Inwagen, "The Problem of Evil, the Problem of Air, and the Problem of Silence," 160.

4. William Hasker, *The Triumph of Good Over Evil: A Theodicy for a World of Suffering*, 133–34. See also Bruce Reichenbach, *Evil and a Good God*, 101; Richard Swinburne, "Natural Evil," 295–301; and Richard Swinburne, *The Existence of God*, ch. 11. C. S. Lewis takes this line in *The Problem of Pain*, 30ff. For more on the physical parameters in question, see John Leslie, *Universes*, chs. 1–3.

5. Hasker, *Triumph of Good Over Evil*, 133–34.

out that it is a vitally good thing that when water freezes it expands so that it floats on top of water, otherwise biological forms that thrive in fresh water ecosystems could not survive—absent God creating another regularity like *no ice ever forms regardless of the temperature.* The omni-god could create water that never freezes. The omni-god could create water that sustains life but does not drown us because God is not limited to what is physically possible given natural regularities. In fact, humans have been able to engineer fluids that mice can breathe without drowning.[6] The omni-god is not subject to natural laws or regularities; rather, the omni-god determines precisely what natural regularities shall be. Thus, the omni-god can have any natural laws of physical regularity *that are logically consistent.* The omni-god could have a world where the speed of light is not the constant C (186,282 miles per second) but some other value (say 148,224 miles per second). If changes in these laws did change physical constants, the omni-god could make just enough adjustment to the initial constants to compensate because such adjustments would be logically consistent.

The God of the tradition that creates *ex nihilo* could have a world *both* characterized by natural regularities necessary to sustain life and moral responsibilities *and* in which deadly tornadoes, earthquakes, and tsunamis never occur. Even though such natural events arise given the equations that govern systems of self-organizing chaos, the omni-god would not need different natural laws to prevent such natural events because they are not the logically necessary features of any natural system regardless of chaotic mathematics functions. Moreover, the omni-god could have such a world even given the types of natural regularities that obtain. He could simply revoke the regularities whenever such events would otherwise occur given the kinds of constants that in fact govern our world—and if He did, then there would simply be different regularities or constants that describe how the natural world in fact behaves. Although the surface of the Earth moves on tectonic plates and collisions of plates cause fissures and earthquakes, it is not a logically necessary feature of tectonic plates that they do so.

The omni-god could have a world devoid of cancer and viruses because they are not logically necessary features of the biological forms that in fact arose in the course of evolution, given the regularities that define

---

6. L. C. Clark and F. Gollan, "Survival of Mammals Breathing Organic Liquids Equilibrated with Oxygen at Atmospheric Pressure," 1755–56.

recombinant DNA and survival of the fittest. Such evolutionary life-forms are random and not an inevitable result of even the natural laws that in fact obtain in our world. The theist has never provided any plausible explanation for why such logically contingent features are necessary even given the natural laws that obtain in our actual world—let alone in a world with different natural laws that would give rise to different possibilities. The key fact is that God need not constantly intervene to make the world massively irregular to prevent the evolution of such viral and bacteriological agents. Rather, God could simply intervene in a very unobtrusive and micro manner to ensure that the single genetic mutation that leads to viruses such as smallpox and AIDs never occurs. God could intervene to ensure that the first cancerous cell never deviates from the cell-division of healthy cells. This type of one-time micro intervention would never be noticed by humans and would not upset any of the constants that govern our space-time universe.

Given the problem of natural evil, the only viable option open to the tradition is that the omni-god contrives these natural evils to serve some higher purpose that we cannot fathom. If the omni-god values regularity, it is still not difficult to consistently conceive of a world governed by predictable outcomes and consequences for our actions that doesn't include things like smallpox, AIDS, and bubonic plague—or cancers of all types. These natural evils must have been contrived for some purpose if one accepts the traditional view that the omni-god's power is not limited by any non-logical constraints entailed by the notion of creation *ex nihilo*. By "contrived," I mean that the omni-god purposely brought them about or allowed them to naturally occur and chose not to prevent them. God is responsible for their occurrence.

6

A MORMON FINITISTIC THEODICY

One prominent trajectory of Mormon thought maintains that God is dependent on a logically and temporally prior universe already characterized by natural regularities before God ever becomes fully divine. This trajectory is represented prominently in John A. Widtsoe's *A Rational Theology* and many current Mormon scientists and engineers,[1] and it arises out of a particular reading of both Joseph Smith's King Follett Discourse and the Sermon in the Grove. It holds that the person who is God is an essentially material entity that was not always fully divine. For purposes of convenience, I will refer to this particular divine person as "El"—though I am not asserting that El is the personal name of the god. On this view, El became fully divine at some first moment by learning to master the natural regularities that govern the universe and the laws of divine relationship (law of love) and morality. If El "learned how" to be fully divine by mastering the natural laws, then the natural laws exist prior to and independently of El's creative activity. When used this way, "God" means that El is one of the members of the council of gods, each of whom has a certain status and particular character attributes that are definitive of being divine. It is not the case that the laws depend on El for their existence; rather, El is dependent on the natural laws for his status as God. I will call this view "Mormon finitism." Given finitism, neither El nor the divine council of gods controls *which* natural regularities obtain or *whether* natural laws obtain. Further, nei-

---

1. John A. Widtsoe, *A Rational Theology*; A Scott Howe, ed., *Parallels and Convergences: Mormon Thought and Engineering Vision*.

ther El nor the divine council of gods controls what the moral laws are that are necessary to become fully divine or godlike.

El himself became fully divine by obeying the eternal moral laws and constraints required for a divine personality and character. At a time (tI), El became fully divine by obedience to eternal laws, but there was an eternity of time prior to tI in which El was not fully divine. Prior to tI, El was in the process of becoming divine by obedience to those gods in the divine council who became divine before tI. El forged his goodness in the crucible of real moral dangers and tests over eons of time. He has developed such steadfast commitment to love and goodness through the process of soul-making that, given His character and proven trustworthiness, we can have faith in Him completely to keep His word and always seek our best interests. Given His trustworthiness and mastery of love, the council of gods assigned El a region of the local universe to organize and govern. In this region, El is supreme and the sole God who is revealed and "with whom we have to do."[2]

On this view, any given individual exists of *de re* necessity—that is, it is the nature of any given individual to exist, and it is *physically* impossible that such a being could not exist. However, it is not El's nature to exist *as God*—or, in other words, as a fully divine being. Further, there have always been fully divine beings on this view. Much of the order that exists in the natural universe is due to the organizing influence of the always temporally prior council of gods. There is an infinite regress of beings who have mastered the nature of the universe and progressed in moral goodness and love to the point that they are fully divine. They have devised a plan to assist us to also become fully divine like them, through the same developmental process. It requires teaching us to master nature as a scientist and learn to be morally good to such a degree that we can share everything that they have learned—just as the gods before them did. Similarly, we must learn from the moral and natural challenges that come our way to create a firm and virtuous character wholly committed to love and goodness.

One of the purposes of mortal life is to prove to God that we are worthy of the kind of ultimate trust implicit in sharing with us all the pow-

---

2. This phrase was first used in Brigham Young, April 9, 1852, *Journal of Discourses*, I:50–51, but it derives from Hebrews 4:13: "All things are naked and open unto the eyes of him with whom we have to do."

er and knowledge that He has. Indeed, it must be established very firmly that we will work cooperatively with God and each other for the good of all so that He can trust us with the fullness of His divine power. Sharing such knowledge with persons who are not proven to be trustworthy would entail a risk that is too great. There may have been innumerable different types of worlds and various types of challenges, tests, and experiences that we have passed through as intelligences or spirits to get where we are at this particular moment in time.[3]

Moreover, El does not and cannot control what creatures will freely choose. The universe is populated by eternal intelligences that are sentient in the sense that they exhibit some degree of creativity and natural regularity, and there is a complete range of these intelligences, from bare power to act in a law-like manner to the fullness of intelligence that characterizes El and the other gods. Moreover, God's intelligence is the sum of all intelligences combined that transcends the mere sum, and El somehow learned to harness the properties of intelligence of all intelligences. The essence of every person's personal identity is an eternal intelligence that is uncreated and has always existed. The eternal intelligences are essentially free, and their choices are up to them; not God. Perhaps God could control the physical ability to make choices given the corporeal nature of a human being the way an anesthesiologist can control whether a person is conscious by administering physical drugs; however, if left free to choose, the choices cannot be up to God. Moreover, given that intelligences manifest their free will in a way that is constitutive of what it is to be an intelligence, taking away the free will of an intelligence is essentially obliterating the identity of the personal agent involved.

God's power on this view is necessarily merely *instrumental*—that is, it is exercised through some means other than direct and immediate control of what occurs. God must act through instrumentalities if God interacts with the natural world the way a scientist would. Now, it may be that El has implanted in His vastly-technologically-augmented-physical brain a remote that transmits His thoughts so that He can immediately send information as fast as it is physically possible for information to travel. After all, we have developed technology that allows brain waves to be immediately transmitted to control electronic devices by mere thought. El may also have a means of

---

3. Abraham 3:25 puts the purpose of life this way: "We will prove them herewith to see if they will do all things whatsoever the Lord their God shall command them."

actuating energy anywhere within a space-time matrix immediately through such devices. However, if God's power and knowledge are technological, they are not a part of what it means to be the person, or even the natural kind, that God is by nature. El is not *essentially* as powerful as it is possible to be through technology. Nor is El *essentially* as knowledgeable as it is possible to be through technology. El is all-powerful and all-knowing contingently and not necessarily. Thus, the doctrine of essential predication must be abandoned, given such a view of God. It is possible for El to not be omnipotent or omniscient and still be the eternally existing individual that He is; it is not possible, however, for El *not* to be all-knowing, all-good, and all-powerful and still be worthy of our worship and devotion, or fully divine and God.

A strange fact emerges for such a view of God. The atheistic naturalist cannot argue that naturalism has an explanatory advantage given such a view of God. For instance, Paul Draper argues that naturalism is much more probable than theism because naturalism predicts a world with a long history of evolution, where the brutal process of survival of the fittest requires millions of years to create our present species. Theism, on the other hand, maintains that God is perfectly good and can create such species instantaneously. A good God, Draper argues, would not utilize such a wasteful and blood-infang approach to creation.[4] However, the view presented by Mormon finitism is naturalistic in its entirety. Moreover, it is precisely what would be predicted given naturalism. There is an evolutionary argument for the existence of God in Mormon finitism. Evolution is the process that governs the development of natural life and that even involves the evolution of more integrated and intelligent beings—including eventually divine beings. Given enough time, it is very likely that superlatively intelligent beings would evolve somewhere in the universe who would learn to use technology to enhance their natural power, intelligence, and knowledge to be vastly greater than we possess. They would progress morally to the point that they have overcome base desires, disunity, and war that would threaten their continued existence and well-being. Such beings would be god-like to us.

Now Mormon finitism has the considerable merit that it simply dissolves the classical problem of evil. On this view, the explanation of evil is that El does not have sufficient technological means to know in advance what will be freely chosen by the creatures that evolved through natural

---

4. Paul Draper, "Natural Selection and the Problem of Evil."

processes. El lacks foreknowledge on this view because He can only access what is available through scientific means—through the causally necessitated results. Yet it appears that we find ourselves in a world governed by indeterminism at the quantum level and non-linear systems and chaos that make such precise prediction of the future technologically impossible in principle.[5] El does not have sufficient technological means to exercise technological power at all places and prevent all evils. El does not have sufficient means to stop hurricanes and tornadoes in at least the instances they actually occur. He cannot stop all viruses immediately because it takes time to work out solutions and cures. As soon as God figures it out, He reveals it for the benefit of humankind. Unlike the God of the tradition, the God of Mormon finitism cannot specially tailor natural laws in just any logically possible configuration. God does not contrive any purposeless evils to somehow bring about a greater good on this view.

Given finitism, God did not allow the murder of a three-year-old girl; rather, He had the will to prevent it but lacked the resources to stop it. Neither could He stop the car from running over my friend's little girl because of the local limitations that confronted Him. God would have prevented it if He could have. God couldn't stop smallpox for five thousand years because He lacked the resources to do so until about 1796 when Edward Jenner, a doctor in Berkeley, Gloucestershire, rural England, discovered that immunity to smallpox could be produced by inoculating a person with material from a cowpox lesion. Perhaps God revealed it to him in some way. Yet, if this is the explanation for evil, it is scant comfort to religious faith and trust. Why pray to a being who can't do better than we could do on our own? This objection seems decisive to me. It may be that there is a more complete theodicy that could be worked out on this view, given considerations, in addition to the lack of power and knowledge—but my point is that if limitation in God's power and knowledge are the sole explanation for the existence of evil, then the explanation still has a lot of explaining to do about other issues for faith. If God is really limited to the natural laws that obtain in such a way that He must figure out how to overcome them—the way we have learned to use an airfoil to create flight and literally lift tons of steel into the air using mere air!—then it seems to me that trust

---

5. Qiwei Yao and Howell Tong, "On Chaos and Prediction in Stochastic Systems," 357–69.

in such a being is greatly attenuated. While a being like this may be a very advanced god-like being compared to us, this kind of finite uber-scientist is unlikely to win devotion compared to the kind of being who can command our allegiance as a moral duty and organize the entire universe.

The problems of such a view are significant. This view begins with a naturalistic commitment, but it must abandon such a world-view if God can do the kinds of things reported in scripture—like resurrecting and raising the dead (John 11:38–44; 3 Ne. 7:19), stopping the rotation of the earth for a day so that the sun stands still (Josh. 10:12–14), or stopping human flesh from burning in the presence of fire (Dan. 3:15–27). Further, it seems to me that naturalism is problematic in many ways with a Mormon understanding of matter. The notion assumed in Mormon finitism that God just happens to find Himself in the midst of an eternal universe with already existing laws seems both antiquated in terms of current cosmology in general and in terms of Joseph Smith's revelations in particular. Current cosmology adopts the notion of an expanding pocket universe with a population of universes in a multiverse. That concept does not get enough recognition because creation occurs on such a view largely by choosing the initial constants of a particular pocket universe that govern which laws will fall out of the asymmetry created at the Big Bang of each pocket universe. Where does a wholly physical El stand in relation to the Big Bang? The Mormon finitism model assumes that the physical universe is infinitely old—but at least our particular pocket universe appears to have had a beginning as a space-time manifold. There could not be an eternally old, physically complex being in such a local universe. Thus, El would have to "stand" outside of the physical space-time matrix that defines our own pocket universe. But if so, then how does He get back into or communicate with our universe—let alone evolve to become a fully divine being within its space-time matrix?

More critically, this view seems inadequate to explain the assumption in Joseph Smith's revelations that the creation and laws governing the regularities of the bodies in the natural world depend on God's immanent power. Doctrine and Covenants 88 reveals:

> He that ascended up on high, as also he descended below all things, in that he comprehended all things, that *he might be in all and through all things*, the light of truth; Which truth shineth. This is the light of Christ. As also he is in the sun, and the light of the sun, and *the power thereof by which it was made*. As also

he is in the moon, and is the light of the moon, and *the power thereof by which it was made*; As also the light of the stars, and *the power thereof by which they were made*; And the earth also, and the power thereof, even the earth upon which you stand. And the light which shineth, which giveth you light, is through him who enlighteneth your eyes, which is the same light that *quickeneth your understandings*; Which light proceedeth forth from the presence of God to fill the immensity of space. The light which is in all things, which *giveth life to all things, which is the law by which all things are governed, even the power of God who sitteth upon his throne, who is in the bosom of eternity, who is in the midst of all things.* (vv. 6–13)

And again, verily I say unto you, *that which is governed by law is also preserved by law* and perfected and sanctified by the same. That which breaketh a law, and abideth not by law, but seeketh to become a law unto itself, and willeth to abide in sin, and altogether abideth in sin, cannot be sanctified by law, neither by mercy, justice, nor judgment. Therefore, they must remain filthy still.

All kingdoms have a law given; And there are many kingdoms; for there is no space in the which there is no kingdom; and there is no kingdom in which there is no space, either a greater or a lesser kingdom. And unto every kingdom is given a law; and unto every law there are certain bounds also and conditions. (vv. 34–38)

He comprehendeth all things, and all things are before him, and all things are round about him; and he is above all things, and in all things, and is through all things, and is round about all things; and all things are by him, and of him, even God, forever and ever.

And again, verily I say unto you, *he hath given a law unto all things, by which they move in their times and their seasons; And their courses are fixed, even the courses of the heavens and the earth, which comprehend the earth and all the planets.* And they give light to each other in their times and in their seasons, in their minutes, in their hours, in their days, in their weeks, in their months, in their years all these are one year with God, but not with man. The earth rolls upon her wings, and the sun giveth his light by day, and the moon giveth her light by night, and the stars also give their light, as they roll upon their wings in their glory, *in the midst of the power of God.* (vv. 41–45)

I have quoted this revelation at length because it provides a view of God's relation to creation of natural law of regularity different than that assumed in naturalistic Mormon finitism. God is universally present to and immanent in all realities as the power by which they are governed and sustained in order. He gives laws to all things. That is, He is the source of natural laws or the regularities of their movements—not subject to them.

God is in and through all things—not a being limited to a particular place from which He engineers the universe. Those who adopt Mormon finitism privilege their reading of the later Joseph Smith they believe is represented in the 1844 King Follett Discourse and the Sermon in the Grove over this revelation (received in 1833) because they adopt an evolutionary view of doctrine such that later doctrinal expressions always trump earlier ones. However, I have argued that this reading of Joseph Smith's later sermons is mistaken. In volumes 2 and 3 of *Exploring Mormon Thought*, I have provided a hermeneutic that brings his later sermons into an alignment with his earlier revelations.[6] Thus, I believe that the supposed prophetic underpinnings for such a view in Joseph Smith's thought must be reconsidered.

Further, Mormon finitism must address the very difficult scientific and philosophical issues that arise from the assumption that God is subsequent to and thus subject to natural laws. How does an embodied being communicate with us given the limitations on the speed of light given the limitation on the communication of information? A material being must be *somewhere* and in *some time*. If El resides on or near another governing star in our universe, then how could He possibly communicate with us? How could He visit us? Even assuming that star is Proxima Centauri, He would be at least 4.2 light years away. Assuming more likely that He would reside near a star hundreds of thousands of light years away, it seems that we must have an absentee God of deism at best. How could a body of any sort move at or near the speed of light? Even assuming it could so move (which is a contra-scientific assumption)—could any such being be the God who communicates with us in an instant of back-and-forth dialog and prayer of the type presented in scripture? I don't see how. If a theodicy is going to trumpet an appeal to scientific credentials, then it cannot abandon the confirmed theories that govern science (such as General and Special Relativity) when they do not serve the theological purposes of such a view.

How could El escape the big crunch if the pocket universe collapses given that (a) He is subject to natural laws, and (b) those natural laws ultimately dictate that the universe collapses on itself? Or worse, how does El avoid the big whimper where He and everything else just dissipates into energy death? If El is subject to natural laws, then how is El the ultimate

---

6. Blake T. Ostler, *Exploring Mormon Thought: The Problems of Theism and the Love of God*, ch. 12; Blake T. Ostler, *Exploring Mormon Thought: Of God and Gods*, 17–26.

ally who can overcome every challenger as presented in the *Lectures on Faith*?[7] How does a physically limited being like a mere human ever become the imminent reality of power residing in all things and the power by which they move and are governed, as Doctrine and Covenants 88 clearly states? I do not see anything remotely suggesting that naturalism as a beginning assumption could be compatible with the view of God and His power as presented in this revelation.

It seems to me that such a view would have to posit some very controversial assumptions about what is physically possible in our material universe. First, it would have to adopt the view that God exists in another dimension of sorts (outside our space-time coordinates) that gives Him access to our present space-time coordinates. Such a view would have to accept that gravity is not an ultimate law that trumps all other forces in the universe over time. It would have to posit something like space-time curvature that creates a wormhole to give access to any particular space-time within our local universe coordinate instantaneously at will.[8] Perhaps there

---

7. The *Lectures on Faith* states that God's power must be sufficient to overcome the threat and challenge of every being that could threaten the stability of our eternal salvation; otherwise, we could not rely on God delivering us from the challenges presented. See Blake T. Ostler, *Exploring Mormon Thought: The Attributes of God*, 69–74.

8. Scott Howe writes in a private correspondence to the author dated April 19, 2010:

"Pertaining to laws and God, I agree that the laws were created by God (or the society of the Gods), but I also feel that God does not live outside those laws—in the same way we create our laws for ourselves, to give our world order, I think God also must abide by the laws so that order can be preserved. Matter and intelligence, coexisting eternally with God, have innate behavior, and the laws are created to channel that behavior into more complex order, all the way to the point where enough complexity provides a seat for selfaware intelligence. I think there is a difference in saying God evolves out of a naturalist universe as opposed to God creating the laws and abiding by them as well. God is perfected by abiding by the laws, not in spite of them. We are currently subject to causality, but all things are present before God, meaning that even though causality cannot be disturbed for the sake of preserving structure, God has a means of perhaps utilizing 'closed time-like curves' for editing and redirecting some causal paths back on themselves for various purposes (perhaps subject to paradox rules, branching in 'many worlds,' etc).

"There are two essays [in *Parallels and Convergences*] that address possible solutions to a communication problem limited by the speed of light—'Spiritual

is technology that could accomplish such tasks, but it is clearly beyond the purview of our present scientific theories. Perhaps there is technology that permits a physically non-local being to prevent skin from burning in the midst of fire and reanimate corpses after they have been dead for extended periods—even after fully decomposed over thousands of years. Perhaps the gods have developed technology that allows them to maintain the information of every person's DNA that can be exactly replicated (eternally preserved at twenty years of age nonetheless!) and also stored all memories of each person in a database to be download to the regenerated body of each person—and this technological process of DNA regeneration constitutes resurrection. I cannot see any reason why we wouldn't identify the regenerated DNA bodies with full memories and personality as just the same person that existed before death. Perhaps they even have a way of accessing the dimensions in which the soul or intelligence resides in the interim state of existence between death and resurrection so that souls can animate or become identified with such DNA regenerated bodies so that the full Mormon view of existence can be preserved. The limits of technology are difficult to foresee. I don't want to underestimate the resources available to such a view to address the issues I have raised, but we could hardly call such suggestions consonant with naturalism and science as we know it.

Further, if we begin to make these kinds of adjustments to our view of God to square this view with the kind of personally-present God revealed in scripture, then it becomes possible that, if God had even the limited power of a mere human, He could have prevented the kinds of evils

---

Underpinnings for a Space Program' mentions Moroni's visit to [Joseph Smith] via a 'conduit' may be referring to advanced transportation technology such as a traversable wormhole. 'Standard Physics Model of Spirit Matter' also mentions the possibility of quantumscale effects within each cell structure, including quantum wormholes. Current literature in physics have stressed that quantum wormholes exist in extremely dense numbers, constantly created and evaporated in every volume of space as part of the quantum foam that makes up reality. Regarding wormholes or 'closed time-like curves,' however, current literature is still debating whether it is possible to send information through without collapsing the opening. If it is possible, then a mechanism would exist for sending information between any two points in time or space without exceeding the speed of light. If we are to believe that Moroni did indeed visit [Joseph Smith] through such a contrivance, then the evidence is there, and the physics will eventually be known to us."

that involved the murder of a three-year-old and the tragic death of my friend's little girl. The problem of evil comes back with a vengeance given the kinds of things God is said to have done in scripture. If we augment greatly what El can do through technology, then we will have to look to additional resources to explain why such beings allow the kinds of evils that confront us when they could eliminate them.

7

A MORMON PROCESS THEODICY

Theism is the view that God transcends the natural order because God is its creator *ex nihilo*. God is therefore logically prior to all else that exists. Pantheism is the view that God is identical with the natural order. Finitism is the view that God exists within a prior-existing natural order to which God is subject. God is logically subsequent to the law-like order already present in the natural universe given finitism. Panentheism is the view that God is immanent in reality and all reality is embodied in God; it maintains that God is as eternal as the universe (or multiverse) and whatever order exists is a result of God's influence. God logically co-exists with the universe.

Precedents in Mormon Thought for a Process Theodicy

A prominent trajectory of Mormon thought concludes that God is *immanent in all realities in the universe* as creative power and the co-source of order in all things. It departs from Joseph Smith's revelation recorded in Doctrine and Covenants 88 that states that God is in and through all things as the power that gives all realities the law of their movements. That is, God is the organizing power of all things by which the universe exists as a cosmos rather than chaos because God's light is immanent in all things. This trajectory of thought draws on the views of brothers Orson and Parley Pratt and B. H. Roberts.

The Pratt brothers maintained that the most basic realities are bits of intelligent matter called atoms, each of which had some minimal degree of mind or intelligence. The intelligences range from very basic, quasi-sentient information structures to more organized entities that exhibit some level of higher intelligence. All are referred to as "intelligences" in the sense that they manifest some level of intelligence in their behavior and experience. They are active and self-moving in the sense that they attract and repel other particles.[1] They have some level of mental properties that allows them to act in a regular and consistent manner that gives rise to natural laws. They develop and evolve more complex structures over time. The Pratts adopted a form of panpsychism, which is the view that mental properties are inherent in all physical realities to some degree. They viewed the nature of intelligences as defined by their ability to be interpenetrated with and given some level of active power by the light of God that is in and through all things. However, the intelligences also eternally have some level of active power of their own.[2]

What they proposed is a form of panentheism. They maintained that every particle of intelligence was endowed with some level of intelligence and that the unitary Intelligence of all of the intelligences constituted the One God.[3] Orson Pratt writes:

> The infinite number of particles of the Holy Spirit moves universal nature as if by the will of One Being; for in fact, though the particles are infinite, yet they all act by one will. . . . So likewise it is with the oneness of the will and other attributes that constitutes the oneness of the great universal Spirit which pervades all things. The particles wherein this one will resides, are infinite in number, extending through all space. The one will that pervades them all, is the same as the will that dwells in the Father and Son. The most perfect unity in all the moral and intellectual attributes of the Father, Son and Holy Ghost. It matters not how distant some parts of the Holy Spirit

---

1. "After a substance had passed through ages of experience in acquiring a knowledge of cohesion and motion, it would be qualified to begin to exert these elementary forces systematically, according to prescribed laws. The next thing, perhaps, in the great school of experience would be for one portion to form itself into an immense number of atoms of the same size and form, and for another portion to form itself into a vast number of atoms of another size and form, and in this way all the elementary atoms of nature could be formed out of the same substance. . . . These atoms uniting by their own self-moving powers, according to prescribed laws, would form all of the various compounds of nature with all their various properties." Orson Pratt, "The Great First Cause," 15.

2. See my discussion in Blake T. Ostler, *Exploring Mormon Thought: The Attributes of God*, 82–88.

3. Ostler, 82–88.

may be from others; nor how far they may be from the persons of the Father and Son, yet they are imbued with the same will, and never act in opposition to each other's desires. And this is the great secret of oneness.[4]

In addition, each of the intelligent particles acts upon and influences each other. Human intelligence and individuality arose only with the organization of these more basic intelligences. Thus, they held that human intelligences had a beginning when they were organized by God to form spirits. These spirits are then embodied in human flesh to become mortals. Orson Pratt recognized that eternally existing intelligences—each of which exercised a form of its own creative power—entailed that God's power is conditioned.[5]

Similar views were later developed by B. H. Roberts, who maintained that God is immanent in every part of nature as its organizing power and also that every part of nature is immanent in God.[6] Relying on Doctrine and Covenants 88:6–13, Roberts distinguished immanence from mere omnipresence by asserting that immanence is "presence accompanied by power; or presence plus power; presence accompanied by doing an act, leading to manifestations of God's power."[7] In effect, God takes the experience of all realities

---

4. Orson Pratt, "The Holy Spirit," 55.

5. Orson Pratt observed that metaphysical necessities conditioned God's power: "There are some things that cannot be performed.... [T]he great God Himself ... has not the power to do that which would be naturally impossible, or in opposition to the great, necessary, and fundamental truths of nature, which ... cannot be otherwise than they are." Orson Pratt, April 6, 1856, *Journal of Discourses*, 3:299–307.

6. Citing Doctrine and Covenants 88, B. H. Roberts stated: "God Immanent in the world—'The Light of Christ'—the 'Spirit of Christ'—is the power creative; the sustaining power; the life-giving power; and the intelligence-inspiring power. It is the active principle in all these respects; and is omnipresent." B. H. Roberts, *The Seventy's Course in Theology: Fifth Year: Divine Immanence and the Holy Ghost*, 8. Roberts went on to conclude that it is as true that God is immanent as creative power in all things in the world as it is that all things in the world are immanent in God: "[T]he conception of Immanence ... enables one to see not only God in nature, but as a necessary corollary, nature in God—Divine Immanence in the world, and reciprocal immanence of the world in God. That is to say, in one view, God's presence and power penetrates and pervades nature—the universe; in another view, nature is received into the all-including spiritual presence of God: as the One indwells in the other, so the other dwells in the One." Roberts, 17.

7. Roberts, 2.

that exist into his being immanently as the basis of his knowledge.[8] He is affected by co-shared experiences of all realities. Unlike the Pratts, Roberts did not discuss the nature of uncreated realities other than human intelligences except to state that unlike human intelligences that act, all other eternal elements are merely acted upon.[9] However, he maintained that "element" in its most fundamental form, space, time, natural laws, and moral laws are uncreated and eternally existing. Unlike the Pratts, who held that individual identity had a beginning with the organization of lower-grade intelligences, Roberts held that each individual human identity was uncreated and eternally existed as an intelligence. Each intelligence eternally had properties of intelligence, moral volition, consciousness of self and the external world, and ability to deliberate, think, and imagine.[10] Further, Roberts clearly saw that the existence of such essentially free eternal intelligences placed conditions on both God's power and knowledge. Thus, Roberts defined the divine power:

> What then is meant by the ascription of the attribute of omnipotence to God? Simply that all that may or can be done by power conditioned by other eternal existences—duration, space, matter, truth, justice, reign of law—God can do. But even he may not act out of harmony with other eternal existence which condition or limit even him.[11]

In addition, Roberts recognized that the fact that God's knowledge depends on experiencing what has and presently exists entails that God's knowledge is progressing and growing as the present unfolds in becoming what was once future:

> So with the all-knowing attribute, omniscience: that must be understood somewhat in the same light as [omnipotence]: not that God is omniscient up to the point that further progress in knowledge is impossible to him; but that all the knowledge that is, all that exists, God knows. All that shall be he will know. The universe is not so much "a being" as "a becoming," an unfolding. Much more is yet to be. God will know it as it "becomes" or as it unfolds; for he is the universal consciousness and mind—he is the "All Knowing One" because he knows all that is known, and all that shall yet be to become known—he will know it.[12]

---

8. Roberts, 13.
9. Roberts, 13.
10. B. H. Roberts, *The Truth, the Way, The Life: An Elementary Treatise on Theology*, 83.
11. Roberts, 418.
12. Roberts, 418.

Roberts thus held that God does not know the future because the world is essentially a "becoming" that "unfolds" into new realities that could not have been experienced until they come into existence. His view of reality as essentially "a becoming" suggests affinities between Roberts and process thought. God does not know the future because it does not yet exist to be known. God cannot do just anything logically possible because there are eternally existing realities that God informs with his immanent power to organize. However, God's experience includes the experiences of all realities in the universe so that God's knowledge is the synthesis of the sum of all that exists (Abr. 3:18–19).

Armed with these clarifications, Roberts constructed a theodicy. First, he argued that God's purpose in organizing the world and allowing the spirits to encounter evil is to deify, or endow with divine glory, not merely the intelligences but every aspect of reality.[13] He argued that evil is inherent in the eternal structure of reality as a part of the total harmony of good and evil. The possibility of evil is inherent in the total harmony of the world because there are eternal intelligences who inherently possess moral volition to choose evil as well as good—and God cannot have it otherwise. He also argued that moral evil is due to the eternal freedom of intelligences that God cannot control. Further, God always does His best to eliminate evil, but His mode of acting through the influence of His immanent spirit on "intractable material" entails that God cannot unilaterally end evil. God is responsible for neither the level of intelligence nor the level of moral development of the intelligences. As Roberts asserted:

> God is not responsible for the inner fact of [intelligences], the entity that ultimately determines the intellectual and moral character of spirits and men, which are but spirits incarnate in human bodies. God is not responsible for their nature as if he had created them out of nothing—intelligences, spirits, men; and created them as he would have them, measuring to each severally as he pleased to have them in intellectual degree and intensity of moral value. Had he so absolutely created them, he could have made the man of lowly degree the same as the man of the highest degree: the man of brute mind and nature the same as the man of refined sentiment and aesthetic instincts. Why this inequality, if God absolutely created men, intelligence and spirit, body; and created them as he willed to have them, and could have had them different had he willed? Why then doesn't he have them all higher grade all

---

13. Roberts, *Seventy's Course*, 10.

around? . . . The answer to this is that God did all that could be done as the immanent, eternally, active, and creating and causing power in the universe under the limitations of other eternal existences . . . including consideration of the intractableness of the material with which the Creator had to work. If that did not eventuate in the best conceivable of worlds, under the limitations of our human thinking, we may be sure that it has resulted in the best of possible worlds. And while the best possible world presents apparent limitation to the power of the Creator, such as he may not create space, nor matter, nor force, nor intelligence; nor annihilate evil, yet all the power that is, creative, or destructive; or controlling is his; he holds it, and hence he is all-powerful; all the might that exists is his; hence he is Almighty; all the good that exists is his, hence he is the All Good; and the All Benevolent, and the All Loving One, for the same reason that he is the Almighty.[14]

Roberts noted that God is not responsible for the evil done by devils any more than He is of free intelligences. The existence of devils presents no greater problem than the existence of persons who freely choose to do evil given Roberts's account. He concludes: "God may not be able to prevent evil and destroy the source of it, but he is not thereby impotent, for he guides intelligences, notwithstanding evil, to kingdoms of peace and security. Evil is a means of progress, for progress is overcoming evil."[15] Thus, God is assured of victory over evil in the sense that progress toward deification in any degree is a victory over evil.

Roberts also made clear that when referring to God's immanent power in the universe, "God" means the immanent influence proceeding from an eternal unity of divine beings. He referred expressly to the type of immanent unity shared by the Father and Son reflected in John 17:21–26. The light that proceeds from God's presence to dwell in all things as power and knowledge is shared equally by both the Father and the Son, according to Roberts. However, this unity also includes "the light of all Intelligences who have participated in the divine nature and become one with the Father and the Son."[16] Roberts affirmed that "God" in this sense is eternal and has always existed as the governing and organizing power of the entire universe: "But there has always been a race of divine beings in existence, an eternal race, from whom such a divine influence or atmosphere has proceeded forth

---

14. Roberts, *The Truth, the Way, the Life*, 338.
15. Roberts, 339.
16. Roberts, *Seventy's Course*, 9.

to "fill the immensity of space... the source whence the God Immanent proceeded is eternal, so too is the immanence eternal, has always existed, and will always exist."[17] Roberts was attempting to reconcile the notion that God created the universe by bringing order out of chaos with the notion that at some point "our god" became divine within the confines of an already ordered universe. He relied on a notion of the immanent influence arising from "an eternal race of divine beings" as the source of such order. For if there is an infinite regression of gods who constitute the divine council of gods, then there is such an eternal entity that acts in complete unity as one "God" to order the universe. The problem is that the ordered universe is logically prior to the unity of the gods to order the universe on such a view. However, Roberts didn't address that problem. Nevertheless, I don't see any uncontroversial reason why it couldn't be true "for all we know."

It seems to me that the better view is that "God" refers to the light that proceeds from the Godhead or unity of the Father, Son, and Holy Ghost as "one eternal God" that is affirmed repeatedly in Mormon scripture. The gods are all subordinate to God the Father, to whom even Christ gave all glory. The Godhead's existence as an indwelling unity of mutual love is eternal and logically prior to all order on the view that I shall present (and have discussed at length in *Of God and Gods*). I would add that there is a general scholarly consensus that there is a good deal of correlation between Mormon thought and basic commitments and process thought.[18]

---

17. Roberts, 10.

18. See my discussion in Ostler, *The Attributes of God*, 43–64; 82–100; See also Eugene England, "How Can God Be Both Good and Powerful?" 93–100; Truman G. Madsen, "The Meaning of Christ—The Truth, The Way, The Life: An Analysis of B. H. Roberts' Unpublished Masterwork," 259–92; James McLachlan, "Fragments of a Process Theology of Mormonism," 1–40; James McLachlan, "Process Thought and Mormonism"; Sterling McMurrin, *Religion, Reason, and Truth*, 67–69, 79–81; Sterling McMurrin, "Some Distinguishing Characteristics of Mormon Philosophy," 35–46; Blake T. Ostler, "The Absurdities of Prayer to the Metaphysical Absolute," 24–38; Ostler, *The Attributes of God*; Blake T. Ostler, "The Idea of Pre-Existence in the Development of Mormon Thought," 59–78; Blake T. Ostler, "The Mormon Concept of God," 64–93; B. H. Roberts, "The 'Mormon' Doctrine of Deity," 81–102; Floyd Ross, "Process Philosophy and Mormon Thought," 17–25; Garland E Tickemyer, "Joseph Smith and Process Theology," 75–85; and Daniel W. Wotherspoon, "Awakening Joseph Smith: Mormon Resources for a Postmodern Worldview."

Basic Commitments of a Mormon Process Theodicy

Given the basic commitments of Mormon theology, we can elucidate a complete, and I believe generally satisfying, process theodicy. The theodicy can be created by adopting (a) the Pratt brother's recognition that all of reality is constituted of basic realities that manifest some level of "intelligence" and therefore have independent power to act on their own that cannot be controlled by God; (b) Roberts's recognition that such limitations condition God's power and knowledge; (c) the recognition by both the Pratts and Roberts that God's power is always exercised as co-creative power so that God cannot unilaterally bring about any state of affairs without cooperation of the eternal realities with which He is working. The basic structure of the process theodicy to deal with the global argument from evil is as follows:

(1) God's purpose in organizing the world is to bring the intelligences to share the fullness of His own glory and thereby to deify both the personal intelligences and the entire world to the extent that each has the capacity to receive God's light in order to maximize the flourishing and enjoyment of experience of each reality in the world.

(2) There are eternal realities with which God must work to achieve His purposes, including a continuum of intelligences that ranges from those essentially having some minimal level of freedom for the simplest "low grade" intelligences to full moral and self-determining freedom for "higher level" and complex intelligences.

(3) God acts in relation to intelligences of all grades by granting the grace of His immanent light, which (a) may be incorporated to a greater or lesser extent into "becoming" in each moment of each entity's existence; (b) provides co-power to each basic reality to become part of an organized entity abiding a law-like governance; (c) provides a vivifying energy to the extent accepted by that entity; and (d) provides an organizing co-power that empowers higher grade intelligences (persons) to organize their experience into a synthetic whole of conscious experience and have capacity for free will to act as self-determining agents.[19]

---

19. These are the activities of God's spirit that proceeds from His presence to be in and through all things in D&C 88:6–13. Roberts identifies this same power of the immanent spirit of God. Roberts, *Seventy's Course*, 6–10.

(4) God cannot, of metaphysical necessity, unilaterally coerce the intelligences of any grade to receive His light, and therefore the action of God's light on the world is necessarily persuasive and alluring rather than coercive and controlling. In addition, persuasive power is generally morally superior to coercive power (D&C 121:41).[20]

(5) There are metaphysically necessary correlations between power and value of experience entailed in "opposition in all things" (2 Ne. 2:11–12) such that (a) the capacity to freely bring about good is correlative of the capacity to freely bring about evil and suffering for others; (b) the capacity to enjoy intrinsic goodness is correlative of power to suffer intrinsic evil; (c) the power to influence others for good is correlative of the power to influence for bad; and (d) the capacity to freely choose to love is correlative of the capacity to freely reject and resist others.

(6) Persons require opposition and challenges to be able to make free choices such that they can grow toward God's likeness and deification.

(7) God acts in the world by seeking to persuade individuals and every aspect of reality to actualize the optimal realization of possibilities that are open for them to co-actualize.

(8) The process of integrating God's light (by which the world is glorified fully with celestial glory and persons are deified with a fullness of divine light) is an eternal process that was ongoing before this life and continues into eternity after this mortal life; it cannot be brought to a fullness of fruition in a single, mortal lifetime because God's glory is an ever-increasing expansion of possibilities, and there is no upper limit to such progress by its very nature.

(9) God's perfection is eternally self-surpassing; however, at any given moment, God is the most advanced of all and incorporates into His being a fullness of experience and knowledge derived from the experiences of all existing realities. (This notion is sometimes called "panexperientialism" by process thinkers.)

---

20. Doctrine and Covenants 121:41–42 states: "No power or influence can or ought to be maintained by virtue of the priesthood, only by persuasion, by long-suffering, by gentleness and meekness, and by love unfeigned, by kindness and pure knowledge."

I submit that these provisions are "true for all that we know."[21] From these commitments it follows that God must act as persuasive power to inspire and persuade the co-eternal realities to accept His light—exactly analogous to the way the "initial aim" of God is offered to actual occasions to be incorporated into the synthesis of each new moment of becoming in process thought. God creates through an evolutionary process, where over immense stretches of time He lures chaos to organize into an orderly cosmos. It took eons to organize the initial chaos of energy to coalesce to form basic elements such as hydrogen, and later to form stars and galaxies to prepare the way for life. The lower-grade intelligences such as quarks, electrons, atoms, molecules, and so forth cannot deviate much from the divine aims for them because their "mental" capacities are such that they exhibit very little power for self-determination. The lower-grade intelligences at this level are pretty much the result of their inheritance of information from their prior moments and immediate environment. They essentially engage in law-like conduct that repeats the patterns of their behavior millennium after millennium. Over millions of years, God lured the amino acids that had developed on the earth to form single cell organisms. Further up the scale of organization we move into very complex living cells largely determined by their DNA structure. The capacity for novel, self-determining responses is greater for lower-grade intelligences but very limited compared to higher-grade intelligences like humans. With greater biological complexity the powers of "mind" and the powers of self-determination increase. Humans have greater self-determination than snakes, and snakes greater than ants, and ants greater than amoebas. Our capacities as eternal intelligences for experience and to integrate our experience into consciousness of a material world were increased by taking on a mortal body.

The upshot is that God cannot unilaterally bring about change without some period of time and some level of cooperation. The possibilities for change among low-grade realities is very limited. God cannot simply suspend the natural laws. This view explains why God adopted evolution as a mode of creation and why it takes such vast time—and why it involves such cruelty to power the engine of creation of more evolved forms of life

---

21. My formulation of a Mormon process theodicy is informed by David Ray Griffin's exposition of a process theodicy. See the Appendix at the end of this volume for a list of works that I have consulted regarding process theodicy.

through the process of survival of the fittest. It follows that if the law-like behavior of these entities in aggregate causes suffering (such as from cancer or destruction in the environment such as tornadoes, hurricanes, and earthquakes), God cannot unilaterally cause the protons and neutrons that support such systems to divert from their natural course. If a cancer develops, God cannot unilaterally move the cancerous cells to instantly return to naturally healthy cell reproduction.

Higher-grade intelligences, such as human persons and higher forms of life, exhibit much greater intelligence and much greater self-determination, freedom, and creativity. God is able to provide a great deal of light and "novel aims" to influence their behavior very quickly—if they are open to such influences and, for humans, provided that we are willing. We have much greater power to deviate from God's aims and purposes for us than, say, earthworms. If we are about to cause harm, God could inspire us to change very rapidly. He can inspire us to find cures for disease and the equivalencies of mass and energy and to discover the structure of DNA. However, correlative with such creative freedom is the power to also invent very serious evils like the Holocaust and mass genocide. Correlative with our power and intelligence to split the atom or fuse hydrogen atoms comes the power to destroy all life on the earth.

God can get a human body to move only by persuading the person to move it. God's light is not like a physical hand in the sky that acts directly on things to bodily coerce their actions like I coerce my children to go to bed by carrying them there. There is no way that God could make my decisions for me. They wouldn't be mine if He did—but He couldn't even if He tried. God cannot unilaterally stop a bullet mid-flight that has been fired from a gun. God cannot stop the car speeding down the highway out of control. Such things could occur rarely depending on amazing and unexpected cooperation of the basic realities involved—but such miracles are few and far between.

This view provides that God has immense persuasive power to act on all things in the universe (multi-verse) as co-creative power. However, God does not have coercive power. God acts by granting the grace of His light, which He offers for incorporation into individuals to the extent freely accepted to a greater or lesser degree. This light conveys knowledge, intelligence, information, vivifying power, and organizing energy. However, it is only one influence among many to be chosen to be incorporated into the experience of the intelligences.

In each moment God is doing the best that He can to lovingly persuade, empower, and inspire every aspect of reality to its greatest possibilities. The best world open to God is one that reflects an optimal response from the realities in the world. God is thus not after the best of all possible worlds that God can bring about alone; He desires the optimal world in which the other realities in the world are willing to cooperate with God to co-create. God is not seeking the best of all *logically* possible worlds; He seeks the optimal realization of inherent capacities of eternal intelligences and the realities that are organized by God to exist from them. God does not create unjustified evils or intentionally bring them about. Nor is every evil necessary to realize some greater good. The possibility of evil is inherent in, logically entailed by, and correlative with the eternal powers of the eternal intelligences.

In fact, this view has advantages even over standard process thought. Those who promote standard process views must address the issue as to why God would lure the higher-order realities into existence when the capacity for such greater evil is inherent in the correlative power of more highly organized realities. God does not have foreknowledge and thus could not know whether the universe would evolve into a reality worth having—a world where evil far outstrips the good sought by God but which could not be guaranteed. On the Mormon version of process thought, God has no choice about the fact that already higher-order intelligences exist. God's choice wasn't whether they should exist; God's concern is over what is the best that can be done for them given that they do. The choice was made for God already in the fact that there was no other possibility for further progress and growth toward divine glory and deification. Further, it was the choice of each intelligence whether to further progress. God gave the choice to each, and it was the decision of each intelligence whether to seek the possibility of increased glory in relationship with God.

Further, the standard process view does not provide a theoretical basis for asserting that there is life after death.[22] If this life is all there is and

---

22. See C. Alan Anderson, "Immortality in a Process Perspective," 21–37; David Basinger, "Process Theism, Evil, and Life After Death: A Response to Griffin," 353–63; Joseph A. Bracken, "Bodily Resurrection and the Dialectic

our subjective existence is snuffed out with death, then it appears that many people have lives that are not good for them overall. The injustices and evils that destroy so many lives are left unresolved except in the higher harmony of God's perfectly preserved "objective" memory of our lives. Young children who die in infancy do not even get a chance to begin to develop their inherent potential on the standard process view. However, if we begin with intelligences that somehow become incorporated into mortal bodies, then life of eternal duration without beginning or end is a background assumption of the metaphysical realities that define the world's possibilities.

With respect to the particular radical evils that I identified, each is easily answered by this theodicy—which is really a dissolution of the classic problem of evil rather than a solution (which I don't believe exists). God could not unilaterally prevent a young girl's murder. Given the combination of the inherent freedom that persons have and God's acting by persuasive power and inspiration, He could not stop the murderer without the murderer's cooperation. If the murderer had been open to the light of Christ offered by God to influence his decisions, the murder would not have occurred. Unfortunately, he was not. However, could not God interfere with the brain function of the murderer to stop this tragedy? The answer is that God may have attempted to do so, but brain activity may not be open to God's persuasive influence with such great speed. Sometimes it may work, but other times it may not. God did not have foreknowledge from eternity that this act would occur, so God's persuasive influence must begin when the murderer's plan becomes clear. There was not enough time, given the evil propensities of her murderer, for God's persuasive power to prevail.

---

of Spirit and Matter," 770–82; Joseph A. Bracken, "Subjective Immortality in a NeoWhiteheadian Context," 72–90; David R. Griffin, "Life After Death in the Modern and Post-Modern Worlds," 39–60; Arthur S. Berger and Henry O. Thompson, "Life After Death, Parapsychology, and Post-Modern Animism," 88–107; David R. Griffin, *Parapsychology, Philosophy, and Spirituality: A Postmodern Exploration*; David R. Griffin, "The Possibility of Subjective Immortality in Whitehead's Philosophy," 39–57; Charles Hartshorne, "The Acceptance of Death," 83–87; Granville C. Henry, "Does Process Thought Allow Personal Immortality?" 311–21; J. Norman King and Barry L. Whitney, "Rahner and Hartshorne on Death and Eternal Life," 239–61; Lori E. Krafte, "Subjective Immortality Revisited," 35–36.

If unable to influence the murderer, could not God have revealed the murderer's intentions to another who has the ability to bring to bear bodily coercion? Perhaps God did try to get through to someone, but tragically no one was open to hear or respond to God's inspiration in time. Whether a revelation is heard is partly up to those that God moves upon to inspire and persuade them. The way the revelation is understood is partly up to the person's own cognitive activities to make sense of the data received. All revelation is co-creative and can be wholly rejected, misunderstood, not fully grasped, or only partially accepted. The degree of light and knowledge we receive is partly up to us and not God alone. I have called this view of revelation and personal communication between God and humans "creative co-participation."[23] It coheres much better with what we actually find in scripture than the notion that God simply controls and dictates divine message to passive recipients.

Why did not God simply stop the smallpox and AIDS viruses before they ever became active infections to kill billions? Given the natural DNA and viral cell structures that evolve due to God's organizing influence over millions of years, the evolution of such viral infections was the natural result of God's light, which brings about order and the responses of the low-grade actualities (things like atoms, organic molecules, and cell bodies) with which God worked. God did eventually get through to mere mortals to inspire a vaccine for smallpox. Before that, we may not have been adequately prepared cognitively to recognize the cure or vaccine when God revealed it. God cannot just override our cognitive and noetic structures to fill them with information. That is partly up to us in the process view. So, God got through to us as soon as we were ready, willing, and able.

Could God have stopped the car that killed my friend's daughter? It was within His power, given enough time—or a miraculous cooperation by the basic material constituents of the car itself to suddenly act in a way contrary to the natural proclivities of a ton of steel and gravity to roll downward. However, God could not unilaterally stop the car. He is not a big hand in the sky that can reach down and exercise such coercive power. He acts by the persuasive power of his light that is given as a grace to all things. But that means that God couldn't even bring to bear in this

---

23. See Blake T. Ostler, "The Book of Mormon as a Modern Expansion of an Ancient Source," 111–15.

particular instance the physical power of a normal man. Why shouldn't we recognize that as merely meager power rather than omnipotence? The answer, or the best that can be done on this view, is that God has perfect power because the nature of God's action in the world is a universally present immanence that acts immediately on all things to organize the cosmos from chaos, to lure the cosmos into an order that evolves higher order life-forms and inspires humans to love one another. It is the *means* of God's power that prevents coercive physical action at a distance, not the *amount* of power that God possesses. God has the power to bring these things about, provided that the realities cooperate in His enterprise and have the capacity to do so. As David Ray Griffin claims,

> Delimitation of the concept of perfect power requires discussion of the nature of the "world." For the power involved in the problem of evil is a relational concept. It is God's power in relation to something distinct from God, i.e., the world.... Put otherwise, to exert power is always to exert power over something (even if that something is oneself). Hence before drawing implications as to what a being with perfect power could do, the nature of the things upon which the power is to be exerted must be considered.[24]

> But let us assume that it is a metaphysical truth that the actual world contains self-determining entities. Then, even if such a world could possibly be free from evil, it would not be true that God could unilaterally prevent all evil in it. Whether the worldly entities would always avoid evil would finally, in Plantinga's words, "be up to them."[25]

Thus, the question of whether or not omnipotence requires that God can bring about a state of affairs itself requires a prior inquiry into the nature of the state of affairs to be brought about. If that state of affairs includes the self-determining decisions of other free entities who exert some power of their own, then God cannot unilaterally control what the state of affairs shall be. However, this view, as William Hasker claims, isn't just an extension of the traditional free will defense to all of nature in addition to humans that are free in a libertarian sense.[26] In that tradition, God can override and control the decisions of any other reality given the nature of God's

---

24. David Ray Griffin, *God, Power and Evil: A Process Theodicy*, 265
25. Griffin, 271.
26. William Hasker, *The Triumph of God Over Evil: A Theodicy for a World of Suffering*, 136–37.

power. Thus, God can both prevent any act by rendering it unfree and also override the natural laws on the view that God creates *ex nihilo*. Neither of these kinds of power is available to God in process thought. Instead, God is limited out of metaphysical necessity so that He cannot coerce a free decision. Thus, God cannot suspend the laws of nature.

But if God cannot even bring to bear the physically coercive power of a human of normal strength in any given situation, why pray for God to change such things as Jesus taught? Why would I ask God, for instance, to heal a friend of cancer? I have addressed this issue at length in volume 2 of *Exploring Mormon Thought*, in the chapter entitled "Providence and Prayer."[27] It seems to me that this is the second greatest difficulty for a process theodicy. Nevertheless, process thought is not without resources to answer this question. It seems that God is always dedicated to bringing about the best for us that He can—even if we don't pray. However, God may have good reasons to wait for us to pray before acting. These reasons may include His desire for us to voluntarily approach Him for help, to wait on our permission before interfering in our lives, or to seek an intimate relationship that can only be achieved by giving us space to act without His immense glory making it impossible for us to reject. Perhaps God withholds the full persuasive power He could bring to bear in any given situation until we ask. That really doesn't solve the problem for the process thinker, however, because the problem is that God doesn't have the unilateral power to answer prayers. Still, in process thought it follows that God's effective power is increased by the cooperation of the persons or entities with which God is striving. Thus, we increase God's power to answer our prayers by opening ourselves to be influenced by God to answer our prayers through our prayers! We open ourselves to become an instrument to achieve God's will. Further, we add our power and light to God's to achieve the petitions we make of God. In process thought, we also add to the "mental pole" of experience of low-grade realities when we seek to persuade them and to be added to the persuasive power of God's initial aim. The mental pole is the primordial nature of God that defines all possibilities; whereas the physical pole is God's consequent nature that consists of

---

27. Blake T. Ostler, *Exploring Mormon Thought: The Problems of Theism and the Love of God*, ch. 2.

God's experience of what occurs.[28] Thus, God's light may be more powerful and persuasive if I add the influence of my own light and will to heal my friend of cancer through prayer.

There is another, more powerful response to this very difficult challenge. God's power is increased by the greater number of entities that cooperate in His enterprise. If we engage in corporate prayer as a body of believers, in the greatest unity of purpose that we can bring to bear, then we effectively increase the light that is offered to effectuate desired outcomes. God's power to influence is literally increased by corporate prayer on the process view. The LDS practice of the prayer circle in the temple therefore makes good sense from this view of prayer. The greater the number of people having a common cause and hearts united as one, the greater God's power and influence in the world may be directed toward any given state of affairs. It is true that neither God nor we knew that the car that killed my friend's daughter would begin to roll. It remains the case that despite our prayers for protection and cooperation in God's plan, the car still began to roll and killed this precious little girl. In the next section I will suggest some added resources of Mormon thought to address this, but I believe that is the best answer that can be given within the limits of the Mormon process theodicy. I do not find it fully satisfying without the additional resources I will discuss in the next section.

The greatest challenge to a process theodicy is that God is revealed to have performed acts that appear to require coercive power in scripture. I say "appear" because it is always possible that such miracles can be explained in terms of non-coercive power. In process thought it is always possible that the constituent realities cooperated in a rather miraculous manner in some instances to accomplish truly astonishing results in a very short period of time to bring about miracles. However, the entire world and its order is a miracle

---

28. The primordial nature is God's envisagement of all possibilities; in other words, it is God's knowledge of all possible worlds. It is called "primordial" because it represents what is logically possible in contrast to the actual events as they occur. The consequent nature is God's prehensions (feeling or experience) of the actual processes of the world. In contrast to the primordial, the consequent nature is the world's influence on God. It is called "consequent" because it is dependent upon the decisions of non-divine actual entities as a consequence of such experience (Whitehead calls them actual occasions). The consequent nature is the record of all achieved facts, a perfect memory of all that has been. See Alfred North Whitehead, *Process and Reality: An Essay in Cosmology*, 13, 19.

on process thought if a miracle is thought of as an occurrence caused in part by God. Sometimes cancers are cured or go into remission in what appear to be miraculous and unexpected ways. Such results could be God's persuasive influence when the cancer cells respond in a favorable and unexpected way. Process theodicy predicts that sometimes such miraculous results can be achieved by God, and that sometimes they cannot. This appears to be just the way things occur in the actual world. A process view defines miracles as something like *the loving persuasion of God remarkably influences a situation or intelligence in an unusual way that is contrary to expectation based on common experience.*[29] The truth is that we are never certain on empirical grounds alone that any given event is a miracle or the result of divine action. We always have some alternative explanation available—such as sheer coincidence or perhaps a scientific explanation beyond our present grasp. That is what this view of miracles predicts we will experience. From time to time there will be truly remarkable and altogether unusual incidents that defy easy explanation. They leave room to see God's hand in the world for those who have faith and eyes to see such possibilities in the events of the world. Thus, sometimes God's loving influence and light is effective due to the cooperation of the realities involved, and sometimes it isn't efficacious because God's offer of light is rejected. Sometimes prayers work to some degree (say, giving comfort and some level of healing) but not to the full degree requested. As Thomas Jay Oord expresses it,

> To say that God's loving activity oscillates does not mean that God sometimes voluntarily chooses to love more influentially. God's nature as love prompts God to exert the most loving influence possible in any situation. God loves steadfastly, and God never takes a holiday from loving us. However, God's causal effectiveness oscillates as creatures cooperate to greater or lesser degree. God's oscillating and diverse love depends in part upon God's own essence as love, in part upon the particular forms and expressions God chooses when loving to the utmost, and in part upon creaturely responses. Jesus responded best—perfectly—to God's loving activity, and for this reason Christians believe that Jesus reveals God's miraculous love.[30]

I would add that this view of miracles through the cooperative faith of those involved is presupposed in the notion that Jesus cannot perform miracles where there is insufficient faith. Miracles are necessarily a function

---

29. See Thomas Jay Oord, *The Nature of Love: A Theology*, 147.
30. Oord, 148–49.

of both God's power to bring about events and the faith of those who are involved: "For if there be no faith among the children of men God can do no miracle among them" (Ether 12:12); "And he did not many mighty works there because of their unbelief" (Matt. 13:58); "So great faith have I never seen among all the Jews; wherefore I could not show unto them so great miracles, because of their unbelief" (3 Ne. 19:35); Miracles are done "according to faith" of the recipient (Matt. 9:29). It is thus a combination of the recipients faith and God's power that results in miracles and healing (Mark 5:34; 10:52; Luke 8:48).

Indeed, process principles provide a metaphysical grounding for the view that God's power is the result of the faith that all existence places in Him. God creates by faith: "Through faith we understand that the worlds were framed by the word of God, so that things which are seen were not made of things which do appear" (Heb. 11:3). God frames the world out of the "things not seen" by the faith of these things place in God. As the *Lectures on Faith* put it,

> By this we understand *the principle of power* which existed in the bosom of God, by which the worlds were framed, was faith; and that it is by reason of this principle of power existing in the Deity, that all created things exist; so that all things in heaven, on earth, or under the earth, exist by reason of faith as it existed in Him. . . . We here understand, that the sacred writers say that all these things were done by faith. It was by faith that the worlds were framed. *God spake, chaos heard, and worlds came into order by reason of the faith there was in Him.*[31]

According to the *Lectures*, order arises because of the responsive faith of chaos to God. Indeed, God's creative power to organize chaos depends on the responsive power of chaos. God does not simply create by *fiat*; He does so by persuading the chaotic realities to trust Him and align with His words. Presumably, if chaos had not trusted God and thereby exercised faith in God, the chaos would not have been ordered on this view.

However, how could God accomplish something like the resurrection unless He could bring to bear coercive power on the physical corpse of Jesus? This is a very difficult question to answer, as I see it, because the resurrection appears to be a violation of the laws of nature if ever there was one. People who have been dead from the torture of a Roman cross for nearly seventy

---

31. *Lectures on Faith*, 1:15, 22.

hours do not just suddenly appear in a closed room with a glorious resurrected body of flesh and bone. However, such a challenge is not beyond possibility in a process world-view. Perhaps the life-long influence of Christ's spirit in relation to his body (I say it this way because I'm not sure what the relation is or was) produced a very powerful effect that "convinced" the structural cells and organs and so forth over the course of his life to respond to Jesus's and the Father's will. Bodies don't die all at once. The structural elements remained sufficiently intact that it was fit for life and responded to the will of God. In the end, who can explain such an event as the resurrection? Jesus's body was not merely a mortal body reanimated; it was a gloriously transformed body that had different properties (such as the ability to never decompose and to hover in the air and go through walls). I think that it is foolish to expect the process theodicist to explain such an event when the traditional view of God's suspending natural law doesn't explain anything except "and then a miracle happened." What is important is that it is possible that there could be a resurrection given process assumptions of persuasive power alone.

Jesus's resurrection is just barely possible given process thought—that may be why it has only occurred once so far. But what about the promised resurrection of our bodies after thousands of years of decomposition and instances of re-composition where the matter of our bodies is incorporated into new types of life and even other bodies? How could such mass resurrection be assured? I'm not sure that a process view has the resources to answer that question in a fully satisfactory manner. Perhaps the resurrection of a gloriously transformed body will take eons instead of an instant. However, it will take less time for those who have conformed their will to God's and had an influence over the matter of their bodies during their mortal lives. That is what seems to be required by this line of thought. Is that enough given scripture? Perhaps.

An Outline of a Mormon Process Theodicy

We can thus provide a comprehensive outline of a process theodicy that also has the resources to answer the challenges presented by the tragic instances of evil taken in all of their particularity. Here is the outline of the global response:

1. God is Almighty, omniscient, all-good, and exists.

2. God is conditioned by the existence of coeternal realities, such as:
   a. Inherently free and self-determining Intelligences (necessarily existing selves).
   b. Chaotic mass/energy.
   c. Metaphysical and moral principles of love that require that God act only persuasively.
   d. Physical laws or regularities defining how low-grade entities act.
3. God is Almighty if He can potentially persuade the optimal realization of potential among states of affairs (i.e., power to bring about all states of affairs consistent with there being other eternally existing realities).
4. An omniscient being knows all that is knowable up until now.
5. A perfectly good being prevents all the evil and promotes all the good it can without thereby preventing a greater good.
6. Moral evils occur, and God is not responsible for them because:
   a. Human nature is uncreated (2a).
   b. Humans are inherently self-determining and categorically free so that God cannot unilaterally bring about human choices (2a).
   c. Humans are morally imperfect and potentially perfectible (2a, 2c).
   d. God's purpose in creation is to provide the opportunity for intellectual and moral development of persons and glorification of the world (2a, 5).
   e. Moral opposition is necessary to moral development (2a, 2c).
   f. God did not create human nature either virtuous or depraved (6a, 6b).
   g. Humans sometimes choose evil (6b, 6c).
   h. God is justified in not contravening evil moral choices (3, 5, 6d, 6e).
7. Natural evils occur and God is not blameworthy for them because:
   a. Chaotic mass/energy is uncreated (2b).
   b. The laws governing mass/energy depend in part on the inherent powers of eternal actualities and on God's concurring light (2b, 2d).
   c. The organization of actualities to reflect stable natural regularities reflecting causal principles is necessary for biological life to evolve and moral choices to be possible (2d).

d. Adverse physical circumstances may enhance moral and intellectual development of intelligences depending on their free response to such challenges (2a, 2c, 6c).
   e. The nature of causal principles is such that many indiscriminant natural evils occur that God cannot prevent (7a, 7b, 7c).
   f. God may justifiably allow some natural evils that He could otherwise prevent (3, 5, 7d).
8. Whatever evils occur are:
   a. Unpreventable by God consistent with individual autonomy.
   b. Unpreventable by God without thereby preventing a greater good.
   c. Unpreventable by God without cooperation of the basic realities in the world.

Here Mormonism manifests its greatest strength in its ability to explain our relationship to God and give meaning to life's challenges. In Mormonism, the concept of inherently free wills possessed by uncreated selves that condition the exercise of divine power absolves God from any complicity in the world's moral evils, while the uncreated realities that inherently exert some power of their own mitigates God's responsibility for physical evils. Indeed, Mormonism views evil as a positive factor in human existence (2 Ne. 2:22–25). The ultimate meaning of mortal existence is found in the struggle to overcome evil and refine the existential qualities of uncreated personhood. The moral gains made in mortality are genuine, and human actions make a real difference in human destiny. In Mormon process thought, God is also confronted by the reality of evil and struggles endlessly against it in a continuing course of organizing the chaotic and enhancing the trivial. God shares humanity's moral struggle, feels genuine sorrow for human failures, rejoices in human moral triumphs, and suffers when humans suffer. There is an earnestness in human experience because the possibility of genuine triumph entails the possibility of genuine defeat. God really loses when humans choose evil over good. Yet, the chance at victory makes mortality an option that justifies its harsh conditions because we freely chose to encounter it. Mormons believe that they are truly laborers together with God, for God has not created evil nor the physical conditions from which it inevitably arises—nor would He allow evil could He end it without thereby making the victory and further progress impossible.

This theodicy has the amazing virtue of dissolving the problem of evil—in its entirety. Note that Mackie's argument that God should have created only persons who always choose what is right cannot even get started on this view. God did not have such a choice open to Him. Further, my argument that God should have created only virtually omniscient beings is completely defanged by this view for the same reason. God never had such a choice. However, the question remains whether the God presented by such a view is one that inspires faith and worship. Is this being properly all-powerful or at least as powerful as a being must be to be worthy of our worship and the kind of obedience that God has requested in scripture?

It follows from this view that God is the most perfect being in existence at all times. However, God's glory is always increasing and surpassing itself. Moreover, God's power derives from the united power of all realities adding to God's power. The efficaciousness of God's power increases with the cooperation of those realities with which God acts as immanent power. Does God's power qualify as omnipotence along lines portrayed in scripture?

Criticisms of Process Theodicy

The greatest resistance to process thought is simply that it is not consistent with the definitively established Jewish/Christian/Muslim tradition that God creates *ex nihilo*. First, tradition itself isn't a sufficient reason to adopt a view. Slavery was allowed by Christians for centuries and was the traditional view, but that doesn't make it acceptable. Second, the argument that God must be able to create *ex nihilo* to comport with scripture is emphatically untrue. God does not create *ex nihilo* in scripture; rather, the creation accounts have Him dividing already existing structures and taming the chaos that constantly threatens the social and cosmic order of the world. Scripture presents a pre-scientific view of creation that doesn't square perfectly with what we know from science, but scripture remains an important source of revelation that is always expressed within the worldview and horizons of those who received the revelations reported therein. The view that God creates by ordering chaos over time is faithful to scripture whereas *creatio ex nihilo* is not.[32] It also comports far better with scientific views of actual evolution of galaxies in our universe and biological evolution of life on

---

32. See Blake T. Ostler, *Exploring Mormon Thought: Of God and Gods*. See also Blake T. Ostler, "Out of Nothing: A History of Creation ex Nihilo in Early Christian Thought," 253–320.

this earth. It comports better with a sound view of revelation and scriptural authority than the notion that God can overpower our noetic structures through revelation to deliver an infallible message with prescient grasp of reality. The process view is vastly superior to the traditional view of *creatio ex nihilo* given scriptural and scientific concerns. These virtues alone make it far superior to the traditional view of God's transcendent omnipotence.

The strongest argument against process theodicy is that God does not have perfect power if He cannot exercise coercive power. Since we know that we can coerce our children by picking them up and putting them to bed when they resist us, we know that coercive power is possible. But if God lacks this power, then He lacks a kind of power that it is logically possible to have. In response, the question of divine power is almost always addressed without considering the nature of the world in relation to God. For example, in the tradition God has all power before (in a logical sense) creation; but if the creation contains free creatures, then God cannot unilaterally bring about the free acts of such creatures. Once God has created the world, God cannot bring about a world inconsistent with the actual historical events in the world up to the time that God acts. What exists prior to God's acts can condition the scope and extent of God's power. Further, God is no less worthy of worship if He creates beings beside Himself who have some measure of autonomy from God. That logically entails that the mere fact that God's power is conditioned by other realities does not, by itself, render God less worthy of worship or less perfect. As Griffin states in response to the "not powerful enough" challenge to his process theodicy,

> One reason [that God of process thought might be seen as unworthy of worship] is that this God is "limited" or "finite." These terms are acceptable if they are properly understood. My God is finite if this means that God is not the totality of reality, that there are other actualities besides God. (The biblical God is clearly "finite" in this sense.) My God is limited if this means that these other actualities have power of their own that cannot be totally controlled by God. (The biblical witness is ambiguous on this point.) But my God is not finite or limited if that means that God's power is imperfect in comparison with that of some other conceivable deity. . . . I conceive God to be perfect in power (as well as goodness), which means having the greatest power it is possible for one being to have. Accordingly, what is at issue is not a God whose power is imperfect in contrast with a

God whose power is perfect; rather, what we have is a conflict between two conceptions of perfect power.[33]

I think that Griffin is correct that given the metaphysical commitments and assumptions of process thought, or of Mormon revelation, such a God possesses the greatest power it is possible for one being to unilaterally exert. Yet, the challenge remains that "the best that God could possibly do was to permit 10,000 Jews a day to go up in smoke. . . . [B]ut remember that God really is doing all that he could to persuade a different outcome of existence."[34] If that is the best that God could do, then it may leave us in despair that we really are at the mercy of evil and God cannot make a decisive difference—ever. How could God ensure the victory of good over evil given the fact that He has only persuasive power? Yet, as Griffin notes, "One of the stranger complaints . . . is that, given the enormity of evil in the world, a deity that is doing its best is not worthy of worship. The implication is that a deity that is not doing its best is worthy of worship."[35] I have to agree with Griffin that the notion of a deity doing less than its best is far less worthy of our worship than the God of Mormon process thought, who always does the best He can.

It is often argued that God should not have lured higher-order beings such as humans into existence through evolution because God lacks the foreknowledge and ability to correct the creation if it goes terribly wrong. Correlative with greater intelligence and greater power to do good is the power to destroy and do evil. Without the assurance of foreknowledge, God should not have lured life to evolve into creatures having such capacities. Of course, such a judgment immediately entails the implicit value judgment that God should not have created humans at all because of the depths of human depravity and that the God of the tradition made a mistake in creating us. I think that this issue is one that must be addressed by standard process thought—and I'm not sure that it has the resources to address it. At most, standard process theism can say that it disagrees with the value judgment: God is in a much better position than we are to make this value judgment, and that is what God decided. However, it may well be that God could be sorry for what has evolved—and indeed that is the implicit

---

33. David Ray Griffin, "Creation Out of Chaos and the Problem of Evil," 133–34.
34. Griffin, 133–34. See also John K. Roth's critique on page 121.
35. Griffin, 135.

message of the story of the Flood and destruction of all human life except Noah and his family—and even they were a rather seedy sort.

As I intimated earlier, it seems to me that Mormon process thought is in a different position than standard process thought on this score. It is true that God lacks foreknowledge and coercive power given Mormon process thought, but it does not follow that God had the same options. God was not beginning with no higher-order intelligences, given Mormon revelation. God was looking for a way that would allow these higher-order intelligences to further progress in their capacity for joy and fulfillment and thus devised a plan for those who freely chose to engage the challenges of evil that are correlative of such increased power. The higher-order intelligences already existed because there is a complete continuum of intelligences in terms of their intelligence and power given in the structure of reality. Thus, the choice wasn't whether to persuade the lower-grade intelligences or realities to evolve into higher-grade realities; rather, God had to decide what the optimal option was, given that such higher-grade intelligences with correlative power already exist.

William Hasker argues that process thought is really in no better position than free will theism of the type adopted by open theists because God cannot bring about or control the free acts of creatures. Hasker argues that both views can absolve God because "God doesn't control the [free] decisions themselves."[36] However, that is not true. The fact that God does not but could control such free decisions means that God is culpable for not controlling them when they should be controlled. For instance, God should have stopped the brutal murder of a three-year-old girl. He should have exercised coercive power to override the free will of her murderer because that is what any decent person should have done who had power to do so without

---

36. Hasker argues: "The reference to freedom points to an area of commonality between process and free will theism. Both views agree that a vast amount of the world's evil and suffering is traceable to the morally wrong actions of human beings. Both views hold that these actions are free in a libertarian sense, meaning that they are not predetermined by any prior circumstances. Both views agree, then, that the primary responsibility for these actions lies with their human perpetrators and not with God, who has in some way provided the circumstances in which the decisions are made but does not control the decisions themselves." William Hasker, "The Problem of Evil in Process Theism and Classical Free Will Theism," 198.

any danger to themself. He is thus culpable for failure to control the misuse of freedom by His creatures given the assumptions of free will theism.

The rejoinder by Hasker is that the process theist is making the value judgment that it would be better if God had such coercive power to bring to bear in certain situations.[37] Thus, persuasive power is not always morally superior to coercive power. However, Hasker is assuming that the process theist insists that persuasive power is not used solely because it is morally superior as opposed to being metaphysically necessary. There are instances where it would be better if God could exercise coercive power to prevent little girls from being kidnapped and murdered. It would be better if freak accidents like cars rolling over little girl's heads did not happen. It would be better if viral contagions did not kill billions. God cannot unilaterally prevent these types of evils, given process assumptions. That is why there are genuine evils—or events that occur that it would be better, all things considered, that they not occur. That is why God is not indictable for them. However, the God of free will theism who creates *ex nihilo* is culpable for them because He could have unilaterally prevented them. The free will theist's view does not provide an explanation for these types of evils—it takes refuge in our ignorance of God's higher purposes just like the all-controlling theist. However, process thought explains precisely why God is not indictable for these evils. They are not on par in terms of explanatory power.

Hasker's next rejoinder is that the process theist's critique of open theism requires God to constantly intervene, and "frequent or routine divine intervention would negate many of the purposes for which the world was created in the first place."[38] However, God easily could intervene in unobtrusive ways that do not upset the natural laws of the world. A small stroke would have stopped a young girl's killer. Holding the car back for five minutes would have saved my friend's daughter. A simple prevention of a single mutation would have prevented smallpox. Further, who cares if God intervenes all the time? As long as it prevents free actions only when they ought to be prevented and does not mess up the natural order, why should we care? Hasker notes that it is better that God does not constantly intervene because the natural evils are necessary to attendant good. He argues, for instance, that hurricanes may kill some, but they may also deposit much-

---

37. Hasker, 199.
38. Hasker, 199. See also Hasker, *The Triumph of God*, 163.

needed rain in areas where there is a lack of rain due to perpetual drought. Well, God could just make it rain where there is a drought. He mentions the fact that evolution produces richer and complex organisms but is also very cruel. Well, the God of the tradition could create such richer and complex organisms without evolution. Hasker responds that such a view entails the value judgment that "the world of nature is a bad thing."[39] However, it does not entail that nature is not good in itself, it merely entails that God could have had this same good without the same amount of evil—whereas the God of process thought cannot.

Hasker also argues that the value of free will "would be negated if God were to intervene each time a wrong action is to be performed."[40] To preserve this value, God must allow at least some evil choices to be brought to fruition. However, Hasker argues that any criterion that could achieve God's purposes for the value of free will and moral motivation "cannot be provided by supposing that God must prevent all 'gratuitous' evils."[41] The reason for this limitation is that if we knew that God prevented all gratuitous or Unjustified Evils, then

> almost all of our incentive and motivation to deal constructively with situations conducive to such evils would disappear. . . . For whatever the evil in question, we could be certain that, if the evil in fact occurs, it has been allowed to occur by God only because its occurrence will lead to some greater good, or to the prevention of some other equal or greater evil. . . . Thus, the claim that God does and must prevent all genuinely gratuitous evils runs counter to God's intention to make of us responsible moral individuals; such a claim should not, then, be endorsed by any Christian believer.[42]

So God must allow gratuitous evils that serve no purpose and are not for a greater good.

Hasker argues that the notion that God only allows evils to obtain in order to realize that a necessary greater good entails that we are morally justified no matter what we do. Such a view does in fact entail the absurdity and impotence of any moral obligation. But what then shall we say of God's goodness? Does it follow that God is good and justified no matter how much

---

39. Hasker, *Process Theism*, 200.
40. Hasker, 200.
41. Hasker, 97.
42. Hasker. See also Hasker, *The Triumph of God*, 163.

purposeless and gratuitous evil God allows but could prevent? Of course not. If God is good no matter what He does, then "goodness" loses all meaning. Hasker cannot consistently take the position he urges. If God has a reason to permit an evil because it will destroy His purposes if He does not, then by definition it isn't gratuitous or unjustified. So if God must permit gratuitous evils to preserve His plan, it follows that it isn't any longer gratuitous. What follows on Hasker's views is that there are no possible gratuitous evils. His position is incoherent. The problem here is Hasker's failure to distinguish between Unjustified Evils and genuine evils as I have done. There may be particular evil choices that, all things considered, don't make the world better but must be allowed for God to achieve His purpose of leaving it up to creatures to freely co-create the world with Him. In order to have a world-type where morally significant free actions are possible, there must be the possibility of morally evil actions that are sometimes allowed to actually occur. What the world shall be cannot be solely up to God on such a view.

So where does that leave us with Hasker's argument that God must allow some gratuitous evils to achieve His purposes to motivate us to prevent any evils and to preserve morally significant free will? It leaves us with a God who arbitrarily chooses to allow some gratuitous evils and not others. It follows that a young victim of murder is in a position to argue justifiably that God sacrificed her life to the good of the world-type that God sought. He allowed a little girl's head to be crushed, which He could have prevented for the purposes of the world-type. He used them as mere cogs in His plan without their consent. God is thus arbitrary and capricious and cannot justify why these particular evils were not prevented. He wronged these individuals by using them as mere things and sacrificed their personal value to the good of the harmony of the whole. He is therefore morally indictable for these failures and thus not perfectly good. The God of process theism who cannot prevent these evils and does not pick and choose among unjustified evils faces no such charges. The process God cannot be indicted for being arbitrary because it is not within God's capacity to unilaterally prevent these particular evils. The process God cannot be indicted for using persons as mere means to fuel his plan. The process God struggles against such genuine evils. He invites us to join him in this struggle. Thus, there is no danger of destroying our moral motivation to rid the world of gratuitous evils.

The real message of this process theodicy is that God cannot do it all alone. He needs our cooperation to accomplish his purposes for the world. The fact that God needs us to cooperate in His project of creating a world worth living in means that something real is at stake in our moral decisions and cooperative efforts to improve the world. We cannot idly sit by assured that God has everything in hand and the world will turn out just fine regardless of what we do. In contrast to the all-controlling deity of Calvin and Aquinas, or the Molinist deity of meticulous providence that deals with whatever the fates have dished out to it, this view does not guarantee the moral impotence and absurdity of moral obligation to act. To the contrary, if adding our action and faith to God's light that acts through immanent persuasive influence in the world increases the likelihood of overcoming heinous moral evils, diseases, natural disasters, cancer, and so forth *ad nauseum*, then we are maximally morally motivated to put down this book and get to work, making the world a better place as co-creators of the world with God.

There is one final consideration that is rarely brought up in the process view that focuses on aesthetic goods such as intensity and novelty of experience rather than interpersonal concerns: God cannot have the optimal world without our cooperation, and God cannot use coercive power to obtain this superlatively valuable world. God must use persuasive power to accomplish his ultimate purpose by the very nature of this ultimate purpose—a world where loving relationships are possible. God has called us to love each other and to return his love with our own. Such loving relationships cannot be brought about by sheer power but require our free response in cooperation—by the very nature of any love worthy of its name. That is the most valuable world conceivable to me. "No power or influence can or ought to be maintained by virtue of the priesthood, only by persuasion, by long-suffering, by gentleness and meekness, and by love unfeigned" (D&C 121:41). That kind of power is not weakness but strength. Loving persuasion is not impotence; it is the greatest power in the universe. A theodicy that incorporates this insight seems to me to be a more persuasive approach to the problem of evil. It is to that task that I now turn.

8

A RELATIONAL AGAPE THEODICY

Agape (ἀγάπη) is the Greek word for charity or love—the kind of love that family members and close friends have for one another. Agape is the type of love that the divine persons in the Godhead have for each other that unifies and deifies them. The agape theodicy differs from the prior finitist and process Mormon theodicies in at least three significant respects. First, it adopts the view that God can exercise maximal power and, for some purposes at least, coercive power. The notion of God's power is inevitably part of a larger metaphysic of the nature of the eternal realities with which God must work to accomplish his purposes. In addition, this theodicy adopts the view of the Godhead that I argued for in *Exploring Mormon Thought: Of God and Gods*. The divine persons of the Father, Son, and Holy Ghost do not become fully divine at some first moment in time after an eternity of not being fully divine. Rather, they are each fully divine from all eternity. Together they constitute the One Eternal God without beginning or end. They are a united Godhead because in each moment of everlasting time they have freely chosen to love each other with perfect love. Their individual exemplification of divine attributes of godliness is the result of their love for each other. Their mutually indwelling light and glory emerges from their perfect unity. This relationship is fully realized, however, only to the extent that we accept the invitation to join them in their unifying love that seeks its fulfillment in the happiness and growth of others.

The biggest difference between this agape theodicy and the other two theodicies is that it views this world as an environment lovingly ordered to serve us. Evil is not outweighed by some greater good; rather, evil is redeemed by giving it meaning in the interaction. Whether evil remains evil or is redeemed because we used it to heal and learn is up to us. The meaning that evil has is not solely up to God in a matter of calculus in weighing evils against the value of greater goods; meaning is instead found in the creative interaction in the world that we bring to it. The point is not to justify evil (as the name "theodicy" would suggest); it is instead a call to action to transform evil by healing it and to transcend evil by overcoming it through love. The point is that evil must be confronted and transformed by our response to it.

In contrast to the other two theodicies that view the world's evils as the result of a hostile and recalcitrant world that resists God's purposes, this theodicy views the world as a result of God's power to order the cosmos to fulfill His purposes. Through the creation, God ordered the world to serve as an environment in which we can learn to love God and each other from our own experiences. While God's power is not absolute and remains subject to the nature of eternally existing realities, God has sufficient power to order the universe in its general purposes. Knowing how to love is not to know about propositions that describe how to love. Knowing how to love is an experiential knowledge. It is a developed way of being in the world based on numerous concrete instances of freely choosing to act in a loving manner—or not. We learn to love by doing concrete moral acts that have real consequences that provide experiential feedback from which we can learn. Love is not something we possess in the abstract. It is a result of character forged in concrete circumstances where we are genuinely free to refuse to love others. The world is set up as a school of experiential learning. It is designed to teach us what can be gained only from experience: learning the consequences of our actions in relation to others and existing in an environment that calls for us to respond with compassion and charity.

However, the world only has this pedagogic character because God has power sufficient to order it in an ingenious manner that challenges us to learn to love. Often we may not see the purpose of certain experiences afforded us until long after they have transpired. Only in retrospect can we appreciate the blessing that our life's experiences have given to us as a sheer gift. The world is filled with loving grace and angels all about us in the guise of other persons who teach us how to love despite ourselves—and despite the fact that they often appear as challenges and problems rather than angels. Only in the fuller context of life's experience can we see that our greatest challenges have been our greatest blessings.

A RELATIONAL AGAPE THEODICY

The nature of the test of our loyalty and love at issue in this mortal probation is portrayed through the drama of the book of Job. In the drama, Job's suffering is explained by a prologue of agreements that occurred in another realm of existence and to which Job is not privy (Job 1:6–12). He remains ignorant throughout the entire story of God's reasons for allowing Satan to test him. The challenges are so grave that it is almost unfathomable that Job remains committed to God. In this story, Satan is not a demonic figure of later Christian thought; he is a "prosecutor" whose job in the divine council is to bring out the truth about people through challenges and examination. The tests placed before Job are explained by the fact that Satan challenges God that Job is not truly known to be loyal and faithful despite his apparent goodness. His goodness is merely innocence and not the kind of faithfulness and loyalty that can only be demonstrated in the crucible of circumstances that test Job's commitment to God. God assumes that Satan's challenge has merit. Thus, God agreed with Satan that until Job is put to the test, whether Job's faithfulness is genuine cannot be fully known. This is both because free actions that will be done in the future are unknowable even to God and because Job is a dynamic, living person who will create and declare whether he is faithful through his concrete lived experiences.

Job knows nothing of the contest between God and Satan. When he questions God why he has been put through such trials as physical pain caused by boils and losing his family, possessions, and friends, God does not explain that He is testing Job's loyalty. Rather, God reminds Job of how little he knows of God's purposes, including how little Job understands about the challenges that even God faces with His immense power. For example, despite that power, God struggles with the sea creatures Leviathan and Rahab that represent the chaos that constantly threaten to overwhelm the creation. God does not reveal the context of the tests that were designed to prove Job's trustworthiness and steadfast commitment notwithstanding any challenge that the Prosecutor (Satan) can dish out. The challenges that confront Job, by any measure, are extreme and seem impossible to fathom. Yet Job remains steadfast in his commitment to God. In the end, Job passes the test. (See Job 2:10–15.)

Job-like tests, however, seem to have little relevance to the radical evils that I have identified. While Job passes the test, what of his children who die as the result of a whirlwind so that Job can be tested? What are we to make of their interests? The story, of course, is silent, because it is Job that

God and Satan are focusing their efforts on to prove him one way or the other. But why are they any less important than Job? How could they justly be sacrificed for Job's test consistent with God's justice?

The reality of these kinds of evils is often starker. The heroes often do not appear to pass the test in real life. Like Job, my neighbor just a few doors away lost his wife and two children in a fire. He never recovered psychologically. He remarried and had a son, but he was paranoid and could not leave his family alone out of fear that they too would be randomly selected for death by some freak event. He worked from home and rarely left the house. He died of alcohol poisoning shortly after his son left to go to college. Was the fire, too, a Job-like test, or was it just a freak accident? We, of course, do not know. We do not know the details of the agreements and covenants before this life. We do not know God's mind and purposes. We do not know whether we even have the capacity to fathom the nature of God's plan and what He is up to. What we do know is that death, both our own and of our loved ones, could come at any time. We know that we have been called to love.

A theodicy must address the complete range of evils that we face, and not merely the "great men of history" approach taken so often in scriptural texts. Job's children, who are mere means in the story to move the plot along, are just as valuable to God—and to us—as Job is. People are more than mere plot points. Forfeiting their lives as a means to test Job seems to devalue them in a way that is truly immoral on its face. In fact, without more context, the bargain struck between God and Satan itself seems immoral. Who would want a friend like that—let alone a God? Thankfully, there is much greater context to make sense of these kinds of tests that mortality throws at us. This plan of agape theodicy focuses on God's purposes and our possibilities rather than on the limitations on God's power and knowledge. It focuses on seeing God's hand in all things and the love inherent in the world that surrounds us rather than the hostile tendencies of nature. It emphasizes the radical and voluntary nature of divine love that seeks to persuade us to return God's love with our own freely given love. It focuses on the extreme circumstances that are sometimes necessary to get us to pay attention to God and our duty to love one another.

We usually do not see what God is up to in our lives. The evils that confront us seem overwhelming and out of context if the world were truly organized by a loving God to serve us. In a way similar to the story of Job, the agape theodicy begins by placing our story in a critical context that begins before this life. It suggests that there are details to which we are not privy as mortals. We do not remember because we have been caused to forget the details of the eternal prologue (see I Cor. 13:12). This prologue is essential context to make sense of our experiences of evil. Unless the experiences of God's glory and goodness were erased from our immediate recall, it would be impossible to put us to the test to prove our faithfulness and to create the possibility of the kind of relationship sought by God.

We are in a position somewhat like the Karate Kid, who is given the task to wash the car and paint the fence by his mentor, Mr. Miyagi. In the story, Mr. Miyagi instructs him to wash the car using specific round-about arm movements: "Wax on, wax off." After a full day of these movements, he is exhausted but sticks with it simply because he trusts Mr. Miyagi to teach him karate at some later time. The next day Mr. Miyagi instructs the Karate Kid to paint the fence using exact arm and wrist movements: "Up, down." The Karate Kid thinks Mr. Miyagi is merely exploiting him to do these meaningless tasks so that Mr. Miyagi can get free labor to wash his cars and paint his fence. He does not see the meaning of the apparently pointless gestures of "wax on, wax off," and "up, down." It is only later that "Daniel-san" learns what his experiences have taught him. Until then, he does not see that he is being taught the most basic moves of karate. To top it off, Mr. Miyagi gives him the car he worked so hard to wax—but certainly not hard enough to buy the car. In an analogous way, we are placed in circumstances with challenges that seem pointless and unjust, but it is only later, perhaps much later, that we realize that these experiences taught us valuable lessons.

The Nature of God's Providence

On the view that I have elucidated in my prior works, God is not unilaterally responsible for the natural regularities that obtain in the natural world. God can determine whether the world is an ordered cosmos governed by natural regularities, but God cannot determine what the natural regularities shall be given that natural laws obtain. (I will use the term "God" to refer equivocally to the individual divine persons or to the Godhead or both.) I have adopted a particular view of natural laws that is characteristically Aristotelian in its assumptions about inherent basic power of natural realities. It may be called the agent-powers-liability view of natural laws. I adopt it because it seems to me to be the view that most naturally falls out of

Mormon commitments that (a) the world cleaves into things that act and things that are acted upon (2 Ne. 2:14–16); and (b) the most fundamental realities (intelligences) have their own basic physical powers to act and to be actuated when moved upon (i.e., they are not further analyzable and cannot be reduced to explanation by more basic levels of existence). For example, two atoms of hydrogen have a basic power to form a valence electron bond with an atom of oxygen to form a molecule of water. Two atoms of hydrogen isotopes have a power to fuse and release energy when in a certain proximity at a certain temperature. Such fusion occurs with regularity in all stars. These are regularities that are explained by the basic powers inherent given the natural kind of thing that hydrogen atoms just are. We cannot analyze these basic powers into yet more basic powers unless we somehow discover that such powers are explained by properties of quarks—in which case the most basic realities will simply be quarks and their powers will be most basic. I am going to explain my view of intelligences and natural laws as a prelude to defending the agape theodicy from objections.

The Nature of Intelligences

On the view presented here, there are two basic types of intelligences: (1) personal intelligences and (2) natural intelligences. Personal intelligences are those eternal sentient beings who have the ability to enter into loving interpersonal relations. This ability requires libertarian free will such that the intelligences can freely choose to accept or reject such relationships. Natural intelligences, on the other hand, express a "naturalistic causal propensity" when they act. This latter term requires some elucidation.

A natural causal propensity is a basic causal power to act in a way that is predictably regular. When natural intelligences act, they do so within a narrow range of behaviors and in a predictable manner that changes very little over time. All things (except perhaps the most basic realities, such as conserved mass of bayrons) decay over time and change their behavior to some degree. That all composed material things decay over time and that material states tend toward greater entropy over time is strong evidence that chaos is the natural state of matter and material states. However, the basic realities that form the world behave with consistent regularity over the spans of time.

Natural intelligences have basic natural causal powers defined by the kinds of things they are. It is a natural causal power of gold atoms to give rise to the properties of gold. Electrons have the basic natural propensity to orbit nuclei in various valances of atomic nucleuses. It is a natural propensity of hydrogen and oxygen atoms to be able to form molecular bonds and give rise to the properties of water when in molecular unity. There are deterministic natural tendencies to the extent that the actions of these basic realities are invariably regular and always follow the same predictable patterns of regularity with exact predictability. However, at a certain level—the quantum level—predictability becomes fuzzy, and there are degrees of freedom in describing how subatomic particles will act.

Personal intelligences, on the other hand, do not act with predictable regularity in the manner described of a natural causal tendency. Joseph Smith taught that the most essential part of humans—the mind, soul, spirit, or intelligence—is uncreated: "Man was also in the beginning with God. Intelligence, or the light of truth, was not created or made, neither can it be" (D&C 93:29). In Joseph's thought, the term "intelligence" minimally refers to "truth" about what constitutes a person's individual essence. Such truth is independent of God's creative power. Thus, the concept of "intelligence" includes minimally what we today would call individual essences or *haecceities*.[1] Such truth or intelligence has an existence independent of God because it includes what is true of persons, given the fact that they are free to act for themselves. Joseph's revelation boldly asserts: "All truth is independent in that sphere in which God has placed it to act for itself, as all intelligence also; otherwise there is no existence. Behold, here is the agency of man" (vv. 30–31).

However, intelligence is not a mind-dependent concept of merely ideal possible persons as it is for Molinism; rather, intelligence is the defining property of actual entities that Joseph later called "intelligences." Individual intelligences exist necessarily in the same way that God's existence as an individual is naturally necessary:

> We say that God himself is a self-existing being. . . . Who told you that man does not exist in like manner upon the same principles? Man does exist upon the same principles. . . . The mind or the intelligence which man possesses is co-eternal with God himself. . . . There never was a time when there were not spirits; for they are co-eternal with our Father in heaven. . . . God

---

1. See Blake T. Ostler, "The Idea of Pre-Existence in the Development of Mormon Thought," 59–78.

never had the power to create the spirit of man at all. Intelligence is eternal and exists upon a self-existence principle. It is a spirit from age to age and there is no creation about it.[2]

Every individual person that can exist in mortality existed eternally prior to mortality as a personal intelligence. These intelligences exist independently of God's creative power because it is their nature to exist. It is fairly discernible from Joseph's sermons and writings that personal intelligences have the following properties: (1) they have delimited and stable personal identity; (2) they have a basic power to be self-determining and autonomous; (3) they are individuated in the sense that one could be "more intelligent than the other" (Abr. 3:18–19); (4) they have the capacity to advance through further organization and integration with material bodies[3]; (5) their individual enhancement and growth is not possible in the absence of moral opposition and genuine moral temptation; and (6) by freely entering into a loving relationship with God, it is the nature of personal intelligences that they can grow in light, truth, knowledge, and power until they enjoy the fullness of unity and glory that the Father, Son, and Holy Ghost share (D&C 132:20).[4]

Though eternal intelligences are not contingent and thus do not depend on God for their existence, there is a sense in Joseph's thought in which the *abilities* of intelligences depend on God. God's spirit or light that dwells in all realities "quickeneth your understandings . . . [and] giveth life to all things" (D&C 88:11–13). By this I understand that the ability of an intelligence to integrate its experience into a unified consciousness of experience seems to be dependent on God's sustaining power. Further, no growth of any kind would be possible for intelligences without God's active power to enhance and actualize the capacities inherent in each individual intelligence.

---

2. Joseph Smith Jr., *Teachings of the Prophet Joseph Smith*, 352–53. The amalgamated text states: "*Man existed in spirit;* the mind of man—the intelligent part—is as immortal as, and is coequal with, God Himself." See Stan Larson, "The King Follett Discourse—A Newly Amalgamated Text," 196.

3. Larson, 203

4. *Lectures on Faith*, 5:2–3

The Ontological Status of Natural Laws[5]

According to Joseph Smith, the most basic "elements" or constituents of matter are also uncreated and eternal. On the view that I present here, all material states are subject to God's power. The "light" of God proceeds from "God's presence to fill the immensity of space" and "is the law by which all things are governed, even the power of God" (D&C 88:12–14). It is an imminent power that is infused in all things to organize matter and give life to all things (vv. 7–10). God's immanent light is thus the co-source of natural laws. The "thingness" of organized material objects depends on God's creative power, for "that which is governed by law is preserved by law" (v. 34). Moreover, God has "given a law to all things by which they move" (v. 42). God's imminent power is the source of all order in the universe.

The natural state of matter is chaos. It is only when informed by God's creative power that order arises from chaos. In Doctrine and Covenants 88, Joseph Smith's revelation described that the natural bodies move according to laws that define how the planets and stars will move. That there are natural laws at all is totally up to God. As the revelation states, God gives a law to all things by which they move with regular patterns of behavior. However, exactly *what* the natural laws will be is *not* totally up to God. On the view of agent causal powers and liabilities as the basis of natural law that I present, material states have certain capacities and natural inclinations that define how they will act. These powers are basic to the natural kind that a basic reality just is. There are certain essential properties that define what causal powers can be exerted by underlying material states.

Perhaps an analogy can help to explain this view of natural laws and their relation to God. Both hydrogen and oxygen may be organized in many different ways, but whenever they are organized as H_2O they exhibit their causal power to produce the properties of water. Moreover, water is essentially H_2O. If something exhibited properties of water but did not consist of H_2O, it would not be water. Similarly, when protons and neutrons are organized having a certain proper atomic number, their causal powers *always* produce the same element. For instance, consider the properties of gold (Au): atomic number=79; atomic mass=196.96655 amu; number of protons/

---

5. I have described my view of natural laws more fully in Blake T. Ostler, *Exploring Mormon Thought: The Attributes of God*, ch. 4.

neutrons = 79; number of neutrons = 118; density= 293 K: 19.32 g/cm3). *That the constituents of matter are organized at all is due to God's power; that such constituent parts have the causal powers they do, which result in particular elements and compounds, is due to the properties of the eternal constituents.* That water is organized depends *both* on God's concurring power or light given to the atoms of hydrogen and oxygen to exercise their power of covalent bonding *and* also on the basic natural powers of hydrogen and oxygen to bond in molecular union.

God has the power to organize matter in any way that is possible for the matter to be organized. He has this power because the intelligences that constitute matter trust God's word unconditionally. Thus, God can produce any results that are possible given the potential properties arising from the innumerable permutations of the most basic material constituents. Joseph Smith's writings presuppose that God cannot bring about natural laws that are contrary to the natural capacities of these material states. For example, although logically possible, Joseph asserted that it is impossible for God to create out of nothing the most basic constituents of matter. Further, God could not create matter that is not located in space-time (D&C 88:36–37). What is physically possible is not limited solely by logical possibility but also by what is *nomologically* possible (*nomos* is Greek for "law"). For example, it may be impossible for God to create matter in a closed system such that entropy does not increase when energy is expended. It is impossible for God to annihilate mass-energy. Neither of these acts is logically contradictory in first order logic, and thus they are logically possible acts. However, they are neither physically nor nomologically possible.

Thus, the most reasonable resolution of Joseph Smith's view is that he conceived of natural laws as a combination of the energy or power to move and act originating with God, and the capacities to move and act as originating with the eternal constituents of matter. Whether that was his view or not, what I propose is a form of divine concurrence—any basic act of a given reality (say an organic molecule) requires God's concurring power to realize its natural propensity to act. The ways in which the law-like natural tendencies of material states are manifested depends on the causal powers of the material states and the various ways it is nomologically possible for them to be organized. God's power is the source of order, but God is not a complete determiner of what that order shall be. The power deriving from God to organize material states is analogous to the electricity necessary to power a computer. The software that organizes data is analogous to God's will as to how things shall be organized. The material state consisting of eternal matter is like the hardware of a computer that defines its capacities to run the software. Not even God could run software on a Mack truck. The nature of the basic realities that make up the constituents of a Mack truck do not have the natural capacity to run software.

God can neither have water that is not H_2O nor H_2O that is not water. God cannot have two atoms of oxygen that are covalently bonded with an atom of carbon that do not have the deterministic natural propensity to form carbon dioxide. However, God could prevent carbon from bonding covalently with oxygen to form carbon dioxide by not lending his concurrence to the atoms to form the compound. God could prevent water from having its causal powers by choosing to not give his concurring power to hold it in an organized form. Thus, God has a form of coercive power with respect to natural intelligences. Natural intelligences are just the various most basic natural substances of the various natural kinds that actually obtain in our universe. God can act on natural substances to bring about all of the results possible given the natural causal powers of the constituents of the universe.

Thus, it is within God's power to "suspend" or "revoke" the natural laws by ceasing to lend his organizing concurrent power to material states. However, the result would not be for matter to suddenly have different capacities or for there to be different natural laws; rather, in the absence of God's sustaining power the universe consumes itself in entropy and the cosmos is reduced to chaos. However, it must also be emphasized that organization of material states adds more than the mere sum of the parts. What material states are possible for God to organize is not limited to mere permutations of matter, because organization leads to new capacities on a new level of existence. Water looks and acts nothing like its constituent parts of hydrogen and oxygen and has a life sustaining power that neither of them alone has. The possibilities of complexity are literally unlimited. The sheer possibilities of complexity arising, for instance, from the DNA strands suggest that matter is infinitely permeable. Joseph Smith's revelation recognized that new levels of organization lead to capacities that are hardly imaginable to human beings: "For man is spirit. The elements are eternal, and spirit and element inseparably connected to receive a fullness of joy; and when separated cannot receive fullness of joy" (D&C 93:33–34).

There are also at least two ways to construe the time intervals in which God can bring about states of affairs. In other words, there are two ways as to how quickly God can realize his purposes through concurring power in relation to organizing the matter in the world. In the "quick results" interpretation God can instantaneously bring about the desired causal results. God grants concurring power to atoms of hydrogen in the vicinity of atoms of oxygen, and they immediately interact to bring about water. If God withdraws that concurring power, the atoms of hydrogen and oxygen would immediately cease to be water because the atoms of hydrogen and oxygen will not bond to form water.

The "slow burn" interpretation, in contrast, provides that God takes time to achieve his purposes. For example, when God withdraws concurring power to atoms of hydrogen and oxygen, they decay over time to revert back to atoms of hydrogen and oxygen that are not in a molecular bond. The disintegration of the atoms is subject to the laws of entropy in their increasing disorder over time. When God grants concurring power to atoms to enter into bonds or express their natural causal propensities, it takes time for the results to be realized. Thus, God's organizing power may require vast amounts of time to be realized. God's power may require vast amounts of time of progressive evolution to bring about a DNA strand that expresses the properties of complex life. As a result, the slow burn view is much more like the process view with respect to God's interaction with the natural world. It is also much more consonant with the theory of evolution. Further, the slow burn model is really an assessment of how long it takes, given the natural laws that actually obtain, for natural processes to transpire. However, the agape theodicy utilizes both models depending on the nature of the realities on which God acts.

Because I have already discussed a process theodicy, I will not elucidate this view further and will assume that God may at times have quick results power with respect to higher order realities like humans and animals that have more developed central nervous systems and slow burn power with respect to many other natural processes in the universe. God at times has quick burn power with respect to personal intelligences—but only if they freely cooperate. God has both quick results and slow burn power with respect to natural intelligences to the extent that they cooperate. How much time is necessary to achieve God's purposes depends on the preexisting configurations and capacities of the material constituents, given their natural propensities. However, over time natural intelligences are much more predictable and subject to divine purposes and power because they act of a deterministic natural propensity.

God's Providential Power and Knowledge

The most common objection to a resolution to the problem of evil that proposes any limitation to God's power is that such a God simply lacks enough power to evoke awe and worship. However, some limitations on divine power are necessary to avoid logical inconsistencies. God does not require power to do the following to be maximally powerful: (a) be able to bring about the acts of free agents; (b) do anything inconsistent with the divine attributes; or (c) have power to alter what has occurred in the past. There is still need, though, for a theodicy to explain why God allows events to occur that He has sufficient power to prevent. Thus, it must be stressed that the ontological commitments of the agape theodicy do not simply dissolve the problem of evil as in a finitist theology. However, the objection that these ontological commitments limit God too much dissolves upon closer examination.

God's Power. Given Joseph Smith's ontological commitments, the maximum possible power consists in all the power that it is possible for any agency having God's attributes to possess that is compossible with the existence of a physical world, including free persons who have actually existed for eternity. It is metaphysically impossible that any single agency possess greater power. Indeed, it is even impossible for the divine persons acting individually to contest the almighty power of the Godhead, because the individual divine persons are not almighty unless they act in perfect and loving unison.[6]

The view that I propose affirms that God possesses the maximum amount of power it is possible for any single agency to possess. God's Maximal Power (MP) can be defined as follows:

> (MP) An agent A is maximally powerful at a time T if and only if A is unilaterally able at a time T to bring about any state of affairs SA such that: (a) SA does not entail that "A does not bring about SA at T;" (b) SA is compossible with all events that preceded T in time in the actual world up to T; and (c) God's power ranges over the maximum range of states of affairs possible that compossible with (a) and (b).

---

6. See Blake T. Ostler, *Exploring Mormon Thought: Of God and Gods,* 311–13.

There are four points that I want to emphasize about this notion of maximal power. First, it is impossible that any single agency existing within an actual world having a real history could have greater power. By a "world having a real history," I simply mean one in which the past has occurred, the present is occurring, and the future does not yet exist. In other words, this view assumes the A-theory of time so that what is open to divine power to bring about is time indexed.[7] Given this notion of reality, what is past is now fixed in the sense of temporal necessity. For instance, not even God can now bring it about that the World Trade Center was not attacked on September 11, 2001. God could have prevented such events prior to and on that date, but He cannot do so now.

Second, maximal power is consistent with the eternally past existence of the constituents of mass-energy and primordial intelligences. That God cannot create mass-energy *ex nihilo* does not entail that God is not maximally powerful. The fact that the constituents of mass-energy and intelligences are not created is consistent with *God's being able at a time T to bring about any state of affairs compossible with all prior events that occurred in the actual world up to T.* Because the existence of intelligences and mass-energy is always prior to any act by God, they are fixed realities that need not be within the scope of God's power to bring about. Thus, God's maximal power need not include the power to create mass-energy or intelligences *ex nihilo*.

It is true that if God creates *ex nihilo*, then His power *initially* ranges over a greater multitude of possibilities. However, that God cannot bring about just any temporally fixed state of affairs after a certain time cannot count against His power or His greatness. In the moment after creation, the range of possibilities open to God's power were reduced to those compossible with the events that had already occurred in the world He had created. Thus, in the moment after creation, God had fewer possibilities open to His power than before. That God creates a world with a fixed past history cannot count against His greatness; indeed, it should count in favor of His greatness. Further, it seems that any consistent account of divine power would have to agree that God has fewer options open to His divine power

---

7. The problem of competing omnipotent beings cannot arise given this position because divine power is necessarily a single agency arising from the loving union of the separate divine persons. I discuss the A-theory of time in Ostler, *The Attributes of God*, 142–43; 320–24; 349; 357.

after He creates persons having free will than if He creates persons without free will. Virtually all human actions are within God's control if He refrains from creating free creatures. However, God is not less worthy if He creates free persons rather than mere automata. On the contrary, God's willingness to take risks inherent in the nature of love by creating a world in which persons are free seems to be a source of divine greatness. God is not less ultimate, less worthy, or less than the Greatest Conceivable Being simply because He creates a world having a genuine history.

Further, judgments that compare what is possible across various ontological systems are precarious at best. For example, the power of God as conceived by Alvin Plantinga ranges over fewer possibilities than that conceived by Thomas Aquinas. Plantinga's God creates quasi *ex nihilo* in the sense that He does not bring about either the individual essences or the properties included in such individual essences. He merely instantiates such properties that "exist" in all possible worlds independently of His creative power. However, given the Thomist view, God brings about the kinds and essences of individuals.[8] Yet any assertion that the Thomist God is therefore a greater being than that of Plantinga's is simply comparing incommensurate systems. On Plantinga's view, creation of essences is not possible and is inconsistent with significant freedom of creatures. Similarly, any assertion that a god who creates *ex nihilo* is greater than the God revealed by Joseph Smith assumes fallaciously that God is greater simply because His power ranges over a greater number of possibilities. On Joseph Smith's view, creation *ex nihilo* of mass-energy and intelligences is not truly possible.

Third, this notion of maximal power is essentially identical to definitions of God's power given by traditional theologians who have sought to eradicate inconsistencies in the concept of omnipotence.[9] The *concept* of God's power implicitly proposed by Joseph Smith is just as robust and complete as any coherent idea of the greatest possible power.

Finally, this view of God's power appropriately places the emphasis on God's love and purposes for Him being an adequate object of worship and source of salvation—and not on merely unlimited power *per se*. The *Lectures*

---

8. See James Ross, "God, Creator of Kinds and Possibilities," 315–34.
9. See Thomas P. Flint and Alfred Freddoso, "*Maximal Power*," 81–113; Edward Wierenga, *The Nature of God. An Inquiry Into Divine Attributes*, 28–29; George Mavrodes, "Defining Omnipotence," 191–202.

on Faith assert: "God had power over all things, and was able by His power, to control all things, and thereby deliver His creatures who put their trust in Him, from the power of all beings that might seek their destruction."[10] God need only possess power and knowledge sufficient to ensure the realization of His purposes. God's maximal power certainly exceeds this minimal requirement, but He is not thereby a more adequate object of faith.

God's Providential Knowledge. Like the process and finitist views that I have previously outlined, the agape theodicy posits that God is all-knowing in the sense that God knows all that exists but does not have foreknowledge of future contingencies such as free acts. I suggest that God's knowledge is providential in that God can use His knowledge to ensure the realization of His purposes in the following ways:

1. God is all-knowing in the sense that, for any state of affairs (SA), if SA is or has been actual, then God knows that SA; if SA is possible in the future, then God knows now the present objective probability of SA, if any.
2. God knows now what His purposes are and that He will achieve them.
3. God knows now how He will respond to whichever contingent states of affairs occur to ensure the realization of his purposes.
4. God does not know now precisely which contingent possibility will be chosen or become actual.

This notion of God's contingent knowledge of all possibilities entails that God knows all things now and possibly existing (1, 2). It suggests that God knows all possible avenues of choices and their present probability of becoming actual (1, 3) and, coupled with the idea of maximal power, entails that God's plans and declarations of future events will be realized (3, 4). The best statement of this notion of providence is expressed by Nephi in the Book of Mormon: "But the Lord knoweth all things from the beginning; wherefore, he prepareth a way to accomplish his works among the children of men; for behold, *he hath power unto the fulfilling of all his words*" (1 Ne. 9:6). In other words, God's knowledge that He will realize the fulfillment of His plan is assured because of His power to fulfill His words rather than His knowledge of what will occur alone.

---

10. *Lectures on Faith*, 4:12.

A RELATIONAL AGAPE THEODICY

The Moments of God's Causal Relation to the Universe

God's Moment in Relation to the Universe	God Before the Universe	God with the Universe	God After the Universe
God's Relation to Natural Law	God concurs with the eternal natural propensities of eternal realities	God influences momentary occurrences to lure order	God uses existing natural laws to bring about order
God's Knowledge	God knows all that has been, all that exists now, and anything determined to come and the present probability of future contingents	God knows all that has been and exists presently and present tendencies into the future	God knows what has been since obtaining divine status, all that is available to know now given natural laws, and what can be predicted given existing causal circumstances
God's Presence	God is immanently present to all realities and can act on all things immediately	God is present to all realities as initial aim and immanent presence	God is present to parts of the universe accessible by existing natural laws
God's Relation to Time	God is omnitemporal and occupies all inertial frames of reference	God is concurrent with each temporal moment	God is bound by a particular inertial frame of reference
God's Relation to gods	The Father is the one God, Father of the council of gods and one in the Son and Holy Ghost	Each divine person is immanently present in each distinct divine person	There are three distinct divine personages who agree with each other in purpose
God's Mode of Creation	God creates by organizing all that exists by acting on all realities as immanent presence	God creates by organizing events through luring them to adopt his purposes	God organizes some regions of matter by using natural laws

Nevertheless, given God's vast power and knowledge, this view confronts the problem of evil in a way that the other views of Mormon thought do not. The problem of evil is not logically dissolved by this view. God has sufficient power and knowledge to prevent the kidnapping and murder of a three-year-old girl, the death of my friend's daughter by the car that rolled over her, and the billions of casualties from smallpox. God can immediately act decisively at will at any place. Thus, this view requires a theodicy to explain how it is possible that God is good notwithstanding permission of such radical evils. However, it also provides considerable resources for a theodicy that are not available in the tradition.

The theodicy that I present is a pedagogical explanation—one that focuses on the person-centered goodness of learning from immediate experience. By "person-centered," I mean that its primary concern is not cosmic harmony or the goodness of some possible world overall as its sole or even primary focus of explanation; rather, the focus is on the goodness of learning from one's own personal experience what cannot be learned or appreciated in any other way. While the view I have presented entails that God has power to prevent many of the radical evils that in fact occur (though not all), it also entails that God has sufficient power to organize the world to function to serve His purposes. The primary importance of this view of providence is that God can plan general strategies for each person to confront the types of challenges that can be useful to foster our growth. Although not all evils can simply be eliminated, God can plan our mortal probation so that good can be brought out of evil, and He can ensure that we will encounter the challenges and experiences that give us the opportunity to learn the lessons we came here to learn.

The Nature of the Challenge of Learning to Love.

The primary focus of the agape theodicy is twofold: (1) loving relationships of fellowship must be freely chosen and thus must also entail the possibility of rejecting such loving fellowship; and (2) we learn to love by facing challenges that call for us to be deeply, morally responsible for each other, face challenges that call for compassion from us, and develop our own souls to grow in greater light toward deification. To better understand this, a relationship of fellowship must first be distinguished from other kinds of relationships. According to the Mormon revelation, we all existed in a filial relationship with God prior to this life (Abr. 3:18–25). Such filial relationships were not freely chosen. Further, filial relationships are not necessarily loving relationships—for example, one could be a son or daughter without loving his or her mother or father. Filial relationships are relations of status—they are causal relationships that obtain without the consent of the son or daughter. However, a relationship of fellowship or *agape* is different. Such relationships are not causal in nature, do not rely upon status, and are mutually chosen. The challenge of this life is not to be in filial relationship with God—we have that status just by being children of God. The challenge is to be fit for a relationship of fellowship such that we can fully share the indwelling glory of God. To be fit for that relationship, we must abide the law of love toward which all of the commandments aim. All of the commandments are given as a means to teach us how to love one another. However, such learning is experiential in nature. We do not learn to love by mastering coursework or memorizing studies. The experiential knowledge of learning to love issues from a virtuous character that is forged in concrete circumstances of free choices made in the face of genuine challenges. The way we respond to the challenges of our lives makes of us the persons that we are.

The challenge of learning to love requires that we be deeply, morally responsible for each other. In other words, we must have personal accountability for each other in the sense that we have sufficient power to do great good for each other out of our love. However, the power to do good for each other entails the correlative power to do great harm to each other as well. It could not be the case that I have sufficient physical power to lift someone off of the ground with my arms without the correlative power to punch them in the face. In addition, to be deeply, morally responsible is to be personally accountable for another in the sense that I am praiseworthy for doing great good to someone and blameworthy for doing great harm to them. Personal accountability for our conduct is essential to such loving, interpersonal relationships.

In Mormon thought, this notion of personal accountability is expressed by the teaching that the degree of light that characterizes our being is correlative of our conduct. The nature of the experiential learning process requires us to forge a certain way of being that abides a law of a degree of divine light. Those who abide a celestial law—the way of being that demonstrates divine love for one another—are characterized by, given life from, and participate in a celestial glory. Those who abide a terrestrial law—a way of being that is honorable but does not enjoy divine perfection—are characterized by, receive life from, and participate in a terrestrial glory. So, also, for the telestial glory—those who are liars, whoremongers, adulterers, thieves or, in other words, who fail to learn the ways of being that define loving conduct toward one another (D&C 88:21–31). Our degree of participation in the divine light or glory is correlative of the degree to which we learn to love each other. Individual acts become habits, habits become character, character becomes our way of being in the world, and our way of being in the world becomes the degree to which we participate in the light of divine glory.

However, those who are incapable of ordering their conduct to conform to moral laws are not morally accountable. In Mormon thought, all those who are unable to get started on the process of developing a moral character in this life because they were born with severe mental disabilities or became cognitively disabled before the age of accountability are covered by the Atonement from the effects of sin (2 Ne. 9:25–26; Mosiah 3:16). They are already celestial beings. So how could there be a person-centered goodness for them by which they benefit from their mortal experience in terms of this theodicy? This theodicy suggests that they are angels who have consented to become mortal so that they may teach us to love by giving us the opportunity to serve them and thus to be served by them. Many of these so-called disabled are able to demonstrate and teach us love as or more effectively than any so-called whole person.

Before getting started on the harder issues, it is also essential to grasp the nature of the experiential learning process. It is often the case that we do not learn from the first opportunity that experience affords us to learn a lesson. This theodicy suggests that the world has been ordered in such a way as to serve us to learn when we do not get the lessons. I do not want to get into pop psychology, but it is important to have some idea as to how the process of learning to love works pragmatically. I suggest that there are (basically) two ways to learn lessons from experience: the easy way and the hard way. I do not know how to define these two ways with precision, but I suggest that our own experience is a worthy guide in this matter. Learning the easy way means that we get the lessons our experience affords us without the necessity of pain or suffering. Learning the hard way is learning through pain and suffering.

I am going to give an example that I believe can be generalized. Often, as we grow from childhood to adulthood, we develop particular "issues" that plague us in our relationships on a continual basis. Take, for example, the issue of attempting to control others in relationships so that we do not get emotionally hurt like we have in the past. Those who are controlling will have difficult relationships with others because no one likes being on the opposite end of that control. If one does not learn to overcome the tendency to control others, it is very likely that the relationships in their lives will be damaged or destroyed on an ongoing basis until the controller learns to let go and let it be. The controller may simply learn from a trusted friend or family member who says something along the lines of: "I don't like the way you treat me. Let me decide for myself." However, if the lesson is not learned, the next time the lesson comes around, in order for the controller to get it when receiving such milder feedback did not work before, the means of teaching may need to be more insistent. Perhaps the controller will be yelled at forcefully, "Leave me alone." If not learned, then the next time perhaps a knock to the head may be more effective. If counseling does not teach the lesson, perhaps going through a painful divorce will. In any event, if a lesser means will not suffice to teach the lesson, then a more forceful means may be the only way to get the lesson. I suggest that the world functions in such a way that our opportunities to learn lessons become more insistent and more forceful over time if we fail to learn them the easy way.

I also suggest that emotional pain, like physical pain, can be an important teacher. If we learn the lessons of love, then the interpersonal pain of alienation, separation, loneliness, and abandonment will cease. Some modicum of physical pain is essential to function in the natural environment in which we live. Those persons who suffer from congenital analgesia (who literally cannot feel physical pain) are unable to protect their bodies from injury because they do not receive the feedback necessary to avoid injury. Now, it seems clear to me that there is excessive pain—pain which does not stop when the pain has served its purpose to detect the danger, disease, or infection. However, some pain is essential to human survival. Similarly, the purpose of emotional pain is to alert us to issues about ourselves that must be addressed to abide in loving and intimate relationships.

Thus, I suggest that the world has been ordered to teach us to love one another. It then functions similarly to the movie *Groundhog Day*. There, self-absorbed and cantankerous TV meteorologist Phil Connors (Bill Murray), news producer Rita (Andie MacDowell), and cameraman Larry (Chris Elliott) travel to Punxsutawney, Pennsylvania, to cover the annual

February 2 Groundhog Day festivities for their Pittsburgh television station. Having grown bored of this assignment, Phil grudgingly gives his report and attempts to return to Pittsburgh when a snowstorm shuts down the roads. He and his team are forced to return to Punxsutawney and stay in town overnight, where instead of waking up the next morning, Phil wakes up to find that he is stuck in an endless repetition of February 2. The day plays out precisely as the day before. No one else is aware of the time loop. At first he is confused, but when the phenomenon endlessly continues day after frustratingly same day, he decides to exploit the situation with no concern for longterm consequences: he learns secrets from the town's residents, seduces women, steals money, and generally acts out a morally depraved sequence of antics. Through all of this, his attempts to get closer to Rita repeatedly fail. He feigns love for her to seduce her, but he cannot quite get the relationship started with her.

Eventually, Phil becomes depressed and attempts increasingly desperate methods to end the time loop. He recounts offensive weather reports on the festival, abuses residents, and eventually kidnaps the groundhog. What can one do who is stuck in an endless repetition of life but kill himself? So he attempts suicide only to wake up and find that nothing has changed. He attempts increasingly creative ways to kill himself each successive same-day, but all are fruitless as he continues to find himself awaking at 6:00 a.m. on the morning of February 2.

Phil finally gives up and decides to learn more about Rita, building upon his knowledge of her and each of the town's people each day. He begins to use his increasingly vast experience of the events that follow every ever-repeated day to assist as many people around town as possible. He uses the time to learn, among other things, to play piano, ice sculpt, and speak French. Eventually, Phil learns to love the people in the town and uses his time to make his life and the lives of each of the town's people richer, safer, and more fulfilling. He befriends almost everyone he meets during the day, using his experiences to save lives, entertain, and make the day better for the townspeople—and to get closer to Rita. Finding himself increasingly fond of the town and its citizens, he gives an eloquent and genuine report of appreciation for Groundhog Day and the people who celebrate it in the small town. After the evening dance, Rita and Phil retire together to Phil's room, but now he is not interested in casual sex or seducing her. He truly cares for her and the town's people. He has learned to love them. He wakes the next morning and discovers that the time loop is broken; it is now February 3 and Rita is still with him. After going outside, Phil realizes that he loves Punxsatawney and its people, and he wants to live there and spend his life with the people that he once detested.

I have taken the time to recount this story because of its profound message: we do not get to move on until we learn to love. We are stuck in an endless repetition of our past, controlled by the same issues that have always plagued our lives until we repent, let go of the past, get over ourselves, and learn to love. A life lived as ever-repeating is so intolerable that only ending that life is bearable—and yet we cannot end it. We are eternally stuck with ourselves. The endless repetition is the denial of the Atonement—a never-ending attempt to fulfill our selfishness. Only when we have learned to love can we stop simply repeating the same mistakes that otherwise show up in our lives over and over again. Moreover, we have an eternity to work on ourselves and on our love of others. Life is set up to give us the opportunity to choose whether we will be bored and disgusted by those around us and totally engrossed in our own self-absorbed world. Such a life of endless repetition will eventually become unbearably painful, and the only way out will be to end it all. Yet even then we cannot escape ourselves. We do not get to move on to the next lesson, to the next glory, and to the profound joy of fulfilling and intimate relationship unless and until we learn that love is a choice and begin to freely choose to love others.

An Outline of the Agape Theodicy

Rather than focusing on the limitations on God's power, the agape theodicy focuses on the nature of God's purposes and the inherent potential that eternal intelligences have to share the fullness of God's glory. A basic outline of the most essential features of the agape theodicy includes:

1. The greatest good possible for us to realize given our eternal nature is to participate in the relationship of loving oneness of the Father, Son, and Holy Ghost, and thereby to be deified in sharing the fullness of God's glory, power, knowledge, and immanent presence.
2. The goodness of realizing the goal of deification by participating in divine love to be at-one in God is a towering good of superlative

value that justifies confronting any challenges and evils of a finite duration necessary to attain it.
3. Without further experiential knowledge, we were not able to love as required to be in this divine relationship because of our inherent self-absorbed alienation and self-deceived individuality.
4. A genuinely loving relationship, by its very nature, must be freely chosen in circumstances where rejection of the relationship is a live possibility.
5. To teach us how to love in a way that we are fit to be in this divine relationship, and to give us an opportunity to freely choose to be in the relationship of divine unity, God has instituted a plan to give us a probationary period during which we can freely choose to return God's love.
6. As a necessary condition to be fit to be in the divine relationship, we must learn from our own experience how to love. To learn from our experience how to love, we must be placed in an environment where we can learn by:
    a. Being placed at an epistemic distance from God (where His power and glory are not readily obvious, and the world can be interpreted as if God does not exist) so that we can freely choose to love God;
    b. Being deeply, morally responsible for others in the sense that we can do both great good and great evil to others for which we are accountable;
    c. Being confronted by others who are challenging and difficult for us to love, including enemies;
    d. Being in a natural environment where bad things can happen to good people, because if calamity befell only evil people we would inevitably be seeking reward and avoiding penalties rather than making genuine, moral choices;
    e. Being given the opportunity to experience godlike powers by being united as one-flesh with a spouse to create children in our own likeness and image or to adopt children who mimic us and thereby reflect back to us our issues, behaviors, shortcomings, and selfishness and who are yet prone to forgive and love us;

f. Being placed in a probationary environment where, unlike eternal duration of existence, there is urgency to choose because death could occur unexpectedly at any time;
   g. Being placed in an environment where there are natural regularities so that physical life is possible and our actions have predictable consequences from which we can learn; and
   h. Being placed in an environment where soul-making and moral development are possible because the natural regularities cause real challenges and dangers that call us to learn to be compassionate and charitable in response to the possibilities of many kinds of diseases, accidents, and disasters and the accompanying pain and suffering of others.
7. God has instituted a rescue plan to overcome our separation and alienation by both becoming mortal to demonstrate divine love through His life and suffering and becoming at-one with us if we are willing to soften our hearts to let Him enter into our lives as a shared life.
8. God has given us an instrument that vibrates in knowing response at the core of our being to subtly detect His loving overtures and spirit if we are willing to soften our hearts—but which can also be disregarded or explained away if one chooses to have a hard heart.
9. God obtained the prior consent of those personal intelligences or spirits who were willing to confront the dangers of mortal life and devised a plan to ensure that each does not suffer without some potential redeeming purpose as follows:
   a. God presented his plan of agape to the personal intelligences and, after explaining the kinds of potential blessings, challenges, risks, dangers, and evils attendant such an endeavor, God gave each the choice whether to confront the physical world with its inherent dangers.
   b. All persons who have ever been mortal freely consented to confront the kinds of conditions presented by mortality; however, those who freely chose not to confront the challenges of this life were permitted to remain as they were at that stage of their progression but without opportunity for further progress.
   c. God promised each who chose to confront these conditions as a necessary means of moving forward in relationship and

progressing toward deification that they would be ensured a genuine chance to learn the lessons they would come to mortality to learn, but none would be coerced to learn, and whether the lessons would be learned in the opportunity given remains up to each.

d. Some of the intelligences had already progressed before this life to the point that all that was needed from mortal experience to be fit for a fullness of celestial glory is to obtain a mortal body that could be glorified in resurrection in order to: (i) gain power over unembodied spirits; and (ii) gain the capacity to access the physical world through bodily senses.

e. Those who had already progressed to celestial glory before this life are fully served by mortal life even if they die in infancy.

f. Once a person has had sufficient opportunity to learn what each came to this mortal life to accomplish or learn, death can occur at any time as a matter of chance—where "chance" means that their deaths are not planned, the timing and means of death are without particular significance, it serves no one's end, and it might very well have been otherwise; thus if someone asks, "Why did that happen?" the appropriate answer is "There is no particular reason, it just happened."

g. Knowing that morally significant free will means that persons must be allowed to actually choose to do evil acts that could harm others, and knowing also that learning compassion requires that there are conditions that call for compassion and charity, some pre-mortal personal intelligences who were willing volunteered and were given the opportunity to express their love for others by consenting to be subjected to pain, suffering, and injustices as a means of providing an occasion for others to potentially learn from these experiences of evil.

h. If a personal intelligence did not consent to suffer evils that do not have the potential to benefit them personally to learn from their own experiences, then, to the extent that He could, God ensured that they would not be subjected to such evils through miraculous intervention.

i. God ensured that we would have no recollection of these agreements and consents, and thus we do not know who among us

are angels of mercy who have agreed to serve us with such love that they are willing to be subjected to suffering and injustice at our hands, if necessary, to give us the opportunity to potentially learn unconditional love from such experience if we so choose.
10. The process of growing into God's likeness so that we have the capacity to love as God loves has been ongoing for eternity and will continue after this life in an eternal progression into new horizons and opportunities to learn from our experiences—just as God does.

9

THE PLAN OF AGAPE

In Mormon thought, evil potentially serves us to grow and learn. We all could have remained in a pain-free environment without any natural evils. We could have remained in an arena of limited freedom to do evil given the obviousness of God's existence. However, we freely chose to confront this world knowing that it presented the possibilities for choices between good and evil and that sometimes evil may actually be chosen. We chose this life knowing that the natural world was designed to stretch us beyond anything we had previously experienced. (See Abr. 3:25–28.) Indeed, I suggest that there is no growth inside the comfort zone and that only by being stretched beyond what we are comfortable with are we really able to learn from our experiences. The evils we encounter are not merely uncomfortable; they can be gut-wrenching and sometimes body- and soul-destroying. Yet we chose this life because we knew that it was necessary to our progression. We desired the enhanced capacities to experience through the senses of a mortal body, to learn from concrete experiences, and to stretch beyond where we were.

God's plan of agape entails the potential of bringing good out of evil as a means to foster our progression. This view of God's plan is expressly elucidated in Mormon scripture. According to the Book of Moses, Satan proposed a plan that would have avoided all moral evil while allowing us to become mortal. However, to realize the pain-free world without evil, it would have been necessary to override every evil decision that would be freely made: "Satan sought to destroy the agency of man, which I the Lord God, had given him" (Moses 4:3), and a revelation to Joseph Smith revealed that a significant portion of the pre-mortal spirits chose not to confront this life (D&C 29:36). This same revelation also revealed the irony that resulted when God beat Satan at his own game. Satan sought to destroy the agency of humans in order to avoid the possibility of moral evils. Ironically, God turned Satan's desire to destroy our agency into the very means by which morally significant agency is made possible: "And it must needs be that the devil should tempt the children of men, or they could not be agents unto themselves; for if they never should have known the bitter they could not know the sweet" (v. 39). Thus, God created this world as a space to choose to enter into a relationship with Him by granting us the opportunity to experience "opposition in all things" (2 Ne. 2:11). The challenges and temptations of this life represented by Satan provide the opposition necessary to make agency possible and to promote our growth in the eternal process of soul-making.

The *felix culpa* (the "happy fall") theme is expressed clearly in the Book of Moses:

> And in that day Adam blessed God and was filled, and began to prophesy concerning all the families of the earth, saying: Blessed be the name of God, for because of my transgression my eyes are opened, and in this life I shall have joy, and again in the flesh I shall see God. And Eve, his wife, heard all these things and was glad, saying: Were it not for our transgression we never should have had seed, and never should have known good and evil, and the joy of our redemption, and the eternal life which God giveth unto all the obedient. (5:10–11)

Mortal experience opens our eyes to the joy of life. Mortal life gives an opportunity to have children who are begotten in our own likeness and image: "And Adam lived an hundred and thirty years, and begat a son in his own likeness, and after his image; and called his name Seth" (Gen 5:3)—just as we are begotten in God's own likeness and image (1:26–27). The power to beget life is a godlike power of creation. The opportunity to learn to love from our children is perhaps unparalleled by any other. In their brutal honesty, our children provide feedback to us about every limitation and shortcoming we have. I venture that our children are our greatest teachers. Nothing can bring us nearer to divinity than parenthood—and nothing can try us more and expose us to greater risk of heartache than our own children. Too often the value that children have to us as our teachers is overlooked in the context of theodicy. Of course, not all have the experience of being a parent. However, for those who choose to take on the challenge of being a father or a mother, the opportunities to learn from such experiences give a glimpse into both the depth of divine love and the width of the most tormenting hell. Family life can give us a foretaste of the eternal bonds of love that characterize those who participate fully in the divine nature.

The agape theodicy is also evident in the story of Adam and Eve as it is retold in Mormon scripture. Adam and Eve do not fall because they are overwhelmed by temptation; rather, they freely choose this mortal life over a life of innocence in paradise because it is a necessary means for them to learn from their own experience to appreciate the good by confronting evil. They thus can become as the gods by learning to distinguish the good from the evil. They can only learn to appreciate and prize the beauty and sweetness of life by confronting its occasional ugliness and the bitterness. The challenges and evils that they will confront are designed to serve their interests because the entire world has been created for their sake. As Lehi explained,

> For it must needs be, that there is an opposition in all things. If not so, my firstborn in the wilderness, righteousness could not be brought to pass, neither wickedness, neither holiness nor misery, neither good nor bad. . . . Wherefore, it must needs have been created for a thing of naught; wherefore there would have been no purpose in the end of its creation. Wherefore, this thing must needs destroy the wisdom of God and his eternal purposes, and also the power, and the mercy, and the justice of God, . . .
>
> And now, behold, if Adam had not transgressed he would not have fallen, but he would have remained in the garden of Eden. And all things which were created must have remained in the same state in which they were after they were created; and they must have remained forever, and had no end. And they would have had no children; wherefore they would have remained in a state of innocence, having no joy, for they knew no misery; doing no good, for they knew no sin. (2 Ne. 2:11–12; 22–23)

Lehi claimed that the entire purpose of this mortal probation would have been destroyed if there were no challenges brought on by the possibility for evil. There could have been no growth without the engine of evil to provide the challenges to move creation forward. Everything would have remained static without the progress that is made possible by confronting real evils in concrete situations. There would have been no good because there would not have been even the possibility of moral agency.

A similar point is made in the Book of Moses, where God tells Adam, "Inasmuch as thy children are conceived in sin, even so when they begin to grow up, sin conceiveth in their hearts, and they taste the bitter, that they may know to prize the good" (Moses 6:55). The point is that tasting the bitterness of evil in the world affords us an opportunity to learn to prize what otherwise we could not appreciate. Moreover, there is also an ontological dimension to "opposition in all things" (2 Ne. 2:11) in addition to the epistemological dimension. There are virtues that require opposition in order to be realized. Lehi argued that God's purpose in creating humankind was to make it possible for us to know joy: "Adam fell that man might be; and men are, that they might have joy" (v. 25). As a condition to experiencing this joy, it is necessary to be able to choose between good and evil and to experience both bitter and sweet. While it is neither necessary to be unkind in order to be kind, nor necessary that we must do evil in order to be good, it is necessary to have genuine choices among good and evil alternatives to be free in a morally significant sense. God did not ordain or plan the actual moral evils that we freely do; he did, however, ordain a plan that made it possible for us to choose to do moral evils. Indeed, F. R. Tennant has argued that our concept of "good" has meaning only when related to concepts such as temptation, courage, and compassion, which require a corresponding opportunity to succumb to temptation, act cowardly, and be self-absorbed.[1]

It is significant that Lehi's discussion of opposition in all things occurs in the context of free will as a necessary condition to allow individuals to be agents who can choose for themselves. The point of opposition in all things is not that we must be evil to be good; rather, it is that in order to be moral agents in any significant sense we must be capable of choosing between good and evil. Indeed, Lehi does not say that we must *do* both good *and* evil; he says that we must *distinguish* good *from* evil: "And the Messiah cometh in the fulness of time, that he may redeem the children of men from the fall. And because that they are redeemed from the fall they have become free forever, *knowing good from evil*; to act for themselves and not to be acted upon" (2 Ne. 2:26). To be free in a morally significant sense, we must be able to discern the difference between good and evil and be able to act for ourselves as self-determining agents. Thus, it is not the *actuality* of evil that is necessary but the *possibility* that persons can make significant choices. If we would all freely choose to learn to love the easy way, without choosing to do evil, then such a result is possible and preferable to having to learn by confronting evil. Further, whether we can learn without confronting greater

---

1. F. R. Tennant, *Philosophical Theology*, 1:188–89.

challenges and evils is up to us. Yet, there is no choice between good and evil unless we are free to sometimes actually do evil.

There are two value judgments implicit in this view. The first is well-stated by John Hick: "The value-judgment that is implicitly being invoked here is that one who has attained to goodness by meeting and eventually mastering temptations, and thus rightly making responsible choices in concrete situations, is good in a richer and more valuable sense than would be one" who is innocent but never had the opportunity to choose evil or confront danger. As Hick states, for the person who forges a good character, "the individual's goodness has within it the strength of temptations overcome, a stability based upon an accumulation of right choices, and positive and responsible character that comes from the investment of costly personal effort."[2] The notion of "opposition in all things" is an essential assumption of the kind of soul-making at issue. Courage is developed through facing real challenges, loyalty grows through being challenged to be disloyal, compassion comes about as a response to the presence of pain and suffering, and temptation exists only where there is the possibility of choosing evil. As Hugh McCann argues,

> True virtue has to be tested and refined. Someone with the virtue of patience must have tasted affliction and disappointment, and seen things through; the courageous person has to have endured danger and risk; the compassionate must have struggled with temptation, sorrow and hardship. The point of such experiences is not merely to strengthen our tendency to act rightly. . . . [Virtue] requires that we know trial and suffering, and human weakness in the face of them, in the only way they truly can be known: through experience. . . . In short, true virtue requires knowledge of good and evil—not just as they are manifested in our own struggle with sin, but as they are played out in the travail of the whole world. As we gain this knowledge, we become more suited for God's friendship.[3]

Such virtues as courage and bravery have meaning only in the context of a world that presents genuine dangers. Courage untested is no courage at all. The courage of one who has never faced fear is simply nonexistent compared to one who has mastered fear in the face of genuine dangers. As the story of Job portrays, the virtues of loyalty and faithfulness have no mean-

---

2. John Hick, *Evil and the God of Love*, 255–56.
3. Hugh J. McCann, "Divine Providence."

ing except in the context of the possibility of being disloyal or unfaithful. Faithfulness untested is really no faithfulness at all. The virtue of one who is faithful though untested is less valuable and praiseworthy than the proven faithfulness of one that has been tested through temptation and concrete challenges to be unfaithful. The development of these virtues as personality traits is intrinsically valuable.

There is a second value judgment inherent in the agape theodicy. Love that is freely chosen in a libertarian sense is more valuable than any love that is not freely chosen. I have argued at length for this view in *Exploring Mormon Thought: The Love of God and the Problems of Theism*. Freely chosen love that is forged in circumstances where it is possible to withhold love and reject others is more valuable than any love that is the inevitable result of the natural causal order or which is coerced. I suggest that love simply cannot be coerced by its very nature. A love that is freely chosen has the value of the free gift of one's self to the beloved. This gift nature of love would not be present if the "love" were inevitable due to circumstances or nature. If the latter were the case, then no gift would be possible, because a gift must be given freely where there is no duty to give and the gift can be freely withheld. Love that is freely chosen is more valuable because love that must be without such choice implies that the beloved may not be chosen if it were left to our free choice. Such a view thus implicitly devalues the beloved as if they would not be chosen if there were any choice about it. If we wanted to prove that what otherwise appears to be loving actions in fact were merely a sham, all that is needed is to show that actions that appeared to be given out of love were in fact due to circumstances beyond our control—such as threats of harm, drugs, manipulation, hypnosis, and so forth. If the beloved were aware that we did the kind actions only because we had no choice in the matter, the "beloved" would be aware that our love is not genuine.

For example, suppose that Archie takes Betty on several dates. Archie begins to spend a lot of time with her and express his affection for her. He does many kind things for her to win her over. Now suppose that Betty discovers that Archie can't help but do what he does. Suppose that Betty finds out that Archie has been doing all of these things because Reggie has hypnotized him to like Betty. Would not such a revelation immediately be sufficient to convince Betty that Archie's show of affection for her is a sham? Such psychological coercion is inimical to any sort of genuine love. Does it make a difference if the reason is not coercive but merely a natural necessity? Suppose instead that Betty discovers that Archie is doing all of these kind actions because he has a certain brain chemistry over which Archie has no conscious control. This chemistry causes him to do all of these things and Archie literally cannot do otherwise. Would not such a circumstance be adequate proof to Betty that Archie does not have a genuine affection for her? Would not any love that Archie expresses because he freely chose to love Betty be more valuable than any love that resulted from circumstances beyond his control? Betty justifiably concludes that Archie is not choosing her for herself or for the person she is, but as the result of causes outside of Archie's control that do not have anything to do with her. His "reasons" are not personal in nature but impersonal. If Archie's actions and feelings are not the choice of his heart, then Archie does not really love Betty at all. Thus, genuine love, or the most valuable kind of love, must be a free choice of our heart.

Yet the stark reality of the nature of freedom involved in the possibility of genuinely loving relationships and deep moral responsibility for one another is that sometimes we must be allowed to actually make and carry out evil choices—even horrendously evil choices that cause devastating harm to others. John Hick states that if "we take with full seriousness the value of human freedom and responsibility, as essential to the eventual creation of perfected children of God, then we cannot consistently want God to revoke that freedom when its wrong exercise becomes intolerable to us."[4] If each opportunity to choose to harm another was prevented from being carried out through some divine intervention (as Satan's plan suggested), then the possibility of freely making genuine choices would be destroyed. God must allow at least some evil choices where others are harmed to preserve the integrity of genuine moral freedom. As John Hick observes, a world where no harm could come to others could not function as an environment in which soul-making is possible; such a pain-free world would require constant miracles:

> In such a pain-free world one who falls accidentally from a high building would presumably float unharmed to the ground; bullets would become insubstantial when fired at a human body; poisons would cease to poison; water to drown and so on. . . . [Any] world in which there can be no pain or suffering would also be one in which there can be no moral choices and hence no possibility of moral growth and development. For in a situation

---

4. John Hick, "An Irenaean Theodicy," 49.

in which no one can ever suffer injury or be liable to pain or suffering there would be no distinction between right and wrong action. No action would be morally wrong, because no action could have harmful consequences; and likewise no action would be morally right in contrast to wrong. Whatever the values of such a world, it clearly could not serve a purpose of the development of its inhabitants from self-regarding animality to self-giving love.[5]

Hick makes precisely the same point as Lehi. The world could not function as a vale of soul-making and growth if it were pain-free and presented no real challenges. There could be no morally significant choices. God's plan for our growth to be as the gods by learning to love as God loves would be destroyed in such a pain-free world.

It is the same story in the book of Job. God can know of Job's faithfulness only to the extent that faithfulness has been tested and challenged. The challenge of allowing Job to grow through the tests he confronts, however, ignores the value of the others devastated in the test: his wife and children. Perhaps we can understand the tests imposed on Job as necessary to prove his faithfulness and loyalty to God—but what of the interests of his children who were killed by the whirlwind as a mean of providing a test for Job?

Can Radical Evils Benefit the Victims as an Essential Feature of God's Plan of Agape?

One of the greatest challenges to any theodicy is the simple fact that even though being free to choose good and evil requires that sometimes we may actually choose evil, it *does not* require that we be allowed to choose any *particular* evil. The fact that free will is necessary for soul-making and that some evils must be allowed to occur does not entail that any particular evil, such as the kidnapping and murder of a three-year-old girl, is necessary to preserve the possibility of soul-making. Thus, while the possibility of some evil action is necessary to permit God's plan of deification to succeed, nevertheless, no particular instance of evil is necessary to a greater good.

Peter van Inwagen maintains that it follows that any particular instance of evil must be arbitrarily permitted by God.[6] God must simply draw an arbitrary line as to which evils He will permit and which He may prevent.

---

5. Hick, 47–48.
6. See the discussion of Van Inwagen's theodicy in chapter 2 of this book.

However, the problem is that God is then arbitrary and rather capricious with respect to any particular evil that occurs. In addition, if we say that a particular young girl's murder and my friend's daughter's death were just flat out unlucky, then we must conclude that God is culpable for their bad luck. After all, God could have prevented the bad luck. Each is in a position to claim that God has been unfair to them as far as their person-centered interests are concerned. God allowed them to be killed when it was not necessary while preventing other instances of evil that are equally (un)necessary in general to the existence and actual exercise of free will. What is required to avoid this arbitrary injustice is a way for God to allow certain individuals to encounter such evils that is not arbitrary, capricious, and unjust. The revelations of Joseph Smith provide a way for God to allow certain individuals to encounter evils while not being unjust and capricious.

Unless their own interests and purposes are also furthered by allowing the evil, then the victims of evils are used as mere means to accomplish God's plan for the benefit of others. God is in the position of the Nazi scientist who attempts to justify his experiments on humans on the basis that many others may be benefitted by the experiments. The person-centered evils remain unredeemed with respect to the victims of evil. In allowing the evils, God must not use individuals as *mere* means to benefit others. Otherwise, God would demean and objectify the victims of evils in addition to allowing them to be dehumanized by their human perpetrators. For example, the interests of a child are furthered by a vaccination that preserves the child's health; they are not furthered by a gunshot that kills the child, even if the parents could possibly learn greater compassion and love for others as an indirect result of such a tragedy.

I suggest that an evil is permissible if it is redeemable. By "redeemable," I mean that it is an event that has the potential to be given meaning because it potentially furthers God's plan of agape and benefits or furthers the interests of the victim of the evil. The evil need not *actually* lead to a greater good in the sense that it is better, all things considered, that this particular evil actually occurred. However, the *possibility* of such evils is essential to God's plan to achieve his purposes. In this case, the possibility that some will choose to murder, or the possibility that cars can roll over little girls, is essential to the viability of God's plan for us. Morally significant choices that are actually evil must be possible for free will to be genuine. Genuine free will is essential to the possibility of loving relationships. A dangerous environment where accidents can occur seemingly at random is essential to empowering us to exercise compassion and develop the virtues of soul that require challenging circumstances. In this particular case, can the murder of a three-year old girl or the death of my friend's daughter serve to potentially serve others as a catalyst to learn to be compassionate and loving and *also* benefit the infant girls as a necessary part of God's plan?

We do not know why God allowed a three-year-old girl to be kidnapped and murdered, and she is far from being the only child to leave mortality early. It is obvious that countless millions have not even had the chance to get started on the process of soul-making while in this mortal probation. If soul-making must be accomplished during this mortal life alone, then it is insufficient in explaining a great deal of moral and natural evil that in fact occurs, including the murder of a child. However, given Joseph Smith's revelations, we can conclude this much: this young victim is assured a celestial glory. In a vision to Joseph Smith dated January 21, 1836, the voice of God declared: "All children who die before the age of accountability are saved in the celestial kingdom of heaven" (D&C 137:10). There are three points that are essential to make about this revelation.

First, it does *not* follow from that fact that children who die before the age of accountability are assured celestial glory that therefore God caused this three-year-old girl or any other child to die before the age of accountability. Rather, it means that if one dies before such an age, then that person is assured a celestial glory. Thus, if a child dies before accountability, that child had already progressed in the pre-mortal life to the point where all that is needed to fulfill the purpose of life is to become mortal.

Second, all persons who have accomplished whatever they came here to learn, or at the very least have had sufficient opportunity to do so, whatever their age, can leave this mortal probation at any time having fulfilled their purpose in life. God simply does not miraculously intervene to ensure that their lives are preserved after they have had the opportunity to do what they came here to accomplish. With their bodies attained and celestial glory assured, God can leave to chance the time and means of their death without being arbitrary.

Third, there may well be many people who live beyond the age of accountability who are nevertheless assured of the celestial kingdom because of the progress they made before this life. Nevertheless, such persons remain free in a libertarian sense to sin in a way that would negate their assured exaltation. However, the likelihood that such persons will lose their exaltation is so remote that it is not a rational concern. First, once a person has accomplished what they came to mortal life to do, they can die at any time. I suggest that without God's constant intervention to keep us from being killed by natural causes, the likelihood of swift death is extremely high. Thus, the likelihood of continuing to live beyond the point of obtaining a mortal body for such persons is extremely remote. Further, the character that a person developed in the pre-mortal life continues to express itself in actions and decisions in this mortal life. Thus, the developed, virtuous character expressed in mortal decisions also makes the likelihood that such persons will act in such a way that they forfeit their exaltation remote.

However, to be an instance of redeemable evil, there are other conditions that must be met. First, the young victim must have consented to confront this life and all of the kinds of dangers and challenges attendant to mortality. I am not asserting that she or anyone else consented to the particular morally reprehensible actions that caused their deaths. That would only be possible if God could have foreknowledge of morally free actions. Such knowledge is impossible. What I am asserting is that she and others who are subjected to radical evils consented to the types and kinds of evils that could occur in this life. Nevertheless, such a requirement obviously assumes that this girl lived in a life prior to this mortal one in which she could consent. This theodicy thus assumes sentient pre-mortal life. While a belief in a premortal existence will reduce its plausibility for agnostics, it is a belief that is well-established in Mormon thought.[7] Thus, before this life in the pre-mortal world, she must have consented to encounter the types of evils that could include the possibility of being kidnapped and murdered—even at an innocent age.

Second, if having already progressed to the point where she did not need mortal experiences beyond the age of accountability to learn to love as others of us do, she and others who consent to be subjected to radical evils are a necessary part of God's plan of agape by giving others the opportunity to exercise their free will to choose even horrendous evils. After all, if such evil acts are never allowed, then morally significant free will would then be impossible and God's plan of agape would be destroyed. The kind of compassion called for by such tragedies is essential to God's plan to teach

---

7. See Blake T. Ostler, "The Idea of Pre Existence in the Development of Mormon Thought," 59–78.

us to love one another and to shoulder one another's burdens. It would be unjust for God to use a victim as a mere means to further His plan without their consent; God would then be treating them as a mere object to fulfill His purposes while ignoring their interests. It would also be unjust for God to arbitrarily use a victim to fulfill His purposes while preventing such victimization for others. They would then be treated unfairly, and God would not be equally fair to all in his justice. However, if the person consents to such victimization as a way to express their love for God and those who are served by God's plan of agape, then their interests and choices are also recognized and expressed in God's plan.

More than mere voluntary potential victims of great evil, those who consented to assist in God's plan in this way become allies with God to express their own love for us and for God to make our soul-making progress toward deification possible. By ensuring that her own purposes are also furthered, God values this victim as more than a *mere* means to an end and thus does not violate Kant's second formulation of the categorical imperative. She is given the opportunity to express her love by agreeing and consenting to be an essential cooperative in the plan of agape.

Further, God is not arbitrary and capricious with respect to which instances of evil He will allow to preserve the viability of His plan of agape. He bases the choice on (a) the prior choice to consent of those who are potentially victimized; and (b) the fact that they will not be deprived of the opportunity for soul-making toward celestial glory as a result of their death. He has a rational and justifiable condition for choosing to allow this moral or natural evil and not others. If the individual did not consent to encounter such radical evils, then God ensures that they are not subjected to dehumanizing and life-ending victimization from which the victim cannot also benefit. The very notion of consent entails the possibility that some could withhold consent. As long as some consent, the purposes of God's plan of agape can be preserved, and we owe a great debt of gratitude to those who do make God's plan possible.

This plan of agape theodicy thus suggests that we are surrounded by angels who have become mortal to serve and give us the opportunity to learn from them. We are in the midst of teachers who express their love for us just by being a part of our lives and being a part of our experience. We are part of a world that has been organized to lovingly serve us by creating challenges that we must meet (even if we do not overcome them all in this life) and to give us the opportunity to move into more perfect relationship with God and each other. Those who die as young children have already realized a celestial glory and have the opportunity to express their love for God and others by consenting to be a necessary means to further God's plan.

Yet it is precisely those who never got the chance to even get a good start on mortal life who are the angels that move the story forward and that make the test possible. They are the essential means of carrying out God's plan. They are God's accomplices. The unnamed, the unnoticed, the little ones. These are the ones who have celestial glory already crowned upon their heads even before the story gets started, according to Joseph Smith's revelation.[8]

Whether an evil that gives an opportunity to learn turns out to actually be an occasion of learning is up to the individuals involved. This life is but a moment in the eternal span of time that we have been progressing and learning through many episodes of various types of experiences. There has been an eternity for the intelligences to work out what they desire to learn in this life. Toward that end, I suggest that each intelligence/spirit in the pre-mortal life may have entered into certain covenants and agreements with others to be the means by which they could learn the lessons necessary to progress in capacity to love.

---

8. It has sometimes been argued that if little children who die before the age of eight are guaranteed celestial glory, then we should kill all children before eight years of age to guarantee their celestial glory. This type of argument fails because it commits the fallacy of misplaced cause. Children who have achieved celestial glory have done so whether they die before age eight or not. What guarantees their celestial glory is the progress that they made before this life and not the fact that they died before age eight. Thus, they will achieve celestial glory even if they die after age eight. Because dying before age eight is not the cause of achieving celestial glory, the proposal to kill children before age eight misplaces the causes of achieving celestial, and instead of guaranteeing celestial glory to at least one person (who achieves it regardless of when he or she dies), the only thing guaranteed is the consignment to hell (the telestial kingdom, according to D&C 76) of the person who killed the child.

10

IS IT JUSTIFIABLE TO PERMIT CONSENT TO PERSONALITY-DESTROYING EVILS?

Of course, issues remain with whether consent can carry the weight that this theodicy posits for those who are subjected to radical evils. Consider the comparison with Alvin Plantinga's theodicy, which posits that God actualizes a world with sinful persons just so that it justifies an incarnate Christ who atones for sin. Plantinga maintains the value judgment that any world with an incarnate Son who atones for sin of others is vastly more valuable than any world with simply perfect creatures who are not rescued from their sins by divine love.[1] In addition to very legitimate questions about the justice and necessity of the notion of atonement that Plantinga posits, I believe that this value judgment is extremely problematic. The problem, of course, is that God is simply using creatures as mere means to their detriment for His own cosmic purposes. The fact that there is no person-centered good undermines Plantinga's claim that this god is loving or merciful to the individuals sacrificed to this god's ends.

Plantinga himself forcefully states the central problem of such a view. God seems "too much like a father who throws his children in the river so that he can then heroically rescue them, or a doctor who first spreads a horrifying disease so that he can then display enormous virtue in fighting it in heroic disregard of his own safety and fatigue."[2] Plantinga maintains

---

1. Alvin Plantinga, "Supralapsarianism, or 'O Felix Culpa,'" 1–25.
2. Plantinga, 21–22.

that one who has gone through a sinful life and comes to God freely has a more intimate relationship with God than one who is created in a perfect condition. However, the value realized by this theodicy is not atonement but the struggle to come to God by overcoming sin—and that raises all of the problems of a soul-making theodicy that cannot explain how mortal life is a good to those who die in infancy and never get started on the process of soul-making. Further, this value judgment in the context of a God who cannot sin by nature and a Christ who remains sinless implies that God and Christ have a relationship that is less valuable than sinners who can come to God after having been redeemed from sin. From the perspective of Christian theology, such a result is absurd.

To get around this problem, Plantinga ultimately proffers that it isn't wrong for God to use these individuals for His own ends, because God knows by means of His middle-knowledge that if the question were put before them prior to them being actualized, they would have consented to the life God unilaterally actualizes for them.[3] However, such an observation proposes that counterfactuals with logically impossible antecedents can have a truth value. The relevant counterfactual seems to be: "If God had asked a possible person X, before X was actualized, if X consented to its life, possible person X would have consented to be actualized in the conditions chosen by God." The antecedent of this counterfactual is logically impossible, however, because not even God can suppose that possible persons can respond to such inquiries before they are actual. The notion that such a proposition could be true is far-fetched at best.

Nevertheless, Plantinga insists that a person's preferences are not always decisive. Take, for example, the notion of consent to a medical procedure by one who is *unable* to consent. When patients are comatose, we inquire of their loved ones whether they will consent on their behalf. However, the desires of the loved ones on behalf of the comatose are not always decisive. It may be that they will not provide consent because they lack sufficient appreciation of the medical benefits and relative risks, lack the cognitive faculties to make a proper decision, or have disordered affections that prevents a competent decision. It may be proper to override their refusal to consent in such circumstances. When patients suffer from mental disabilities that render them incapable of appreciating the consequences

---

3. Plantinga, 23.

of their own decisions, it is not inappropriate for us to disregard their own personal desires. Rather, what is relevant is whether an ideal observer who possesses perfect knowledge and mental faculties would consent. Plantinga suggests that God is that Ideal observer for purposes of consent—and He chose this life for us knowing that we should consent.

A significant problem with Plantinga's thesis is that it has God setting up the cosmos without care for person-centered concerns. Such a view entails that God has determined that a rational person would consent to our lives even if He is unjust to us. Plantinga's view entails that in the actual world, a person—let's call him Paul—is damned, but that there is some possible world in which God could have actualized Paul being saved. The problem is precisely that God sacrifices persons for the benefit of the goodness of a possible world as a whole. Allowing God to consent for us to His own use of us to further His plan thus entails that God uses us as a mere means to benefit others. The problem is that to get the world that God wants that requires incarnation and atonement, God has actualized us in a literal hell of a mess needing rescue. God must disregard the person-centered goodness inherent in Kant's maxim: "Do not treat any person as a means only and not also as ends in themselves." What Kant was getting at is that there are moral limits on how a person can be used by another. It is morally permissible to use a person as a means only when we respect their dignity and inherent worth as persons.

For example, we allow an employer to use an employee to make a profit because the employee also benefits, can freely consent to the relationship, and is not degraded in the relationship. If the employer uses a child as labor, even if the child can benefit, such arrangements are inherently morally impermissible because the child cannot assess her own best interests. We allow employment to be consented to when it does not involve a risk of great bodily harm, amount to immoral demands on the employee, or may result in the psychological destruction of the employee's personality. Yet, for Plantinga, God has actualized persons in circumstances knowing that they will be used and abused, degraded and undone, and morally, physically, and spiritually destroyed.

The central problem is that we do not allow individuals to be used as a means to be degraded and depersonalized as mere objects—*even if they consent.* That a person would consent to such degrading consequences is strong evidence that they do not appreciate the consequences of their own actions and do not know what they are really doing.[4] God cannot be considered loving and merciful even if He were to obtain prior consent to use persons as *mere* means to demonstrate how great He is when He rescues us from the suffering and dangers that He Himself created to save us from.

However, such a view also presents problems for the plan of agape theodicy that I present. Is it morally permissible for God to allow the intelligences or spirits to consent to be used and abused so that others can learn the lessons essential to be fit for exaltation? I suggest that in the context of the theodicy that I present, the situation is very different than that posited in Plantinga's view of an omni-god that actualized all things *ex nihilo* with middle knowledge. God does not create the plight of the pre-mortal spirits so that an atonement is needed. Unlike the omni-god posited by Plantinga, God never had the choice of perfect possible persons to actualize. He never had a choice of a possible world that, if it were actualized, would result in a better life for possible person than if it were actualized in this actual world. God isn't merely using the spirits to move His plan along. Rather, God begins with the spirits as they are by their eternal nature, and He lovingly works with them from there. Moreover, God is limited in the kinds of natural laws that govern the world He organized as opposed to the unfettered discretion of the omni-god.

Nevertheless, it seems open to question whether it is morally permissible for God to allow spirits to consent to be used and abused, degraded and traded, and demoralized and depersonalized—even if they express immense love by consenting so that others may possibly benefit. The key difference, however, is that in the plan of agape, the spirits are not *only* a means to God's ends. Their own purpose of expressing their love by being allowed to serve others is also realized in God's plan of atonement. Further, let me suggest that the circumstances warrant such a momentous choice to consent.

Consider an analogy. Suppose that a nuclear weapon has just recently been discovered in a location that threatens the lives of millions, and it is unknown exactly when it may detonate. To disarm the weapon requires at least five people with sufficient competency to enter a zone of extreme radiation. If no one enters the radiation zone, the weapon may kill literally millions of people. Anyone who enters the zone of radiation will suffer

---

4. See Marilyn McCord Adams, "Plantinga on 'Felix Culpa': Analysis and Critique," 131.

radiation poisoning that slowly and very painfully disintegrates the cellular structure of the body. What can be done except to ask for volunteers? Such dire circumstances warrant the remarkable request for some to sacrifice their well-being for the sake of others. However, these persons must be volunteers who can consent. Simply appointing five people would be both arbitrary and unjust. However, if five persons volunteer, I believe we would say that those who approve such actions would be just to allow the volunteers to confront the danger involved because of the number of lives at stake. In fact, we ask something similar of service men and women in the armed forces on a regular basis.

Suppose further that the volunteers who would be subjected to radiation would experience only a period of pain and then a period of coma, after which they would recover fully. It seems to me that this would make consent more viable as an option. For example, when a person has experienced catastrophic brain damage that causes his brain to swell, doctors often induce a coma to allow the brain time to heal. If the coma would be permanent for the remainder of mortal life, then such a procedure would not be a viable medical option. Similarly, the fact that our mortal probation is limited in duration implies that whatever suffering and evils we are subjected to are limited. Moreover, there is an inherent limit to the level of pain we can endure. Humans lose consciousness when pain becomes overwhelming. Critically, the key component of this theodicy is that God has ensured that those who suffer as innocent children (and others who have already realized a celestial glory who live beyond the age of accountability) will not be deprived of the opportunity for soul-making and progress toward deification. They are the perfect volunteers because they have much less to lose from being deprived of a lifetime of mortal experiences from which they may learn. They have already learned the lessons necessary for celestial glory and exaltation.

It seems to me that a situation similar to the emergency needing to eradicate a looming nuclear threat is presented as a given by the eternal realities presupposed in the plan of agape theodicy. God has not created the need for challenges necessary to our growth. He created neither our status of progress nor our capacities for love and virtue. As long as God Himself has not created the dire circumstances that lead to the need for some to take risks, it is difficult to see how God could be culpable or blameworthy for allowing volunteers to undertake the rescue operation represented in the plan of agape. If some do not consent to be used and abused by others to offer the possibility of morally significant choice, the entire creation will be wasted and God's plan will be frustrated. Moreover, there is no other way to achieve the progress required of us to realize the magnificent good of interpenetrating glory in eternal life with God. The value of experience gained in the struggle to overcome challenges cannot be realized without such consenting volunteers. As long as it is our choice to confront the evils, it seems that such a choice is justified.

Moreover, it seems that whoever is asking the volunteers to confront the danger of radiation poisoning to effectuate the rescue mission must themself be willing to confront the same dangers. At the very least, the one who requests volunteers has greatly augmented authority and is far more persuasive if they are willing to join the volunteers in confronting the suffering and pain entailed in such a rescue mission. If the one requesting volunteers gives themself the most dangerous part of the mission, then those who volunteer will more readily detect the urgency of the situation and the nature of the bravery requested of them. I suggest that this is precisely what Christ did. He is the primary volunteer without whom the entire plan would be wasted and impossible to accomplish. Without his willing consent to confront the greatest pain and suffering of all, to take on the deepest anger of enemies and the most profound rejection and alienation possible, the plan of agape would be impossible. Jesus Christ is the exemplar and chief instance of a volunteer who expresses love for us by making the Father's plan possible. Thus, we owe him an even greater debt of gratitude than we do to those who lay everything on the line for our well-being.

It seems that God is in a position something like that of the Trolley Paradox. This paradox arises from our conflicting moral intuitions in response to the following story: Suppose a person controls a switch for a train that is running down a track. She sees that the train will inevitably kill five people if she allows it to continue down the track it is on. However, a child is playing on the track to which she would switch the train. If she does nothing, five people die. If she acts, the train will kill the child. What should she do? There are of course variations. What if the child is her own child? What if she could be charged with manslaughter for the death of the child due to authorities being unable to determine that others were saved because they had left the scene, unaware of what transpired? What if the scenario involved a thousand people instead of five—or two instead of five?

IS IT JUSTIFIABLE TO PERMIT CONSENT TO PERSONALITY-DESTROYING EVILS?

All of these situations call on conflicting moral intuitions. If the switcher reasons in a consequentialist way, she will save the five people on the track. If she considers her own parental duties, she will not. If she values abiding by laws, then she will not save the five people. If she values passive guilt to active culpability, then she will not save the five people.

The point is that the issues related to consent in this theodicy also involve such conflicting moral intuitions. Should God allow some to suffer—even as innocent children—for the benefit of many others? Or should God preserve the innocents and deprive all others of their opportunity for free decisions essential to the process of soul-making and deification? However, the key difference is that the innocents can consent to this life before they are children with limited cognitive capacities. Is the moral situation changed if the innocents consent having full capacity to consent? I believe that it makes a world of difference. If the person on the tracks were an adult who could consent, it seems to be a very different story.

Consider the Trolley Paradox a bit differently. Assume that the five people on the track have become stuck in the train rail. They cannot extricate themselves for at least thirty minutes, but the train is due in ten minutes. Likewise, the person on the alternative track is also stuck in the rail and cannot be extricated for thirty minutes. The track switcher has time to inform each of the impending doom and the necessity of a decision. When the proposition is put to the person on the alternative track to which the train would be switched, he consents to have the train switched to his track. He maintains that his life's purpose has been fulfilled and that he is ready to go at any time. However, when the switcher speaks with the five people stuck in the rail on the main-line track, they will not consent. They each insist that they are not ready to die and have a great deal left to accomplish before they will be ready for death. In this situation, does it now appear that the proper choice is to switch the train to the rail where the one person who has consented is found?

I suggest that obtaining the consent of the intelligences to be used as a necessary means to make free will and the plan of agape possible is the most rational and the morally preferable course of action God would have open—at least given the constraints of the eternal realities with which God is endeavoring. Further, it must be kept in mind that God does not have foreknowledge of what free agents will choose. When a person is born, the magnitude and kinds of evils any individual may actually endure are mere possibilities and not given certainties that God chose. Thus, God's plan of agape is one of general purposes and resources to respond to whichever contingent realities occur to ensure the realization of those purposes. The point of this theodicy is not that it is better, even all things considered, that a young girl was murdered or my friend's daughter was crushed by the neighbor's car. The necessity that some must consent to potentially experience such crushing and heinous evils does not transform the evils into greater goods—such evils remain truly and implacably evil when such evils actually occur. It would be better that they not occur—even though the possibility that such evils may occur is essential to God's plan, and this plan is in our best interests. It is justifiable for such individuals to consent to express their love to be subjected to such evils, but it is not better that such evils actually occur. Ultimately, the real tragedy occurs when we refuse love and fail to learn the lessons of love and soul-making from our experiences made possible by their loving consent.

I believe that it is also important to point out that God as presented in the plan of agape is not culpable for the risks in the way that God in traditional open theism is. In the latter, God creates a world out of nothing, not knowing how it will turn out. The risks in the world are due to God's choice of creation as one containing open possibilities. However bad things are in our world, they could also be much worse. God took the risk, hoping that all would join Him in loving relationship but knowing that very likely some and perhaps most—possibly even all—would not. In contrast, given the commitments of this plan of agape theodicy, God did not set up the risks. God is working with eternal realities and offering the best options that are available to them, given where they are in their level of progression. The nature of the risks is inherent in reality, and the nature of the best options available are already delimited by the nature of the eternal realities. The only risks are those the personal intelligences freely chose to take on. Contrasting this, in open theism the risks are foisted onto mortals who are thrown into the world without their consent.

Nevertheless, it must be admitted on both of these views that when a child is born into a family that has a long history and propensity for child abuse, alcoholism, or dysfunction, that God certainly knows that history and that there is a certain probability that such evils will be visited on the child. God certainly knew of the plans of the September 11 terrorists long before they were carried out. After the first plane struck the first tower, He clearly knew that the plan was afoot and had power to stop both the plane that flew into the second tower and another that flew into the Pentagon. God is not exonerated simply by a limit of foreknowledge necessitated by the existence of free agents. However, it mitigates His responsibility that He did not plan for and concurrently enable the very evils that occurred. God did not cause the acts of a young girl's murderer. He did not cause the car to start rolling or the driver to fail to set the brake that rolled over my friend's daughter. Because they had already fully realized the purposes of their lives, their deaths were a matter of chance, pure and simple.

Further, even if the spirits consented, it seems that they would be unable to give *informed* consent due to their having no experiences of bodily pain and suffering to understand what such consent may entail. The spirits are becoming embodied as mortals precisely so that they can gain the capacity to appreciate such experiences. If they cannot know what pain and suffering are unless and until they become mortal, how could they have the capacity for consent? I admit that this prospect leaves me uneasy. However, there are several considerations that suggest that such consent is effective. The notion that a person can consent to a medical operation only if that person has already experienced the kind of pain that may be involved is way too stringent as a criteria. No one could ever consent if it were adopted. Indeed, the very notion of consent would be logically impossible if we had to experience what we consent to before we consent to it. Rather, what is required is the ability to imagine the circumstances and the kinds of experiences that might be involved. We just don't know what the capacity for a pre-mortal personal intelligence to consent is in concrete terms. While I will never know what it is like to experience childbirth, I have at least experienced a wide variety and intensities of bodily pain in my life that I can look to as analogous to what childbirth my feel like. Even though they lack experience of any bodily pain, I can see no reason to suppose that spirits/intelligences lacked any analogous spiritual pain nor the capacity to imaginatively project from that pain the potential experiences that they might have in mortality.

Ultimately, the decision for the pre-mortal spirits came down to their trust in God, just as it does for us. They had to express trust in God when He laid out the plan and explained whether the endeavor would be worth the risk. Trust in God is like trust in experts in our culture. When we cannot fully assess a matter because we lack the training or ability to assess the evidence, we rely on trusted experts who have a better grasp of matters than we do. It is morally acceptable to defer to another who has expertise in matters that are beyond our ability and training. The trust is even more justified when we know that the persons on whom we rely care for us and desire our best interests. Sometimes we must just defer to another with greater wisdom and knowledge to make key decisions. There is no one in the universe more knowledgeable, more caring, or more competent than God. Thus, trust in God's directions whether this life was worth the risk is supremely rational and morally appropriate.

Is General Consent Sufficient or Must There Be Specific Consent to the Particular Evils That We Will Actually Experience?

It is essential to distinguish between two types of consent. *General consent* is the view that we all consented to the same extent and in the same way to confront all of the various types of experiences (including all types of radical evils) that we could possibly experience in mortal life. The advantage of the general consent view is that it is easier to see how a God with maximal knowledge who does not know what will be freely chosen in the future could order the world in a way consistent with the consent given. The general consent is essentially the commitment that (1) God explained in sufficient detail to the premortal spirits the kinds and types of conditions that may be encountered in mortality without any specific details about what would actually occur to us; (2) the spirits had the capacity to grasp the kinds and types of experiences with enough clarity to have sufficient grasp of what was entailed in these types and kinds of experiences to consent to them; and (3) the premortal spirits considered the disclosures and consented to confront them.

The general consent view was well-stated by American philosopher William James:

> Suppose that the world's author put the case to you before creation, saying: "I am going to make a world not certain to be saved, a world the perfection of which shall be conditional merely, the condition being that each several agent does its own 'level best.'" I offer the chance of taking part in such a world. Its safety, you see, is unwarranted. It is a real adventure, with real danger, yet it may win through. It is a social scheme of cooperative work

genuinely to be done. Will you join the procession? Will you trust yourself and trust the other agents enough to face the risk?[5]

The primary challenge to the general consent view is whether such a minimal disclosure is adequate in light of the actual evils we will all almost certainly confront. Two examples should suffice. At the time a baby is born into a family, God already knows the likelihood of genetic abnormalities that will confront the child. Assume that a child will, with certainty, be born to a mother addicted to drugs, and the likelihood of deformities is very high due to the drugs in her system. An adequate disclosure would require assessing the risk and fully disclosing it.

Or consider a situation in which a child will be born into a family where the father is an alcoholic with a generational history of alcoholism due to genetic and environmental factors and who has in the past engaged in physically abusive acts. An adequate disclosure would require disclosing the details of existing conditions and the genetic proclivity to alcoholism and abuse that the child will be subject to—together with details about the kinds of issues presented in growing up in a home with an alcoholic, how difficult it will be to avoid the same problems, and what challenges such problems may present in one's life.

It seems fairly transparent that another condition to the consent obtained by God is necessary to render the consent adequate: (4) to the extent specific details were known to God about the conditions that a particular premortal spirit will in fact encounter, God must disclose those details and obtain consent. However, these kinds of cases present little challenge to the consent model because they are based on conditions known to God at the time a child enters mortality. Such disclosure and consent differs significantly from the type of divine intervention, planning, resourcefulness, and competence necessary to disclose what conditions will be experienced by the child many years after birth.

Thus, we may contrast the general consent view with *specific consent*, in which God explains more than the general types and kinds of evils that may be experienced throughout mortal life. On the view that I have argued for, God lacks knowledge of the specific events that will result from free choices. However, God knows all of the possibilities that could occur in a mortal life. God also knows, at any given time, the probability of each event

---

5. William James, *Pragmatism*, 290–91.

occurring, including free choices (to the extent there is such a probability) at the time of disclosure. Thus, we may add a fifth condition to consent: (5) God must not only disclose the general types and kinds of evils that all mortal may experience, but He must also detail the possibilities for each specific human life and the probability of occurrence of each such possibility. Further, God must obtain consent to each of the possibilities and probabilities to the extent known.

God could specifically disclose each of those possibilities and obtain consent to each of them. But what if the premortal spirit expresses a desire to have certain kinds of experiences from which it may learn and grow? For example, a premortal spirit may express a desire to know what it is like to grow up without a father and is thus willing to go to a family where the father will die when the child is three years of age. Or the premortal spirit may desire to learn what it is like to experience a life in a body that presents extraordinary challenges, such as a body that will contract multiple sclerosis at the age of twelve. The benefit of such a view is transparent: each spirit could have a detailed and specific tutoring program to assist it to learn from the specific experiences that would most assist it to progress toward the purposes that the spirit has adopted in a cooperative venture of growth and progress. God would have to arrange events so that the father dies when the child is three or bring it about that the child suffers from multiple sclerosis when they are twelve. On the model that I have presented, God has sufficient power to bring about these conditions because He can do so through divine power. Could God grant such desires to the premortal spirit for a particularized tutoring program? To the extent that the request involves only the consent or request for experiences of that premortal spirit, the answer seems to be straightforward—yes, because the experience was requested by the premortal spirit. However, it would require the consent or request also of the mortal father and all others affected by the premature death.

But what if the premortal spirit desires to know what it is like to be married to a specific person or to experience a divorce or to be rejected by a friend? Each of the conditions is contingent on free choices that God does not know with certainty beforehand and that God cannot bring about without obliterating the very free will essential to His plan. For instance, imagine a person who desires to learn through mortal experience what it is like to be cheated on by a spouse. The responses of the spouse are based on numerous free decisions that are unknown to God at the time of their birth into this world. The free decision of the family to move to be in spatial proximity to a spouse, the free decision to date each other, the free decision to marry just the right person, the free decision to create circumstances ripe for marital infidelity, and the free decision to cheat. All of these decisions are unknown at the time of birth and cannot be brought about unilaterally by God without destroying free will. Thus, God cannot customize specific experiences into a mortal teaching environment without destroying free will. It is possible for God to obtain specific consent for each possibility that He foresees may occur, but He cannot obtain consent for actual specific events that are dependent on free choices.

Further, the logical challenges of obtaining consent are also quite obvious. The primary question is how God could both disclose and ensure that the spirit encounters the specific circumstances envisioned, many of which are up to free agents to decide and control. A general disclosure and consent are not adequate in light of the specific possible evils that God knows may occur. Rather, specific disclosure and consent are required for each possible evil that may be encountered. Further, the entire point of a theodicy that leaves us free cannot provide a customized learning experience that guarantees that we will confront specific experiences in our lives to which we have consented.

However, the notion of specific consent does not require God to guarantee that specific circumstances will occur that are tailored for us individually. What the notion of consent entails is not that God must prearrange circumstances to occur that we have consented to; rather, it merely entails that God will only permit specific circumstances to develop that have been specifically consented to. While God can disclose every possible experience that we could encounter in mortality, He cannot guarantee that a premortal spirit will consent to every such instance of evil. A spirit may consent to some but not all possibilities of evil that we could experience. In fact, that is just what the notion of freely given consent entails. If we do not consent, then God must either accept that we have rejected the opportunity to experience mortality because we did not choose to confront the risks of evil, or He must ensure through divine intervention that we do not confront evils we have not consented to. However, consent is more nuanced than merely refusing to give consent when we would rather not confront particular experiences of evil. Let me explain.

What the consent model requires is that if a premortal spirit has not consented to specific circumstances disclosed by God to us, then God will ensure by means of His divine power that we are not born into those circumstances. (Doctrine and Covenants 29:36 posits that roughly one-third of all premortal spirits refused consent.) If we have not consented to some of the possibilities for evil that were disclosed to us, then God will intervene to ensure that we do not confront those evils *to the extent that God has power to do so*. A part of what God must disclose to us is that He may not have sufficient power to stop some kinds of natural occurrences in time to prevent tragedies. He must disclose that He will not intervene in most circumstances to take away free will and the consequences of evil actions that are freely chosen. We may confront tragedies both through free choices and also through natural occurrences that by their very nature God cannot fully control. Given that disclosure, God would then be required to obtain "secondary consent" that even though we would rather not confront such experiences, we still agree that the overall value to be realized through a mortal experience is of such great value that we are willing to confront these possibilities. Secondary consent is that which is given after a spirit initially refuses to give consent to an experience but then agrees to consent after the further opportunities for growth and progress afforded by confronting mortality are explained to them and the spirit is asked by God to trust Him in the endeavor—and the spirit chooses to trust. Thus, it may be that even on the consent model we may experience evils to which we did not give initial consent, but we were willing to confront the possibility of suffering because we desired the growth and possibilities offered by experiencing mortality in this world—and primarily because we trusted God when He told us it would be for our ultimate good.

Nevertheless, it is still possible for God to set up a world where the issues that beset us will be presented to us as learning opportunities. God can use His knowledge and divine power to set up a world where natural consequences follow from choices and conduct. For example, if I choose to protect myself from being hurt again and thus refuse to be open and trust others in order to protect my tender heart from the pain of rejection, I will likely engage in protective behaviors like pushing others away, becoming defensive, and trying to control others to avoid that kind of pain. In return I will receive feedback from others through predictable and natural responses in several forms. If I try to control my wife through anger, shutting down,

IS IT JUSTIFIABLE TO PERMIT CONSENT TO PERSONALITY-DESTROYING EVILS?

becoming childish, or—heaven forbid—becoming violent, then she will likely push back. My anger will likely beget her anger in return. My controlling will likely beget pushing away to create space and reassert control in the relationship. She may point out how much she dislikes it when I get angry and controlling. In the end, she may refuse to further our relationship if I do not learn the lessons her feedback has to teach me.

In all of these ways that I act out to protect myself from being hurt, I am reflecting my own issues about my fears, being hurt again, feeling rejected, and never being enough. It is up to me to learn to overcome or otherwise work through my issues. Such interpersonal issues are the types of experiences that come up for us over and over again, repackaged and represented as a natural result of human nature not yet transformed by love. The response and feedback become more and more insistent over time. If we do not learn the lesson and deal with our issues, then we will destroy our relationships and create the very pain that we seek to avoid. Life is set up so as to grant us opportunities to learn from our behaviors so that over time we learn that forgiveness heals the pain we have caused to ourselves and others. We learn that we flourish and grow in dignity individually and in our most valued interpersonal relationships when we love others as we love ourselves. We learn that loving others is not just the highest expression of our uniqueness, of the gifts that we alone have to give; loving others fulfills the purpose of our very existence.

God can adopt a natural consequences approach to His plan that does not require Him to intervene constantly to ensure that we will have the opportunities to learn to love from our experiences. Rather, given human nature, the very structure of the world and the way that we interact with others in relationships is sufficient to set the stage for the learning process. In fact, the entire point of our mortal experience is to overcome our human nature so that our inherent divine nature is augmented. It does not require that we consented to every particular experience; rather, it entails that we consented to the world into which we were born and gave secondary consent to confront the world even though we may experience evils that we would rather not—and that God would rather not occur. However, the value of human life remains something that we chose and freely consented to encounter, trusting in God when He asked us to trust His word that "all of these things shall give thee experience, and shall be for [our] good" (D&C 122:7).

How Can the Purpose of Life be to Become United with God When Most Never Hear of Christ in this Lifetime?

It could also surely be argued that the agape theodicy cannot explain the purpose of life for the vast majority of those who inhabit this earth because they never get the chance to progress toward a relationship with God through Christ. It is obvious that the vast majority of mortals have neither learned of Christ nor worked toward a relationship of a unity with Father, Son, and Holy Ghost. The vast majority of mortals have never even heard of Christ during their lifetimes. Thus, if God's purpose for all of our mortal lives was to teach us about Christ and to enter into a relation with God through Christ, then this mortal lifespan fails miserably in its purpose for the vast majority of persons who have inhabited the world. It must be recognized that each person's purposes in this life are not the same. Rather, each person is at a different level of progress in degree of light and will be served by a different set of challenges necessary for that particular person to learn to love. The person born in the deepest reaches of New Guinea in 2,000 BC had as much purpose and meaning to their lives as we do. It is just that their purposes in life were different due to the fact that their interests and degree of progress in the light prior to this life were different. However, the purpose of learning to love in fulfilling relationship is a universal purpose of human life—even if that purpose is not fully accomplished in this life alone. Those who do not have the chance to learn of Christ and progress specifically in relationship with God through Christ in this life will be given that opportunity after this mortal probation.[6]

Does that not entail, then, that the purpose of mortal life is not really to fulfill God's plan of agape? If one cannot begin to enter into relationship with God because one is totally unaware of even the notion of the Judeo-Christian God, is that not enough to prove that entering into such relationships cannot be even one of the primary purposes of mortal life? It is not necessary that we are all privy to God's plans for the plan to work. It is not even necessary to function as a theodicy. God undoubtedly has all kinds of details about His plans to which we are not privy and perhaps cannot even begin to fathom—as expressed by God in Job 38:4–7. Thus, the fact

---

6. See Blake T. Ostler and David L. Paulsen, "Sin, Suffering, and Soul-Making: Joseph Smith on the Problem of Evil," 237–84.

that there are many who will never hear of Christ and thus never know of the plan of agape in this life does not count against it as a theodicy. What is essential is that each can learn from experience to love and move forward in capacity for greater intimacy and fulfillment in relationships. Further, any learning from this life's experiences is inherently valuable even to the extent it involves simply learning about the beauty of the earth, how it functions and operates naturally, and the infinite additional types of experiential knowledge that we can gain. Human experience is, in itself, inherently valuable. The value of life is not dependent on knowing the details of God's plan or the details of this theodicy.

It must not be assumed that those who were born into non-Christian or non-Mormon families were, for that reason, less righteous or diligent in the pre-mortal life. Each of us has come to this life to learn the lessons that will serve us to progress. Which circumstances will best give us the opportunity to learn these lessons varies. The lessons that will serve us depend on how we each individually learn. It may well be that already-celestial beings chose to experience life in a non-Christian world to experience what that would be like. We do not know what level each of us had accomplished in progress in the light prior to this life. We do not know what circumstances will best serve our opportunity to learn. We cannot presume to judge righteousness of another based upon their station or circumstances in this life. However, I venture that those who are born with bodies that are broken or non-functional have agreed to take on the amazing challenges and opportunities to learn afforded by such challenges. Those born into dysfunctional families have similarly agreed to learn what living in such circumstances offers for experience. It may well be that those we look down on most are the ones who took on the greatest challenges to learn.[7]

---

7. I will discuss the issues presented by competing secular and other religious beliefs in the fifth volume of *Exploring Mormon Thought*.

11

ARE RADICAL EVILS ESSENTIAL TO THE PLAN OF AGAPE?

It may of course be objected that it is improper to allow anyone to confront such vile evils as the kidnapping and murder of a three-year-old girl. Such evils are too extreme, it seems. Could not God preserve a free will that allows us to steal and cheat but disallows the brutalization of little children? The answer is that of course God could preserve free will with respect to these kinds of actions without anyone ever being murdered. Such actions are surely morally significant and, if we are left free to do them, then morally significant free will is preserved without more extreme kinds of evils actually being committed. However, God would then also have to truncate our power to do good actions. Power to do good entails a correlative power to do evil. However, to prevent only extreme evils and allow others less extreme, God would have to intervene to prevent us from exercising power every time we used our power to do evil while permitting our correlative power to do good. Yet, if God intervened every time we were about to harm little girls, the world's natural stability would be severely compromised. For instance, it would require something like a world where baseball bats are solid when used to hit balls but soft as putty when used to cause harm to a person.

Is the preservation of the natural order worth the pain and suffering it entails when God could still preserve morally significant free will for evils like cheating and stealing while preventing mayhem and murder? I suggest three reasons why a world with power to do great good but not power to do great evil is not a real option. First, it seems that God's existence would have to be rendered obvious to us with the kind of constant and dramatic intervention called for. Yet such obvious intervention would destroy our ability to freely choose to enter into a loving relationship of fellowship with God. If God's existence were obvious, surely we would feel forced to accept any relationship of any nature just to be on his good side. Second, it is not possible for God to simply gerrymander natural laws in the ways suggested. As I have elucidated the nature of God's power, God cannot have any natural laws except those that actually obtain without reducing the world to chaos. Third, confronting radical evils is essential to God's plan because of the nature of love at issue. Let me explain.

There is a very remarkable fact about the kind of love we must learn to be as God is. It is presaged in the uncomfortable ethics that Jesus taught in the Sermon on the Mount. It is not enough to learn to be kind to those who are loveable and kind to us. The challenge is precisely to repay evil with good. It is the kind of love that loves in spite of the evil visited on us. It is the kind of love that commands us to love our enemies. It is the kind of love manifested by those who consent to be subjected to radical evils in order to elicit love both for and from those who carry out such evils as rape, mayhem, and murder of innocent little girls. It is, as Jesus taught in the Sermon on the Mount, a perfect or complete love:

> Ye have heard that it hath been said, An eye for an eye, and a tooth for a tooth: But I say unto you, That ye resist not evil: but whosoever shall smite thee on thy right cheek, turn to him the other also. And if any man will sue thee at the law, and take away thy coat, let him have thy cloak also. And whosoever shall compel thee to go a mile, go with him twain. Give to him that asketh thee, and from him that would borrow of thee turn not thou away.
>
> Ye have heard that it hath been said, Thou shalt love [Gk. *Agape*] thy neighbour, and hate thine enemy. But I say unto you, Love [*agape*] your enemies, bless them that curse you, do good to them that hate you, and pray for them which despitefully use you, and persecute you; That ye may be the children of your Father which is in heaven: for he maketh his sun to rise on the evil and on the good, and sendeth rain on the just and on the unjust. For if ye love them which love you, what reward have ye? Do not even the publicans the same? And if ye salute your brethren only, what do ye more than others? Do not even the publicans so? Be ye therefore perfect, even as your Father which is in heaven is perfect. (Matt. 5:38–48)

What is essential to grasp from Jesus's radical *agape* ethic is that the kind of love that perfects us to be as God is cannot be just for the loveable or those who love us. It is not enough to love those who are easy to love. Anybody can do that—even the IRS. The real challenge of love arises with those who literally mistreat us as enemies. That is the kind of love manifested by those who consent to be subjected to radical evils at the hands of others in the trusting hope that such experiences will shock them into seeing their own evil and desire to change. It is the kind of love that Christ demonstrated when he asked the Father to forgive those who nailed him to a Roman cross. It is the kind of love that goes not just one mile but goes the extra mile. Instead of responding with retaliation when hit in the face, this kind of love meekly turns the other cheek to teach by not resisting evil. It is the kind of love that the Anti-Nephi-Lehis expressed when they refused to take up weapons and submitted themselves to death rather than kill their own brothers—which so shocked their attackers that they eventually refused to continue war against them. It is the kind of love that gives not merely an extra coat to one who is cold, but takes the coat off of one's own back in addition to make sure that the beloved is not cold—the way a parent would care for child. The divine love is thus the commitment to do good for others in spite of their rejection of us and the harm they have done to us.

If we are to learn this kind of love and demonstrate it in action, then there must actually be people who are allowed to mistreat us. To learn to love enemies, there must be enemies. For there to be genuine free will that gives us the opportunity to freely choose to love, we must also be free to reject love. There is no other way. It is the kind of love that requires us to love not only those who are merely kind of bad, like thieves and cheaters, but also those who commit radically heinous evils, like murderers. I know that this kind of challenge suggests a stretch that is so morally uncomfortable that it is naturally repulsive to us. How can we love such a reprehensible person as the murderer of children? Yet God does. It is precisely our mortal nature that naturally seeks retaliation and that refuses to ever forgive that must be conquered. If we are to learn to love as God loves, then so must we. God has a universal love for all by which He desires the best interests of all of His children. We are called to learn to love even those who commit such monstrous crimes.

Thus, those who consented before this mortal probation to be misused and abused if necessary to allow others the opportunity to learn from experience express immense love. They serve us by allowing us the opportunity to experience what we came to mortality to experience. This type of love promotes good despite the evils visited on us. Indeed, this kind of love responds with love in spite of the evil done to our beloved children in order to bring good out of evil. Such radical evil can only be conquered and given meaning by responding to it with love. For in this way not only is the evil defeated by giving it redeeming value, but the evil persons are given a chance to reform and transform into a different kind of person. I would also point out—we have seen the enemy, and the enemy is us.

God's plan provides that, at least potentially, no suffering is pointless or unredeemed. The atheists who argue that the kinds and amounts of evils that occur in the world cannot be explained by their redeeming purpose focus on instances of pain and suffering that no one even knows about—say, the suffering of a fawn after a forest fire. But that rather begs the question, because in the believer's world view there is always someone who notices: God. Further, we know about the possibility for such events and are challenged to address even the mere possibility of evil. It is true that no particular instance of such animal suffering is necessary. However, the possibility of such suffering is inherent in a world that is ordered by natural regularities necessary for God's plan to be achieved.

The problem of evil is thus not answered by an argument that calls evil good or that justifies God in allowing evil so that evil is justified; it is answered by a response that transforms the evil with love. Evil remains implacably evil and not a greater good. There are genuine evils because the world is not better, even all things considered, that these horrendous evils occurred. Rather, the world is made better by our loving response to evil. When we respond to our enemies with love, when we respond to violence with love, when we are moved to love and care for others because of the evils they encounter, then, and only then, can we redeem the evil because it has served its purpose to wake us to our own evil and our potential for good. Then the evil is redeemed, because through it we have learned something we could learn in no other way that has such great value that it transforms the evils into mentors of gods.

God and Natural Evils

The necessity of enemy love may justify God in His permission of some to freely choose to be enemies. Yet such love seems limited to moral evils that require the exercise of free will and does not justify the kinds of radical natural evils that are so devastating. Over a billion people dying from smallpox not only seems like mere overkill; it is an unnecessary trial, given the fact that we now know that smallpox is not necessary to any greater good. However, a similar analysis may be provided with respect to such radical natural evils as was provided for moral evils. Instead of enemy love, there is another type of love that is developed by facing natural evils: a love of united effort and oneness of purpose. These are the very characteristics of love that are essential to abide in the unity of the Godhead. We must learn to be one in all things. Toward that end, only the kinds of challenges that require a united response will function best to accomplish God's purposes of the plan of agape.

We are called to unite and come together to battle such natural evils as plagues, pandemics, tsunamis, hurricanes, and tornadoes. God is forging not merely an individual with virtuous character but a kingdom of saints who are united as one body to accomplish what cannot be accomplished alone. Only a community of persons united in compassion to assist and heal others can address these kinds of radical natural evils. Only evils that require such united action can forge a united response to overcome them. For example, the battle against smallpox was not the battle of one person who discovered a vaccine but of the whole world that united together to distribute and educate regarding the vaccine. It required the efforts and initiative of the United Nations' World Health Organization and virtually every country in the world to effectively wipe out smallpox. The vaccine was known for over a century before smallpox was eradicated. God is seeking not just people who dedicate their lives to overcome cancer, AIDS, and bacteriological diseases; He is seeking entire communities and nations who will unite to do his will.

Further, we all consented to confront a world that presented such challenges. We could have remained in a world free of such diseases and natural disasters; yet we chose to confront this world so that we could be stretched beyond our self-absorbed and ego-centric existence. Just as with any given instance of moral evil, no particular natural evil is necessary to a greater good. Smallpox is not necessary to a greater good. AIDS is not necessary to a greater good. However, *some* instances of natural evils that present a genuine danger and call for our united response and individual compassion are necessary to God's purposes of giving us an opportunity to learn to love one another. If we lived in a world free of any challenges, then the purposes of our mortal probation could not be realized.

So how does God choose when and where such disasters occur? I don't believe that He does. He chooses to allow the natural order to devolve as an organized cosmos to give us an opportunity to confront such challenges. However, He does not plan or cause them. If God could always act in the natural world with instant response from natural elements, then He would have power to prevent all such natural evils. However, it does not appear that the natural elements can respond to divine power immediately. It may well take time even for God to work through the natural order to control the elements. Even if God could immediately prevent the occurrence of all natural evils, He could not prevent them all and still accomplish His purposes in organizing this world as cosmos to serve as an arena for soul-making and progression toward deification. However, He can justly allow indiscriminate natural evils to confront all of us because we have all consented to a world where such overwhelming challenges are possible.

The indiscriminate and seemingly random nature of natural evils also fulfills a purpose. Diseases, natural disasters, and pandemics strike without respect to individual goodness or justice. Yet if the natural disasters occurred only to really bad people and the good people were all rewarded with consistently great weather, wealth, and impeccable health, then we would *not* do what is right and good because it is right and good. Instead, we would do them to receive the rewards and avoid the punishments of our behaviors. Moral commitment would lose its meaning because we would not do anything out of commitment to what is good for its own sake. Dangers and disasters that strike indiscriminately are an essential feature of a soul-making world. The very fact that natural disasters are unfathomable, haphazard, and unpredictable is a necessary characteristic of a world that calls forth united effort to mitigate their effects and fosters caring, compassion, and love.

Further, such indiscriminate randomness calls for our humility in assessing the world. Given that God is justified in allowing *some* natural evils, but where the exact amount, type, distributions, and intensity of God's interventions to prevent such evils that would be necessary for the divine purposes is impossible for us to assess given our cognitive limitations, we are called to trust God. We cannot charge God with allowing an unnecessary evil in any particular instance, given that some natural evils are in fact necessary to God's purposes. Such a view does not entail that just any amount, kinds, and magnitude of evils is therefore justified. It is just that we are not in a very good epistemic position to judge the matter. We can see that

ARE RADICAL EVILS ESSENTIAL TO THE PLAN OF AGAPE?

smallpox is not necessary to God's purposes, but we cannot conclude that neither are any other instances of disease. Moreover, we are not in a good position to determine what kinds of effects the changes to the natural order would have if this particular strain of bacteria or that particular kind of virus were eliminated.

The agape theodicy entails that God will miraculously preserve those who have not had a sufficient opportunity to learn the lessons they came here to learn. Nevertheless, God's miraculous intervention must be discreet and sparing to avoid defeating the purposes of the mortal probation. If God's intervention were obvious and constant, then it would require little faith to be loyal to God. Any rational being would always seek to have such a powerful ally against natural evils. We would be deprived of the opportunity to detect God's subtle hand in all things. Instead, we would be constantly tempted to try to use God as our ticket to prosperity, consistently favorable weather, and good health. It seems that our freedom to act wrongly would be severely truncated if God's existence were obvious.

Moreover, God must act sparingly in intervening to prevent natural evils because divine interventions may have unintended harmful consequences in other respects of the natural order. On the view that I have presented, God brings about miracles by withdrawing His concurrence from the natural intelligences so that they cannot manifest their natural propensities that account for the regularity of the world. When the atoms and molecules that form a weather system would devolve into a tornado, God could intervene only by withdrawing His concurring power so that they do not form electron valence bonds and thus atoms of water and other compounds would not form. Yet the result of such action is not merely to stop a tornado, but to leave chaos in the wake of ordered structure. God cannot make it so that the oxygen and hydrogen atoms suddenly act like gold atoms and thus fall to the ground under their own weight instead of swirling at high speed in the atmosphere. He cannot make it so that these atoms suddenly act any way He wants.

Given the nature of the eternal realities with which God must work, God must choose between a natural world characterized by chaos or a cosmos governed by exactly the natural laws that obtain in our world. God is responsible for the fact that there is an ordered world, but not for the fact that the world has the precise order that it does once it is ordered. Thus, it is not possible for God to have water that quenches thirst but cannot contribute to drowning. God cannot have electricity that conveys power to homes but does not kill when emitted as lightning in the atmosphere. God can only stop the inertia of a speeding car by introducing new and unpredictable consequences into the natural order. God could not have mass that does not convert to energy or a car that develops speed without inertia that has enough force to maim a physical body when it is hit. God cannot have bodies that feel no pain and still provide an environment where persons can negotiate the natural world without destroying their bodies by the numerous small bumps, bruises, and scratches that become enormous gashes and debilitating broken bones without the natural feedback of physical pain. Some pain is biologically necessary for our survival. The point is that if God grants His concurring power to the natural realities, they manifest their inherent natural propensities as dictated by their eternal natures. God does not create the eternal nature of the most basic realities or how they can be organized.

An ordered world is essential to God's plan of agape. In the absence of God's concurring power that enables the natural intelligences to express their natural propensities, there would not be any necessary causal relations. There would be no possibility of rational creatures in such a world. Plans would be frustrated because like causes would not always lead to like effects. Thus, rational expectations based upon natural regularities would be impossible. Predictions about the behavior of the natural world would never be accurate. Our bodily movements would not lead to predictable outcomes. There would be no chance for the accumulation of ordered experience or character, and thus the goal of soul-making would be impossible. Habit, character, and culture could not be formed, and intellectual development would be impossible. Technology would be impossible because it relies on natural regularities to predict how various elements will always act. In effect, the possibility of rational beings who are morally accountable for their decisions would be destroyed in such a world. For this world to be a fitting place for the emergence of rational creatures through an evolutionary process, the world must be characterized by natural regularities.

Moreover, unlike the God of traditional thought, the God of Mormonism (as I have developed the implications of Joseph Smith's revelations) cannot simply decide to have different natural laws than those that in fact obtain. That entails that God cannot simply decide that the DNA information of each person's genetic code will have a different result than it does. The deterministic natural propensities of DNA entail that God must organize through a process of evolution and gradual building of structure through mutations within the possibilities of existing DNA structures. God cannot determine what the properties of the basic biochemistry of alleles and mitochondria shall be if they bond according to the deterministic naturalistic propensities of electron valences and molecular bonds. They will have those properties that are eternally inherent in the kind of realities that they just are.

In addition, the kinds of viruses and bacteria that develop are the natural result of the causal powers of the basic realities that constitute the genetic structure of these kinds of life—or proto-life in the case of viruses. God does not so much intervene as chooses to withhold the grace of his concurring power to these eternal realities. God's concurring power is necessary to enable them to express their inherent capacities. Thus, when God acts to prevent events from occurring, the world is threatened by chaos. The world becomes disorderly and unpredictable when God does not grant His concurring power. Thus, the world tends toward greater entropy and breaks down in its regularity. God can prevent events from occurring by essentially cutting off the power supply necessary for them to exercise their causal powers in relation to each other. Thus, God can prevent fire from burning flesh, for instance, by withdrawing his organizing power to the realities involved. However, the world will be characterized by disorder and chaos in the localized area of the events. The world would be massively irregular if God withdrew His concurring power.

God's miracles leave the world open to unpredictable and unintended consequences elsewhere in the natural order. With respect to natural evils such as smallpox, God could prevent the development of the smallpox virus by withdrawing His concurring power from the organization of the viruses that form it. However, God would lose whatever benefits flow from viruses in doing so. Viruses appear to be necessary to the transposition of DNA in the process of mitosis and played a major role in enabling genetic mutations. Mutations are both good and bad, but without them there would have been no evolution. God could not have organized DNA structures to form human bodies through the process of evolution without the mutations that make genetic change possible. God similarly cannot have a world with good bacteria but no bad bacteria, given that the development of both is entailed in the same biological processes—yet some bacteria are essential to digestion and other bodily functions. The point is that withdrawing the grace of God's concurring light and power from a localized region creates unpredictable consequences elsewhere in the world that are unpredictable even for God.

Consider the nature of the sun's light in the world that is the ultimate basis for all life. The energy that the cougar uses to jump onto the deer is derived from eating meat from animals like the deer. The deer derives its energy to escape from the cougar from the plants that it eats. The plants derive their energy from the process of photosynthesis of the light of the sun. Thus, the sun is a necessary and general concurring cause of life and sentient movement in the world. If the process of photosynthesis were prevented by withdrawing this general concurrence, it would have consequences not merely for the plants but for deer and cougars as well.

With respect to animal pain, I believe that we must be careful not to anthropomorphize such pain. We use Demerol not so much to block pain as to block the memory of pain. However, it appears that an integral memory is essential to the experience of pain. If one were in pain a few seconds ago but cannot remember it, then there is no integrated consciousness of having been in pain. It is therefore very doubtful that animals, especially less complex forms of life, experience pain anything like humans experience it. Moreover, while an integrated unity of consciousness gives rise to consciousness of our experience and the ability to reflect and deliberate, it is doubtful that animals can exercise "downward causation" such that their mental states have a causal influence on their behavior. It is much more tenable to view animal consciousness as merely epiphenomenal so that whatever could be said of the mental state of humans likely is not true of animals.

The prevention of all instances of evil by God's ubiquitous miraculous intervention in nature would wreak havoc on the natural order. For example, where there is a scarcity of food, some animals die of hunger while others survive. In instances of scarcity of food, only a miraculous intervention could save all animals in both groups. However, such miraculous intervention leads to metaphysical impossibilities. The survival of one group of animals entails the death of others. If all animals survived, all carnivores would die. Thus, God would have to eliminate all carnivores to ensure that all animals live without suffering and pain. Evolution could not proceed on basis of survival of the fittest. The delicate balance of ecosystems would be destroyed and could not function as such. The consequences to other aspects of the natural order from small changes are difficult for us to assess. So, some instances of animal suffering must be allowed in order to have a world that functions as an autonomous natural order. We thus encounter the same issue with natural evil that plagues moral evils. No particular instance of natural evil is necessary to the function of nature as an arena where rational creatures capable of love could evolve and have expectations regarding the regularity of behavior. However, some instances must be permitted to achieve God's purposes for the world. Some natural evils must be permitted to have a world that functions as an ordered cosmos rather than merely chaos. Which natural evils will be permitted would appear to be a random decision. If God randomly allows animals to suffer, then some will be used as mere means to achieve God's purposes. However, it is questionable whether God must treat animals as ends in themselves and never as merely means to his ends. Such duties are owed to humans—but it is very unclear that such duties are owed to animals.

If we accept that a person-making and character-building environment capable of supporting persons in the process of learning to love must contain natural causes that result in pain and suffering, then we must accept that whatever level and amounts of pain and suffering are allowed will be intolerable for us. If smallpox is intolerable, then when it is eliminated there will remain something that is the next most deadly viral killer in the world and that too will be intolerable. However, when that is eliminated, then the next most viral killer will also be intolerable and so forth. We will not be satisfied with any level of pain and suffering—nor should we. Yet in removing all pain and suffering from the world we would have created a world that is converted from a person-making world to one that is merely a paradise for pleasure seekers. There cannot be a person-making world that is devoid of all pain and suffering.

12

ATONEMENT IN MORMON THOUGHT

God's participation in our lives by sharing humanity with us in all of its dirty, grimy, painful, and messy reality is God's answer to the problem of evil. However, He seeks to share more than just our humanity with us; He also seeks to share His full divinity with us as well. The beauty of life lived in self-realizing wonder, growth in light and knowledge, and fulfillment in truly intimate and loving relationships is the balm that heals the pain. God has invited us into the divine relationship to be as He is. But to be fit for that kind of glory and power, we have a great deal to change in ourselves and in the world. Christ's atonement is the means of healing the evil, blessing the oppressed, and overcoming the evil with which we all struggle. However, the Atonement itself seems nearly incomprehensible. Most of the expressions or pictures of atonement in Christian history are not merely inadequate, but they are also clearly misleading and often outright incoherent. Even worse, the theories of atonement are often morally repugnant in many ways. Thus, to complete the agape theodicy an explanation of the way the Atonement functions to heal evil and bind our wounds is essential.

The Christian doctrine of atonement teaches that it is because of Christ's life, suffering, death, and resurrection that forgiveness of sins is possible. Sin consists of injury to human relationships and resulting alienation. Atonement consists in eradicating from our lives whatever gets in the way of loving relationships with God and each other. Atonement thus heals our alienation. Why is it that healing, reconciliation, and unity are not possible without Christ? The traditional answers have focused on various metaphors and images that do not seem to answer this question. They instead seem to imply that Christ must overcome the anger of an unjust and unloving father, make a deal with the devil, or appease some realm of cosmic absolutes. Further, they don't really explain why simply forgiving and being forgiven are impossible without these punishments, dealings, and cosmic contraptions.

Mormon scripture suggests a departure from the traditional explanations of the Atonement, signaled by including Christ's experience in Gethsemane as a focus of the beginning of his atoning sufferings. In preparation for the experiences to follow, Christ prays to be one in unity with the disciples just as he is one with the Father. He also prays for a return of his pre-mortal glory that he enjoyed with the Father, as the second divine person of the Godhead, before the world. Further, Christ experiences surpassing spiritual anguish in Gethsemane for human sin as a prelude to the path to death on a Roman cross. It is in Gethsemane that the purpose of atonement is initiated: achieving a relationship of loving and interpenetrating unity of the type enjoyed by the divine persons in the Godhead. The added emphasis on Gethsemane in Mormon scripture is the story of how the alienation inherent in mortal life is overcome and healed through the compassion that God learns by suffering as a mortal. Atonement is the story of God's gracious offer to both accept us as worthy of covenant relationships with Him just as we are and also to enter into relationships with us where the energies of our lives and His are literally mingled as one, enabling us to grow and be made over in the divine image.

A. Desiderata for a Theory of Atonement

The *doctrine of atonement* is the claim that through Jesus's incarnation as God into mortal life, death, and resurrection, we are saved from sin and reconciled to God. It is the core of the Christian gospel. The notion that Christ suffered excruciating pain in Gethsemane and took the pain of our sins upon him is central to Mormon claims about atonement. However, it is important to distinguish between the *doctrine* of atonement—which is a claim of faith—from a symbolic or *metaphorical expression* of atonement, and both of these must be distinguished from a *theory* of atonement. One can believe something without understanding it. I believe that quantum physics is more or less accurate, but I do not fully understand quantum theory. Nevertheless, one must have some grasp of what is asserted to have faith that it is true. If the center of one's faith happened to be that "bliks can jump over the moon," such a claim literally cannot be believed because we have no idea what is being asserted. Is the Atonement like that? Is it something that we believe without having an idea of what is being asserted when we say that "Christ atoned for our sins"?

A *symbolic or metaphorical expression of atonement* tells us something about what atonement is like. There are at least five dominant metaphors for atonement in the earliest Christian scripture: (1) acquittal in a court of law (the doctrine of justification by faith—Rom. 3:21–4:25; I Cor. 1:30); (2) payment for one's release from slavery by a charitable benefactor (the doctrine of redemption—Eph. 1:7; Col. 1:14); (3) reconciliation from alienation and healing a breach of relationship between friends (2 Cor. 5:18–19; Col. 1:20–21); (4) a sacrificial offering of a paschal lamb or other offering that expiates or eradicates sin (Heb. 10:12; I Cor. 5:7); and (5) a military victory over forces of evil (Gal. 1:4; Col. 2:15). The challenge with these metaphors, however, is that they give rise to numerous views that often do not work well together and cannot be adequately answered by such metaphors.

The notion that the suffering of a man who lived in Palestine two millennia ago somehow enables us to be forgiven of our sins today—or more technically, to have our sins eradicated through expiation—is puzzling to say the least. How could this man's suffering and death two thousand years ago still have some relation to my present repentance? How is it possible that the sins I commit now could cause him pain two thousand years ago? Yet, it is as clear in the scriptures and asserted in many varied ways that Christ suffers pain because he takes our sins and infirmities upon him. Such statements are ubiquitous in both Old and New Testaments and Mormon scripture.

A *theory* of atonement, in contrast, is an explanation of how Christ's life, death, and resurrection save us from sin and reconcile us to God, and why Christ's life, death, and resurrection make a difference for us. Such theories attempt to make sense of the various scriptural metaphors and symbols and to defend the basic faith claims against arguments that atonement is unintelligible, immoral, or just plain unnecessary to explain being forgiven. Atonement is often called a solution to a problem where there is no problem. Indeed, it looks like Christianity erroneously asserts that we need a Savior who can be appropriated for salvation only within the confines of the Christian faith tradition. Do we even need an atonement to be forgiven or to forgive?

It seems to me that a theory of atonement ought to answer—or at least cast some light upon—the following questions:

1. How is Christ's life, death, and resurrection either necessary or uniquely beneficial to expiate or eradicate the effects of sin in our lives so that we are reconciled to God?
2. Why can we not just be forgiven without someone suffering?
3. Why does Christ's suffering and experience atone for our sins in a way that the Father and the Holy Ghost do not?
4. How could Christ "bear our sins" or "take our sins upon him" that we commit in the here and now in a way that caused him to suffer?
5. How do the ordinances of sacrament and baptism (among others) signify what occurs in atonement?
6. In addition, does the theory meet "Abelard's constraint" that requires a model of atonement to be "nothing unintelligible, arbitrary, illogical, [nor] immoral"?[1]

Why should a theory of atonement be required to answer just these questions? A theory is judged by its ability to best explain the relevant data: our own experiences of salvation through Christ, release from sin, reconciliation to God, and forgiving and being forgiven.

However, the primary data for any theory of atonement are the scriptural claims about the Atonement and experiences of atonement expressed in scripture. It seems to me that few claims are better attested in the LDS canon of scripture than these:

(A) Christ takes upon him and into his being the effects of our sins.

"[B]ecause Christ also suffered for you, leaving you an example, so that you might follow in his steps. He committed no sin, neither was deceit found in his mouth. When he was reviled, he did not revile in return; when he suffered, he did not threaten, but continued entrusting himself to him who judges justly. *He himself bore our sins in his body on the tree, that we might die to sin and live to righteousness.* By his wounds you have been healed" (1 Pet. 2:21–24); "For Christ also suffered once for sins, the righteous for the unrighteous, that he might bring us to God, being put to death in the flesh but made alive in the spirit" (1 Pet. 3:18).

---

1. Phillip L. Quinn, "Abelard on Atonement: Nothing Unintelligible, Arbitrary, Illogical or Immoral About It," 292.

(B) As a result of bearing our sins, Christ suffers physically and spiritually.

"And lo, he shall suffer temptations, and pain of body, hunger, thirst, and fatigue, even more than man can suffer, except it be unto death; for behold, blood cometh from every pore, so great shall be his anguish for the wickedness and the abominations of his people" (Mosiah 3:7); "[H]e has borne our griefs, and carried our sorrows; yet we did esteem him stricken, smitten of God, and afflicted. But he was wounded for our transgressions, he was bruised for our iniquities; the chastisement of our peace was upon him; and with his stripes we are healed. . . . The Lord has laid on him the iniquity of us all" (Mosiah 14:4–6; Isa. 53:4–6); "He took upon himself our infirmities and bare our sickness" (Matt. 20:28); "[H]is sweat was as it were great drops of blood" (Luke 22:44); "Christ was once suffered to bear the sins of many" (Heb. 9:28); "And he shall go forth, *suffering pains and afflictions* and temptations of every kind; and this that the word might be fulfilled which saith *he will take upon him the pains and the sicknesses of his people*; And he will take upon him death, that he may loose the bands of death which bind his people; and *he will take upon him their infirmities, that his bowels may be filled with mercy*, according to the flesh, that he may know according to the flesh how to succor his people according to their infirmities" (Alma 7:11–12).

(C) Because Christ bears our sins, we are released from the effects of our sins and our alienation and we are therefore reconciled to God and found "in Christ."

"[M]y blood was shed for many for the remission of sins" (Matt. 26:28); "[J]ustified by his blood, we shall be saved" (Rom. 5:9); "Therefore if any man *be in Christ*, he is a new creature: old things are passed away; behold, all things are become new. And all things are of God, who hath reconciled us to himself by Jesus Christ, and hath given to us the ministry of reconciliation; To wit, that God was in Christ, reconciling the world unto himself, not imputing their trespasses unto them; and hath committed unto us the word of reconciliation" (2 Cor. 5:17–19); "But now in Christ Jesus you who once were far off have been brought near by the blood of Christ" (Eph. 2:13);

"For behold, I, God, have suffered these things for all, that they might not suffer if they would repent" (D&C 19:16); "For, behold, the Lord your Redeemer suffered death in the flesh; wherefore he suffered the pain of all men, that all men might repent and come unto him" (D&C 18:11); That he came into the world, even Jesus, to be crucified for the world, and to bear the sins of the world, and to sanctify the world, and to cleanse it from all unrighteousness" (D&C 76:41).

(D) Christ's mercy shown in taking upon himself our iniquities satisfies the demands of justice for those that repent.

"For the atonement satisfieth the demands of his justice upon all those who have not the law given to them" (2 Ne. 9:26); "Therefore if that man repenteth not, and remaineth and dieth an enemy to God, the demands of divine justice do awaken his immortal soul to a lively sense of his own guilt" (Mosiah 2:38); "And thus mercy can satisfy the demands of justice, and encircles them in the arms of safety, while he that exercises no faith unto repentance is exposed to the whole law of the demands of justice; therefore only unto him that has faith unto repentance is brought about the great and eternal plan of redemption" (Mosiah 15:9); "Having ascended into heaven, having the bowels of mercy; being filled with compassion towards the children of men; standing betwixt them and justice; having broken the bands of death, taken upon himself their iniquity and their transgressions, having redeemed them, and satisfied the demands of justice" (Alma 34:16); "And now, the plan of mercy could not be brought about except an atonement should be made; therefore God himself atoneth for the sins of the world, to bring about the plan of mercy, to appease the demands of justice, that God might be a perfect, just God, and a merciful God also. . . . For behold, justice exerciseth all his demands, and also mercy claimeth all which is her own; and thus, none but the truly penitent are saved" (Alma 42:15, 24).

I suggest that no theory in the history of Christianity to date has actually met the burden of explaining how Christ's suffering somehow eradicates our sin in the here and now. I submit that no theory to date has adequately answered the questions raised by the claim that because of Christ our sins are forgiven. None has adequately explained how Christ could possibly bear the pain of sins that haven't even occurred yet—and might not occur because sin is necessarily the result of free choices that could be otherwise. Finally, no theory that I am aware of meets Abelard's Constraint of providing a non-arbitrary explanation for Christ's Atonement that is both coherent and morally acceptable.

B. Does Mormonism Add Anything to the Penal-Substitution Theory?

Mormon discussions of atonement usually assume the Penal-Substitution Theory (PST) that is the mainstay of evangelical thought.[2] This theory maintains that sin is like a debt that someone must pay, and so Christ pays it as a third-party benefactor. This payment is made by Christ because he has amassed super-abundant credit by his mortal life. God's justice is seen as necessarily retributive in nature so that someone has to be punished to satisfy God's just nature. However, for some inexplicable reason, it doesn't have to be the sinner that is punished for his or her own sins. Rather, someone else can be punished to satisfy the demands of justice. Thus, the Father punishes Christ in our place.

However, there are numerous problems with PST. These problems include:

1. It erroneously assumes that justice is a personified platonic absolute that makes demands;
2. It posits a conflict between the wrathful Father who must be persuaded by his loving Son not to punish us;
3. It erroneously assumes that it is just to punish an innocent person in the place of a guilty person;
4. It assumes that guilt and righteousness can be imputed or transferred from a guilty person to an innocent person and vice versa;
5. It provides no reason that guilt must be punished and why God cannot just forgive us without requiring a third-party who committed no sin to suffer;
6. It erroneously analogizes sin to a monetary debt.

---

2. See, for example, Hyrum L. Andrus, *God, Man and the Universe*, chs. 15 and 16; Boyd K. Packer, "The Mediator"; Ronald A. Heiner, "The Necessity of a Sinless Messiah," 5–30.

As I have argued in *Exploring Mormon Thought: The Problems of Theism and the Love of God*, I believe that these reasons are decisive. However, the question remains: Does Mormon thought have the resources to explain or mitigate these problems with the Penal Substitution Theory? Hyrum Andrus provides perhaps the most sophisticated version of PST in Mormon writings. He argues:

> As a divine being, Christ made an infinite sacrifice in order to pay the debt of sin and give life and truth and light to man. . . . The doctrine of the atonement expressed in Latter-day revelation is centered in the immutable requirements of eternal law. The Nephite prophet Alma taught that both penalty and reward are established for each law that god ordains, and that each penalty and reward must be "eternal as the life of the soul." Otherwise, neither justice nor mercy could have "claim on the creature." . . . To satisfy the demands of divine justice and institute a plan of mercy, an atonement had to be made. The Father is a God of justice; and justice had to be paid. The Father's will in this regard had to be fulfilled. The honor and integrity of the Man of Holiness had to be sustained. . . . Justice required the Father to cause the chosen redeemer to suffer. It had to be; truth and consistency made it so. Having fulfilled the will of the Father, Jesus therefore declared: "I have drunk of that bitter cup which the Father hath given me, and have glorified the Father in taking upon me the sins of the world, in which I have suffered the will of the Father in all things from the beginning" (3 Ne. 11:11; see also John 18:11).[3]

To this point in Andrus's discussion, he offers a straight-forward argument based on assumptions in PST. He smuggles in the notion that "justice had to be paid," even though not a single Mormon scripture mentions anything about a money payment in connection with atonement. He posits that the "demands of justice" require that someone must suffer for sin—even if it is not the person who is guilty of that sin. There is nothing here to distinguish the discussion from the standard PST. He even drops in the Anselm's notion that God's honor demands payment to be satisfied. None of these assertions have any scriptural backing.

However, Andrus makes a subsidiary argument that differs from traditional PST. Andrus argues, "For Jesus to take upon Himself the consequences of sin required that He suffer spiritual death for all men, and to this end the Spirit of God was withdrawn from him."[4] Spiritual death in

---

3. Andrus, *God, Man and the Universe*, 396–97.
4. Andrus, 441

Mormon thought means to be fully cut off from God's presence. Andrus also argues that such withdrawal of the Spirit was necessary to test Jesus's

> integrity commensurate with the light and truth He had received from His Father.... [T]he withdrawal of spiritual powers enabled Christ to descend below all things so that He could comprehend all things, and thereby obtain experience and prepare Himself to rescue the fulness of the Father's glory in the resurrection. Having acquired the fulness of the Father's glory, Jesus could then develop in their fulness the divine attributes and powers of truth, and light, and life in others.... [I]n His earthly experience, Jesus learned by direct contact with mortal weakness and spiritual darkness how to succor his people.[5]

The notion that the Atonement was necessary for Christ's growth and experience is revolutionary. Rather than a self-sufficient God who dispenses supererogatory merit to others so that the Father regards them as righteous when they are really sinners, Christ's suffering is a learning experience to enable him to empathize with broken humans. The notion that Christ suffered spiritual death—that he was completely cut off from the Father—is also fairly novel. Andrus follows Brigham Young, who taught that God withdrew his spirit from Jesus in the moment of greatest agony and need so that Christ could learn from his trials to the greatest extent conceivable.[6] However, these observations by Andrus suggest an approach to the Atonement radically different from PST and not merely an amendment or addition to it. Andrus's observations suggest a kenotic view of atonement in which Christ empties himself of the fulness of the divine glory to experience firsthand the vicissitudes of mortal life. The fact that Christ's capacity to succor his people increased because he gained experiential knowledge of the depth of human pain and suffering entails that Christ's capacities to love us were increased by the Atonement rather than merely our capacity to repent and be forgiven. I believe that Andrus offered valuable insights into the nature of Christ's atonement—however, those insights have nothing to do with paying a debt of sin owed by another to the Father.

---

5. Andrus, 441–42
6. Andrus, 441

C. Mormon Theories of Atonement

There have been several theories of atonement that are both historically unique and inherently interesting. I think that it is safe to say that most Mormons accept a form of PST. New theories have been suggested largely out of dissatisfaction with substitutionary theories and the unique beliefs and resources of the revelations and teachings of Joseph Smith.

1. The Demand of Eternal Intelligences for Justice

A novel and interesting theory was introduced by Cleon Skousen. According to Skousen, all material reality consists of intelligences that act as they do because of their trust in God. God's power and glory depend upon the faith and trust that the intelligences place in God. If they did not honor and trust God, then "God would cease to be God" (Alma 42:13, 22; Morm. 9:19). The fact that we have sinned and not been punished for it calls into question God's governance and justice. The intelligences demand justice. If the intelligences are not satisfied, then they will rebel against God's governance and God will cease to be God. The intelligences demand that someone must suffer for the wrongs that have been committed. To satisfy the demand for justice, God sends his own Son because the intelligences respect and trust the Son as much as they do God. However, when they see the suffering of a person they love who is entirely innocent and without sin, they are revolted by their own demand for justice. They see, in effect, that their demand for justice is itself a form of injustice and refusal to forgive. Their demand for justice is thus appeased and replaced with a change of heart that leads the intelligences to be merciful.[7]

There is a lot to like in this theory. It makes progress in answering some of the questions that form the basis of a theory of atonement. There is no eternal law that prevents God from forgiving us from sin. He could just forgive us. However, there is an unjust demand from subjects of the kingdom that requires that someone must pay the price for sin by suffering. There is a reason why the suffering must be done by Christ or at least someone like him: the intelligences must respect and love the victim of the unjust crucifixion. Further, the extent of the suffering must be so excessive and unjust that

---

7. W. Cleon Skousen, *The First 2,000 Years: From Adam to Abraham*, Appendix A.

it shocks the conscious and awakens feelings of outrage and reconsideration of one's own unjust demands and refusal to forgive without someone giving a pound of flesh. The suffering is related to forgiveness because it occasions a decision to let go of unjust demands for retribution and thus leads to forgiveness and repentance. This theory exposes our own unjust demands for justice and refusal to forgive others. It exposes our own unjust refusal to let go of demands for retribution. All of this is very enlightening.

However, the theory doesn't account for the scriptural data that must be explained by a theory of atonement. It doesn't connect with the scriptural sense in which Christ actually bears our sins. According to scripture, the pain that Christ suffers arises from taking our sins upon himself and indeed into his own person (see I Pet. 2:21–24). My sins do not seem to be involved in anything that Christ does because the intelligences were persuaded to give up their unjust demands two thousand years ago. What I do in the present seems totally disconnected from this explanation for atonement. Perhaps it could be said that Christ bears the brunt of an unjust demand for retribution and in this sense bears the sins of the intelligences. However, our sins are not limited to just making unjust demands for retribution. Moreover, the Atonement functions by God giving in to unjust demands and thus entails that God is, in fact, complicit in unjustly requiring His Son to suffer to appease these unjust demands. Moreover, the biggest question it raises for me is: why doesn't the Father himself undergo the punishment to assuage the unjust demands? This view seems to entail that the Father is both unjust and a coward. Wouldn't the intelligences lose faith and trust in the Father for failing to take accountability for the solution? Perhaps it could be argued that it was tougher for the Father to stand on the sidelines and watch His Son suffer. However, that merely emphasizes that the Father had every reason to undergo the unjust suffering himself.

Moreover, is God's status as God really that precarious—that if the intelligences simply fail to honor Him, God ceases to be God? If that is so, why would such a god inspire us at all—or even be in a position to command our total allegiance as He does throughout all scriptural texts? Moreover, the scriptural warrant for this view is obviously questionable. Alma's discussion of the "demands of justice" in Alma 34 and 42 clearly has nothing to do with the demands of intelligences for someone to pay the price of violation of the law.

2. The Self-Rejection Moral Theory of Atonement

Eugene England gives an eloquent expression to his view of atonement. What is unique is that England presents the "demands of justice" spoken of by Alma as our own demand for justice to be meted out to ourselves for our own moral failures. We are estranged by our own sense of moral responsibility for what we have done that is beyond our power to repair. Because of this we are unable to accept ourselves:

> Paradoxically, our moral sense of justice both brings me to the awareness of sin that must begin all repentance and yet interferes with my attempts to repent. I feel that every action must bear its consequences and that I must justify my actions to myself; since there is a gap between belief and action I am in a state which brings into my heart and mind a sense of guilt, of unbearable division within myself. As Alma taught his sinful son Corianton, "There was a punishment affixed, and a just law given, which brought remorse of conscience unto man" (Alma 42:18). This same moral nature, this sense of justice that demands satisfaction, causes me to want to improve my life but also to insist that I pay the penalty in some way for my sin. But of course there is no way I can finally do this. . . . God pierces to the heart of this paradox through the Atonement, and it becomes possible for us personally to experience both alienation and reconciliation, which opens us to the full meaning of both evil and good, bringing us to a condition of meekness and lowliness of heart where we can freely accept from God the power to be a god. And Alma also taught his son this other essential role God plays in the Atonement. Besides giving mortals "remorse of conscience" by giving the law and judging us, "God himself atoneth for the sins of the world, to bring about the plan of mercy, to appease the demands of justice" (Alma 42:15).[8]

However, God intervenes through Jesus to assuage this sense of moral responsibility that leads to estrangement from God and ourselves. He penetrates our refusal to accept ourselves by showing us that because God accepts us unconditionally, we are worthy of our own self-acceptance:

> Christ is the unique manifestation in human experience of the fullness of that unconditional love from God which Paul chose to represent with the Greek term *agape*. As Paul expressed it, "While we were yet sinners, Christ died for us" (Romans 5:8). Christ's sacrificial love was not conditional upon our qualities, our repentance, anything; he expressed his love to us while we

---

8. Eugene England, "That They Might Not Suffer: The Gift of Atonement," 85–86.

were yet in our sins—not completing the process of forgiveness, which depends on our response, but initiating it in a free act of mercy. This is a kind of love quite independent from the notion of justice. There is no *quidproquo* about it, . . . and that is precisely why it is redemptive. It takes a risk, without calculation, on the possibility that we can realize our infinite worth. It gets directly at that barrier in us, our sense of justice, which makes me incapable of having unconditional love for myself—unable to respond positively to my own potential, because I am unable to forgive myself, unable to be at peace with myself until I have somehow "made up" in suffering for my sins, something I am utterly incapable of doing. The demands of justice that Amulek and Alma are talking about, which must be overpowered, are from *our own sense of justice*, not some abstract eternal principle but our own demands on ourselves; those demands which bring us into estrangement with ourselves (as we gain new knowledge of right but do not live up to it) and thus begin the process of growth through repentance, but we cannot complete that process.[9]

Ultimately, England's theory must be seen as a form of moral influence theory. The effect upon us is a psychological realization that we are worthwhile. As England expresses it, "That the Atonement is performed by Christ, the son and revelation of God, is, of course, crucial. He represents to us the ultimate source of justice and is the one whose teachings and example bring us directly to face our need for repentance; he awakens our own sense of justice and stands as a judge over all our actions and thus only he can fully release us from what becomes the immobilizing burden of that judgment, through the power of mercy extended unconditionally in his Atonement."[10] However, when pressing his own theory with the question as to why Christ must suffer and how this suffering is supposed to link up with our sins today, he ultimately begs off giving an answer because, according to England, the New Testament is not a book of theology and we are best left with a kaleidoscope of various metaphors:

> The question "Why is man's salvation dependent on Christ and the events surrounding his death?" is the most central and the most difficult question in Christian theology. The answers (and there are many) are, as I have said, the chief scandal of Christianity to the nonbeliever. Attempts to define logical theories of the Atonement based on New Testament scriptures have

---

9. England, 86; emphasis in original.
10. England, 86–87.

been largely contradictory and ultimately futile—mainly because the New Testament is not a book of theology, a logical treatise, but rather gives us the reaction, the varied emotional responses.[11]

England does claim, however, that the Atonement is necessary because only Christ can motivate the kind of change to accept ourselves with our own self-love:

> The Atonement is a necessary, but not sufficient, factor in salvation from sin—necessary because only Christ can fully motivate the process in free agents, and insufficient because an agent must respond and complete the process. There is no condition in which we can imagine God being unable to forgive. The question is what effect will the forgiveness have; the forgiveness is meaningless unless it leads to repentance.[12]

It seems to me, though, that England is mistaken in his assertion that *only* Christ can motivate "the process" of self-love in agents—or even the kind of repentance that can be accomplished without any unique atonement. There are numerous examples of persons who have suffered unjustly with forbearance and love. Why wouldn't the sufferings of Peter, who was supposedly crucified upside-down, or Mahatma Ghandi suffice? According to England, only Christ will do "because he is the ultimate source of justice." However, what it could mean for Christ to be the "ultimate source of justice" is left vague. Certainly such an extravagant metaphysical and metaethical claim requires some support. England's observations provide us with nothing more than an inspiring example of loving acceptance. Numerous examples from history show that Christ was far from being a uniquely inspiring example of love. Similarly, one hardly has to look only to Christ for an example of a human suffering injustice and dying at the hands of others.

Furthermore, with England's view there does not seem to be any sense in which Christ bears our sins. His suffering is unrelated to our actual sins or to forgiveness of those sins. Indeed, what is necessary is not suffering but merely God's loving acceptance without any prior conditions. Such loving acceptance surely can be given and manifest without Christ bearing our sins and suffering. Far from needing a savior, all of the benefits of atonement given in England's theory seem to be obtainable without anything done by Christ at all. All I have to do is give up my own unjustified demand for

---

11. England, 87.
12. England, 89.

self-rejection. He provides no reason why I cannot simply do that on my own. This is, of course, a general criticism that applies to all moral influence theories. There is nothing immoral or illogical about such a view, and it meets Abelard's Constraint. Instead, it simply fails to explain what a theory of atonement must explain. Perhaps England would suggest that he was not attempting to give a theory at all (since he disclaims any such enterprise). Rather, he just wanted to illuminate some aspects of our human experience of atonement—and in that, he undoubtedly succeeded.

3. The Empathy Theory of Atonement

Kelli Potter presented a novel theory of atonement that focuses on qualifying Christ to be our judge. Potter argues that justice can be equally satisfied by either punishment or forgiveness. However, forgiveness instead of punishment is only appropriate in certain circumstances. God should forgive us only when it is best to do so. The judgment as to when forgiveness is best depends on considerations such as what best serves the sinner, the remorse and repentance of the sinner, and whether the sinner has truly reformed. However, according to this theory, God does not have a sufficient basis to judge us because He has not shared our mortal experiences of alienation and sin firsthand. Potter asserts:

> The suffering in Gethsemane is a miraculous event in which Jesus experiences exactly what each of us experiences in our sinning. Only then can he fully understand why we do what we do. Only then can he fully understand the circumstances of our crimes. Only then can he know our remorse, and know whether our hearts have changed.... Being one of the judges himself, this understanding of our hearts allows him to justly pardon us in the event that we feel remorse for our sins.[13]

Christ can judge justly because he can empathize with us. The "demands of justice," which the Book of Mormon says are "satisfied" by Christ's sacrificial atonement, are met because God will not forgive where mercy is unwarranted.[14] Mercy is also granted when it is warranted by the best judgment based upon considerations of the sinner's contrition, reparations, and

---

13. R. Dennis Potter [now Kelli D. Potter], "Did Christ Pay for Our Sins?," 83.
14. For references to how mercy exemplified in the Atonement "satisfies the demands of justice," see 2 Nephi 2:26; Mosiah 2:38; 15:9; Alma 34:16; 42:15, 24.

reform. But this theory goes far beyond that. The Empathy Theory seems to adopt the Buddhist view that to understand all is to forgive all. However, it seems to require that Christ actually knows exactly what we do and the reasons that we do it before we do it. How does he know such things? Such claims seem odd because Potter accepts, as I do, that foreknowledge is incompatible with free will.[15] Thus, God cannot know our free acts before we do them. Yet this theory seems to require that Christ precisely knows what we do and why we do it—not only for sins that occurred prior to his suffering in Gethsemane, but also for the sins that we are committing two thousand years later. Indeed, he would have to know our reasons for sinning as well. How could Christ know that about us in Gethsemane? Because of His omniscience, God certainly comes to know our reasons at the time we actually sin, but that means that Christ does not need to have the miracle in Gethsemane at all.

Perhaps we should understand Potter to be asserting that Christ knows only what it is like to be subject to temptation and the reasons that one could sin. He has empathy for us in Gethsemane and not actual foreknowledge of what we will do. There is something that seems right about this assertion: Christ is better qualified to judge us, it seems, if he has shared our same mortal condition and suffered with us. But how does this account explain the extreme pain that he experienced as recounted in scripture? This theory fails to account for the scriptural claims that Christ actually bears our sins and suffers for them. It fails to account for the claim that because of his suffering we are released from our own suffering and reconciled to God. While we might have more confidence in God to be fair to us, does this account do anything to explain how we become "sanctified through the atonement" as the scriptures claim (2 Ne. 2:8; D&C 74:7)?

Further, this theory implies that God does not forgive us until after we repent, and it doesn't explain how atonement enables us to repent as Mormon scripture claims (see 2 Ne. 2, Alma 34, 42). Why do we need atonement at all if we can repent on our own and are deserving of forgiveness because of that repentance? It seems that we have earned the right to be forgiven on such a view. It might account for why Christ is in a position to be our judge, but it does not fully meet the requirements of an adequate theory of atonement.

---

15. Blake T. Ostler, *Exploring Mormon Thought: The Attributes of God*, 187–99.

4. The Divine Infusion Theory

Jacob Morgan has presented what he terms the divine infusion theory. Morgan begins by distinguishing two kinds of laws of justice.[16] The first is punitive justice, which demands a punishment if someone sins regardless of whether or not they later change. The second type is what he calls deserts punishment, which punishes a person according to what is deserved. Deserts punishment is not as worried about what a person did as to what a person presently is. Its goal is reform, and if a person repents there is no reason to punish the sinner. According to Morgan, many have taken the "demands of justice" spoken of in the Book of Mormon as the demands for punishment of punitive justice. However, Morgan rejects that view. He asserts that there is another law that applies to those who repent: the Law of Restoration, which is a deserts-based sense of justice wherein everyone gets what they deserve—either based on their works or on the principle that everyone naturally reaps what they sew. There is a natural result for our actions that dictates that we receive mercy for mercy, light for light, and so forth (D&C 88:39–40).

The purpose of punitive justice is to motivate us to repent. If we do not repent, then we are punished. However, mercy can "overpower justice" (Alma 34.15) when repentance based upon true reform has taken place. He states: "There is no need for suffering (vicarious or otherwise) once we have reformed from our sinful ways."[17] To be saved in the celestial kingdom, we must learn to live the celestial law. God cannot decide which kingdom of glory we will receive because that determination follows naturally from the kind of law we live. "Justice is ultimately concerned with what we are—not merely that we obtain forgiveness from God, but that we become like God if we want to live where he does."[18]

Morgan contends that, according to Mormon scripture, we would be in a "super-fallen state" except for the Atonement—that is, we would not be able to repent.[19] We would be unable to choose to repent because we would lack a conscience that allows us to discern between right and wrong. However, as a result of the Atonement, every person is enlightened with the

---

16. Jacob Morgan, "The Divine Infusion Theory: Rethinking the Atonement," 57–81.
17. Morgan, 69.
18. Morgan, 69.
19. Morgan, 64.

light of Christ, which provides to every person the ability to discern between right and wrong (2 Ne. 2:26, Moro. 7:16, 19). Thus, the Atonement is the basis of human agency:

> Without conscience, we would have no practical hope of choosing the right and overcoming temptation. We rely on borrowed light for our recognition of goodness. We could not progress through the exercise of agency if our environment was full of temptation toward sin without anything tempting us toward righteousness.[20]

Morgan summarizes his view of atonement: "The atonement was not a matter of satisfying justice's relentless thirst for suffering. Instead, it was a matter of pulling the universe far enough out of the darkness to make repentance and growth possible."[21] God does that by giving His light to give life to all things. This light is the law by which all things are governed. Morgan concludes that "atonement brought life to all things by infusing the light of Christ in all things. Surely that makes the resurrection more at home in the divine-infusion theory than in any of the other theories."[22]

It seems to me that all of this is correct. My observation is that Morgan does not present a complete theory of atonement. Rather, he presents a theory of prevenient grace that is a necessary condition to accept the grace made available through the Atonement. He does not address many of the crucial questions that a theory of atonement ought to address. Not once does he mention either Gethsemane or the cross, nor does he even reflect on why Jesus suffers or how Jesus bears our sins in atonement. Morgan admits that the Divine-Infusion Theory "does not answer the question of why suffering is necessary to infuse the light of Christ in and through all things, but such is the testimony of modern revelation."[23] Indeed, it is clear that Jesus does not need to suffer in order for his light to be in and through all things—it was in and through all things before he suffered. Any theory of atonement that fails to address the need for Christ's suffering is not a complete theory of atonement. Regardless, the claims that Morgan makes in his Divine-Infusion Theory seem correct to me.

---

20. Morgan, 75.
21. Morgan, 76.
22. Morgan, 77.
23. Morgan, 76–77.

D. A Brief Summary of the Compassion Theory of Atonement

I suggest that Mormon scripture presents a view of atonement that radically differs from the historical theories and has the resources to avoid all of the problems of the other theories. The (barely) essential features of the Compassion Theory of Atonement are as follows:[24]

1. *Sin is self-absorbed alienation.* As we grow from childhood, we all freely (though innocently at first) make the choice to hide ourselves from God and each other by hardening our hearts. We betray ourselves by violating the law of love and choose to harden our hearts against God and others. In doing so, we alienate ourselves from authentic existence and engage in numerous behaviors that injure our relationships with others. We engage in a self-deceived way of being where we convince ourselves that remaining alienated will bring us the greatest happiness.

2. *Atonement persuades us to give up our alienation.* In the absence of atonement, we would be "super-fallen" in the sense that we would be angels to the devil, stuck in our sinful nature and unable to freely choose to repent. However, God gives us our agency by (a) giving us the light of Christ, which actuates our conscience and provides for us a knowledge of good and evil; and by (b) offering to enter into relationship with us as a matter of unconditional grace and unmerited love. Because of the Atonement, we are made free to choose between a relationship in eternal life with Him or suffering pain of alienation and spiritual death. He offers to accept us into this covenant relationship through the sign of baptism. At the moment we freely accept this free gift, we are, as a matter of grace, "justified" or in a right covenant relationship with God. In the moment of opening our hearts to accept Christ, we are redeemed from our alienation and reconciled to God. It is through realization that God both loves us unconditionally and regards us as worthy to be in covenant relationship with Him that we can persuaded to soften our hearts and be open to relationship once again.

3. *Repentance heals and maintains the relationship.* In order to be in relationship with a perfect being, we must be willing to abide those

---

24. A more complete expression of the theory can be found in Blake T. Ostler, *Exploring Mormon Thought: The Love of God and the Problems of Theism*, 189–284.

conditions that are inherent in a close and abiding relationship of fellowship—the provisions of the law of love. The conditions of the law of love define the terms of the covenant necessary to remain in relationship with God and the community of God's kingdom. We must be willing to let go of our past and all of the behaviors that, by their very nature, create alienation. That is, we must repent by ceasing to engage in behaviors contrary to the law of love, making reparation for the harms we have caused, and asking forgiveness of those we have treated with less than love.

4. *Union with Christ results in new life and light.* When we repent and open ourselves to accept Christ, we accept his light into our lives to commingle with the light or life's energy of our lives. We become a new person "in Christ," living a co-shared life in which his light shines in our countenances. We become "new creatures" who are born again into this newness of life in Christ. He takes up abode in us, and we take up abode in him. We take his name upon us, and his image is renewed in us. In this sense, we are at-one with Christ. Prior to entering into union with Christ, our lives are burdened by the darkness of sin. When we overcome our alienation by entering into a union of life in Christ, the darkness of our lives that we share with him is transformed by the light of his love to a greater brightness that grows in the process of sanctification. That is, sanctification is the process of growth in the light toward deification. Deification is the fullness of glorification in union with the divine persons of the Godhead.

5. *A condition of entering into union is willingness to be vulnerable to the other in a relationship.* Love, by its very nature, entails vulnerability to the free choices of the other person in the relationship. The Compassion Theory maintains that our sins cause pain for those who would choose to be in a relationship with us as a natural necessity of the way that authentic relationships function. It is painful to be in a relationship with those who violate the law of love in many ways. In addition, divine union entails the co-inherence or indwelling of our lives in each other. According to Mormon scripture, we share our light with each other in union (D&C 88:45–58; 93:28–40). The Compassion Theory posits that when the darkness of our sins is mingled with the perfect light of Christ, we are enlightened, but the darkness that is in us causes him to experience momentary but excruciating pain. The darkness is a cause of momentary pain that is turned to joy through repentance and healing relationship. Christ is not punished for our sins, nor does he bear our shameful guilt or moral culpability; rather, what he experiences is the pain and subsequent joy of entering into relationship of shared life and light with imperfect humans.

6. *Christ is uniquely able to accomplish atonement.* To enter into the union of life in a way that expresses not merely empathy and omniscient knowing but experiential sharing of our alienated condition, Christ learned compassion by the things that he suffered. According to Mormon scripture, Christ learned how to succor us and share our lives fully by the things that he suffered as a mortal (Alma 7:10–13). Christ is uniquely qualified by his experience because he achieved a fullness of union and glory with the Father while in the Garden of Gethsemane and knew firsthand the pain of omniscient empathy of all the sin that had occurred in the world. Further, fully divine beings, as such, cannot experience firsthand the alienation that is the essence of our human condition, because they abide in a relationship of complete union with the divine persons. Only by becoming mortal and experiencing alienation firsthand can such experiential knowledge be possible. Christ suffered the essence of spiritual death while on the cross when he experienced complete abandonment by the Father following his complete union with the Father. Only he, in all of history, knew the fullness of the loss of that union and the depth of pain of complete abandonment. These experiences uniquely qualify Christ to succor us in pain and to persuade us to overcome our alienation by choosing to repent and enter into relationship with him. Only Christ had the fullness of experience to transform our darkness with his light, in virtue of his experiences in Gethsemane and on the cross. His forgiveness of those who nailed him to the cross while in this state of alienated abandonment is the completion of divine love necessary to render at-one-ment and overcome our alienation.

Christ is also uniquely able to effect atonement because he has power in himself to lay down his life and take it up again. Christ is able to resurrect and to grant the power of resurrection to us as well. The resurrection overcomes our alienation by bringing us back into the presence of God to be judged according to our works. We are judged according to the desires of our hearts by the Law of Restoration, which returns to us what we truly desire, as shown by our works (Alma 41). The Law of Restoration is also recognized by the fact that the degree of light or glory that "quickens" or gives life to our bodies in the resurrection is dependent on whether we abide a telestial, terrestrial, or celestial law (D&C 88:20–32).

7. *Atonement is the mode of relationship God seeks to have with us.* To be at-one is to be in divine union. Being at-one is the very mode of being that Christ seeks with us at all times. He seeks to have the greatest possible unity of loving relationship. He seeks for us to relate to him in the very same unity of oneness with which he relates to the Father and Holy Ghost. Through our union with Christ, we shall thus also be at-one with the divine persons in the Godhead in the same sense that they are one.

8. *Christ satisfied the demands of justice of the Law of Restoration.* Christ suffered as the first person ever to join together the fullness of capacity for experience as God with mortal experience intimately acquainted with human suffering firsthand. The magnitude of suffering was so great that Christ initially shrank at the prospect, but he nevertheless willingly experienced the pain to fulfill the will of the Father so that he could be fully moved by compassion: "And thus he shall bring salvation *to all those who shall believe on his name*; this being the intent of this last sacrifice, to bring about the *bowels of mercy*, which overpowereth justice, and bringeth about means unto men that they may have faith unto repentance" (Alma 34:15). "Having ascended into heaven, having the bowels of mercy; *being filled with compassion towards the children of men*; standing betwixt them and justice; having broken the bands of death, *taken upon himself their iniquity and their transgressions*, having redeemed them, and satisfied the demands of justice" (Mosiah 15:9). The "demands of justice" are the demands of the Law of Restoration that each person shall have returned what she or he has sent out, reaping what has been sown. If we repent, then Christ willingly and lovingly accepts into his being what we would have suffered

so that we will not have to. If we do not repent, then we must suffer for our own sins (Alma 41). The purpose of the law that decrees that we shall receive according to our works in judgment is to awaken us to the suffering we will endure as a natural result of our actions if we fail to repent.

The demands of justice are answered in Christ's Atonement because we each receive the very life that we freely choose—nothing could be more just (see Alma 41). If we choose to repent, then we receive mercy by letting go of our past and forgiving all others. As we forgive and show mercy, we are forgiven and receive mercy. If we fail to forgive, then we suffer the full weight of justice for our sins by bearing the pain ourselves as the *natural consequences* of unloving conduct.

Thus, the Compassion Theory rejects the retributive notion of justice that demands that someone must suffer and pay a price in order for someone to be forgiven. The demand of suffering and payment is replaced by the condition that one must repent and have a genuine change at the core of one's being—one's very heart—to meet the demands of justice. Because the Atonement meets the demands of justice—rather than executing justice immediately—we need not be punished to satisfy the demands of justice. Instead, God has demonstrated His mercy by placing us on probation and giving us time to repent before the final judgment (see Alma 42).

The primary merit of the Compassion Theory, in my view, is that it answers the important questions and explains the basic scriptural claims that must be met by a theory of atonement, without being unintelligible, arbitrary, illogical, or immoral. I believe that it has the added merit of doing so in a way that is not merely faithful to, but explanatory of, the various scriptural metaphors and claims about the Atonement. Not only does it explain how and why Christ bears and suffers for our sins of which we repent, it explains how Christ does so without suffering needlessly nor unjustly. He does not suffer to appease the wrath of a vengeful Father or to satisfy the unjust demands of some platonic ideal of justice. Neither is his suffering a retributive price for a debt owed.

With the Compassion Theory God can forgive us without requiring someone to suffer. Christ's suffering is directly related to my sins because he actually bears the pain of my sins for which I repent but does not unjustly suffer for those which I do not repent of and must then suffer myself. By letting go of the pain of our sins that is in us through repentance, we are released from further suffering the effects of our sins. Moreover, according to the Compassion Theory, the Atonement is directly related to our justification and sanctification because the union of our lives creates a new person through the eradication of our sinful being with the light of Christ. It puts in bold relief the compassionate and sacrificial love that Christ manifests in justifying, redeeming, and aiding us in our progress. Thus, the Compassion Theory has the incredible virtue of being the first theory of atonement that actually answers the relevant questions and explains the scriptural data.

Moreover, the Compassion Theory also has the benefit of illuminating and interacting with the best Pauline scholarship. Our union in Christ's life—being at-one in him—is symbolized by baptism through which we enter into covenant, die with Christ, and rise to resurrection of life with him. We take his life into ours, making him the energy of our lives and bodies, by symbolically eating his flesh and drinking his blood in the sacrament. The New Perspective on Paul, a growing scholarly understanding of Paul, explains that Paul's focus was not on an imputation of Christ's righteousness to make those who are unrighteous righteous; instead his focus was on being found "in Christ" through covenant faithfulness. Consider how the Compassion Theory corresponds with a summary of Paul's thought by New Testament scholar Morna Hooker:

> The sin of Adam was reversed and the possibility of restoration opened up when Christ lived and died in obedience and was raised from life to death. Those who are baptized into him are able to share his death to sin (Rom. 6:4–11) and his status of righteousness before God (2 Cor. 5:21). Since Adam's sin brought corruption into the world, restoration involved the whole universe (Rom. 8:19–22; Col. 1:15–20). . . . [Christ] shared our humanity, and all that means in terms of weakness, . . . in order that we might share in his sonship and righteousness. To do this, however, Christians must share in his death and Resurrection, dying to the realm of flesh and rising to life in the Spirit. Thus Paul speaks of being crucified with Christ in order that Christ may live in him (Gal. 2:19–20). The process of death and resurrection is symbolized by baptism (Rom. 6:3–4). By "baptism into Christ," believers are united "with him," so that they now live "in him." These phrases (in particular "in Christ") express the close relationship between Christ and believers that is so important for Paul.[25]

---

25. Morna Hooker, "Paul," 522.

Instead of pointing to a punishment that God imposes on Christ to satisfy His wrath, the focus is instead on the incarnation and Christ's sharing our mortal condition in an indwelling unity of life. Perhaps the best summary of the Compassion Theory is Paul's statement in 2 Corinthians 5:21 (ESV): "For our sake he [God] made him [Christ] to be sin who did not know sin, so that we might become the righteousness of God in him [Christ]." That is, he takes the effects of our sin into himself to be healed, and thus the sin in us is transformed into life and light in Christ. We become the righteousness of God in Christ by accepting the light of Christ into our hearts in the Atonement. Thus, our alienation is healed, and we are reconciled to God.

E. Response to Critiques of the Compassion Theory

Like most theories, the Compassion Theory is not without criticism. The measure of a theory is its ability to respond persuasively to trenchant criticism from able critics. I believe that it has the resources to respond to the most serious criticisms.

1. The Problem of Causing Christ Pain for Our Sins when We Repent.

Deidre Green maintains that the Compassion Theory is vastly unacceptable because of the manner in which it focuses on suffering and its implicit suggestion that those who repent sadistically impose pain on Christ. She states:

> If Christ's suffering for an individual's sins does not occur until that individual repents, two problems arise. The first is that atonement becomes a matter of conscious and volitional sadism on the part of the repentant sinner; the second is that because of this, human individuals themselves who have compassion and empathy for Christ would be highly unmotivated to repent. If, as Ostler states, "the purpose of the Atonement is to overcome our alienation by creating compassion, a life shared in union where we are moved by our love for each other," then this object is largely subverted by creating a model in which human persons either selfishly and sadistically transfer their pain to Christ in an immediate sense, or choose to refrain from participating in repentance and atonement for the sake of sparing Christ more suffering. This may be especially true for women who are so-

cialized to place the feelings of others before their own and to choose to suffer themselves in order not to impose suffering on others.[26]

It is a fact that, given the commitments of the Compassion Theory, Christ will experience pain if and when we enter into healing relationship with him—as well as with the Father and Holy Ghost through Christ. However, we do not foist any such pain on him, as Green contends. He willingly chooses to enter into relationships that entail momentary but excruciating pain in order to realize the joy of healing and indwelling union. Although Green repeatedly decries any view that involves God in pain as a result of relationships, she admits that it

> does seem that from one aspect of the LDS perspective, Christ suffers in order to experience solidarity with human beings and that human individuals at times experience suffering for the purpose of empathizing with the suffering of Christ. This points to the fact that suffering is a natural part of both human and divine realities and that simply cannot be avoided. . . . Experiencing suffering helps individuals appreciate what Christ did for them and allows them to relate their own sufferings to his.[27]

Nevertheless, Green argues that the Compassion Theory is morally repugnant because it entails that we foist pointless pain upon Christ in the act of repenting, and no sensitive person would ever choose to do that as a means of repentance.

What this critique apparently finds appalling is that Christ cannot avoid suffering if we choose to repent. However, Green's critique is mistaken on many different levels. Green repeatedly describes the pain that Christ suffers according to the Compassion Theory as a form of sadism or deriving personal benefit from causing others to experience pain. Her argument that feminists should be especially repulsed by such a view because they often willingly take on pain of others for no reason underscores this point. Such a view vastly distorts the Compassion Theory and engages in the most uncharitable view of suffering possible as a basis of critique.

To proceed, I will make a few basic distinctions. First, I will distinguish different ways in which the divine persons may be aware of our pain and participate in it:

---

26. Deidre Green, "Got Compassion? A Critique of Blake Ostler's Theory of Atonement," 15–16.

27. Green, 9.

Empathetic Sharing of Experience: Empathy is sharing another's experience by attempting to imagine how the other must feel based upon one's own experience.

Omniscient Sharing of Experience: Omniscient beings participate directly in the experience of others in the sense that they know from a third-person perspective what the other is experiencing.

Compassionate Sharing of Experience: Participating in another's experience from a first-person perspective by having the same experience and sharing the very experience that is experienced by another.

I have argued that the divine persons united as one Godhead share in our experience in the sense of empathetic and omniscient sharing of experience. However, they cannot have a first-hand experiential knowledge of alienation, rejection, isolation, and aloneness while united as one Godhead. This limitation on the divine knowledge is inherent in their mode of being at-one with each other or being united in coinherence or indwelling unity. The Compassion Theory claims that Christ's experiential knowledge qualified him uniquely to atone in two respects. First, his experience includes firsthand experience of the fullness of alienation on the cross in contrast with the full divine union he had with the Father in Gethsemane. Second, he shares with us the very pain of our sins because whatever energy it is that causes that pain in us is transferred to him in union of our life's light to be transformed and "quickened" by his light.

Thus, the Compassion Theory posits that in Gethsemane and on the cross, Christ experienced (1) empathetic suffering for all who have and will suffer under the weight of sin; (2) omniscient suffering in knowing all the sins that had been committed to that point in time; and (3) compassionate sharing of experience for all who had repented to that time. Further, Christ suffers a momentary pain when we are joined to him in the moment of justification by faith through the grace of unconditional acceptance in love. However, this momentary pain is transformed into greater light and enduring joy through the healing power of his life's light. Both Christ and we receive mutual joy through atonement by being joined in healed relationships of intimate union.

This critique rests on the false assumption that we cannot be justified in choosing to create pain for another or that we could do so out of love. However, I want to distinguish between pointless suffering and redemptive suffering to demonstrate how far off her critique is. This distinction is critical to discussing the Compassion Theory, and it is Green's failure to attend to this distinction that challenges her critique.

Pointless Suffering: Causing another to suffer psychological or physical pain for the sake of experiencing the pain or for no reason at all.

Redemptive Suffering: Giving occasion for another to freely choose to suffer psychological or physical pain so that suffering further pain can be avoided or for some benefit that outweighs the disvalue of the pain.

It is of course commonplace that we may justifiably choose to cause another to suffer some physical pain because of the benefits that may be derived from doing so. For instance, parents may choose justifiably to cause pain to their children to become vaccinated through a shot. Could a person choose to allow another to voluntarily experience pain to benefit one's self as well as the one for whom pain is caused? To answer this question, I'll tell two stories.

In the year 1850, a husband had been discussing with his wife whether to have children. He knows that pregnancy appears to be beyond uncomfortable and that childbirth is extremely painful and perhaps deadly. He has (limited) empathetic understanding of the pain she may experience if they choose to have children. He, however, wants to be a father. He wants to beget new life and participate in raising children. His wife says that she also wants to have children. Could he justifiably choose to engage in intimate union with his wife to create new life even though he knows that it will cause great though momentary pain for his wife and could even result in her death? Could he do so out of love? I submit that the answer to both questions is clearly "yes."

Now, this scenario may seem patriarchal because it approaches the question from the male's point of view. However, consider the roles. By analogy to the Compassion Theory of Atonement, he is cast as the sinner and she as the savior. She also wants to have a baby. She knows that by entering into intimate union with her husband to create new life, she will be exposed to great pain and hardship. But out of her love for her husband and her unborn child, she is willing to undergo that pain. Is that remotely sadomasochistic? I trust that even a feminist could see the point of this analogy—and perhaps it is precisely the feminist who will appreciate it most.

Consider another story. A husband has committed adultery. He has hidden the truth from his wife because he does not want to hurt her. He knows that she will feel pain if he reveals his secrets. He is truly sorrowful for the injury he has caused to their relationship. However, he desires to have an honest, authentic, and truly trusting relationship with his wife. He loves her and wants to realize true intimacy and a deeper relationship with her. He realizes that he cannot achieve his desire for more intimate and authentic relationship with her unless he confesses. Indeed, he realizes that by withholding the truth he deprives his wife of the freedom of choosing to be in relationship with him as he truly is. He has made the judgment that if she truly knew him, she would reject him—and thus his secrecy is a form of failing to trust her. While it is possible that she may reject him, he realizes that is her choice to make. He realizes that he is being paternalistic by attempting to shield her from the pain that the truth about his sins will cause.

Is the husband a sadist if he chooses to confess the truth about his affair to his wife and ask her forgiveness? Hardly. It seems to me to be the most loving thing that he can do. Given the fact that he has sinned against her, it demonstrates genuine trust to honor her freedom to choose by facing up to the truth about what he has done. Perhaps a relationship that is a facade can be endured for a small amount of time, but who could endure such a relationship for an eternity? I suggest that such constraints on authentic and loving relationship are exactly the same for a faithful, trusting, and authentic relationship with God.

Both of these stories demonstrate redemptive love—willingness to allow another to willingly experience pain for the benefit of authentic relationships and new life. I submit that they show that the critique is based on an approach to suffering that fails to recognize the distinction between pointless pain and redemptive suffering. Is an eternal and fully loving union with us worth the pain that Christ suffers in the Atonement? I suggest that the answer is, once again, clearly and resoundingly "yes." Moreover, Christ has already voluntarily made the choice to undergo such suffering in order to be reconciled to us. He has already fully prepared himself through his incarnate experience to heal our stripes and salve our wounds with his loving light. He has already said "yes" to us and accepted us as worthy of relationship with him as a matter of loving grace. If we refuse to repent and accept his offer of relationship, then the pain of his mortal experience is meaningless in our lives, and we reject his own demand to repent.

Perhaps more importantly, the truth is that our sinful actions cause pain to those in relationship with us. Indeed, sin consists in precisely the evil of pain committed when interpersonal relationships are injured and alienation is created. Given the commitments of the Compassion Theory, the *only* way to avoid the pain inherent in sin is to refrain from sinning in the first place. The *only* way to stop the pain once we have sinned is to trust Christ and repent. Green thus misses the central motivating point of the Compassion Theory: to avoid creating pain for Christ in atonement, one must avoid sin.

It is ironic that Green critiques the Compassion Theory by arguing that it fails to recognize that an unjust double punishment could motivate us to repent. Green argues:

> While double punishment significantly challenges the concept of justice, it could prove efficacious in motivating persons to repent. Since Ostler's theory focuses on compassion, it might allow for the possibility that when a person believes that Christ has already suffered for sins, she may be motivated to repent by the desire not to allow that previous suffering to go in vain. Ostler's solution presented in order to preserve justice, fails to recognize how the concept of double punishment could serve as impetus for repentance for a compassionate person.[28]

Yet this suggestion seems both backwards and morally reprehensible. Green admits that double punishment is in fact unjust, but this injustice can motivate us to repent because we can give meaning to the pain that Christ has already suffered. How? He has already suffered, and he suffers regardless of whether we repent. What could be less motivating than the fatalistic realization that Christ has suffered and there is nothing we can do about it because he has already fully suffered whether we sin or not? That seems to be maximally un-motivating to me. In contrast, the Compassion Theory entails that if we don't sin, then he doesn't feel the pain of our sins that never occur. Thus, we are motivated to refrain from sinning in the first place, and we realize that there is no cheap grace that frees us with no one suffering. It also entails that his suffering is given meaning *by our repentance*, because our repentance has achieved Christ's purpose in suffering—minimizing sin through avoidance and true repentance, reconciliation, and transformation to new life in union with Christ and God in the greatest joy possible. If that is not motivation to repent, what could possibly motivate us?

---

28. Green, 5.

2. Critique of Scriptural Exegesis.

The scriptural basis that I claim for the Compassion Theory of Atonement has also been questioned. In particular is my use of Doctrine and Covenants 19 to support the theory. The published revelation states:

> Therefore I command you to repent—repent, lest I smite you by the rod of my mouth, and by my wrath, and by my anger, and your sufferings be sore—how sore you know not, how exquisite you know not, yea, how hard to bear you know not. For behold, I, God, have suffered these things for all, that they might not suffer if they would repent; But if they would not repent they must suffer even as I; Which suffering caused myself, even God, the greatest of all, to tremble because of pain, and to bleed at every pore, and to suffer both body and spirit—and would that I might not drink the bitter cup, and shrink—
>
> Nevertheless, glory be to the Father, and I partook and finished my preparations unto the children of men. Wherefore, I command you again to repent, lest I humble you with my almighty power; and that you confess your sins, lest you suffer these punishments of which I have spoken, of which in the smallest, yea, even in the least degree you have tasted at the time I withdrew my Spirit. (vv. 15–17)

According to Green,

> The canon, to which Ostler wants to give primacy, states that Christ has *already* suffered for our sins and that we will suffer for them *in futurity* if we do not repent of them while in mortality. Scripture is clear that this is a suffering we have not yet experienced and that we cannot comprehend. Yet Ostler claims that Christ feels our pain through our volitional transference. . . . Ostler is correct that the transfer is real, but not that it happens in real-time in the act of repentance. Moreover, section 19 implies that God does not consider double punishment unjust."[29]

Thus, Green reads Doctrine and Covenants 19 to state:

> (a) God suffered these things (in Gethsemane) for all who have been, are now, or ever will be mortal regardless of whether they repent.

I accept that Green's reading of section 19 is one possible reading—and perhaps may be the standard interpretation. However, I pointed out four problems with this standard reading: (1) *Problem of Backward Causation*.

---

29. Green, 10.

It creates a problem of backwards causation because Christ suffers for sins that have not yet been committed; (2) *Denial of Free Will*. If Christ has suffered for our sins that we will commit, then we cannot be free to not commit them. Nothing could be surer than the logical entailment that we do not have power to avoid performing acts that have already had causal effects in the world before we commit them; (3) *Double Punishment*. The standard reading creates a problem of double punishment because Christ suffers for sins that we do not repent of, and thus we both suffer for the same sins; (4) *Violation of the Innocence Principle*. The notion that Christ suffers for our sins violates the principle that it is unjust to cause an innocent person to suffer for the actions of the guilty person. To avoid these problems, I offer another reading of section 19 that I believe remains faithful to the text:

> (b) God suffered these things (i.e., empathetic pain in Gethsemane, on the cross, and of our sinfulness) for all those who repent; and those who don't repent must suffer these pains personally.

Given the fact that the original revelation did not have any punctuation,[30] the statement in Doctrine and Covenants 19:16–17 is actually: "Behold I God have suffered these things for all that they might not suffer if they would repent but if they would not repent they must suffer even as I." The referent of "all" is thus to "all those who repent" and not to all that might exist at any time. I suggest that this reading has two overriding virtues: (1) it avoids the four problems with the standard reading I have discussed; and (2) it makes more sense of the two conditional clauses of the text.

Green agrees that the problems I have pointed to are real problems that deserve due consideration. To accommodate these problems so that Christ's suffering does not involve backward causation and implicit denial of free will, Green suggests that there is a better reading:

> There is a better way around the problem of God's limited foreknowledge by relying on LDS scripture. . . . While for Ostler a negation of absolute foreknowledge precludes an infinite atonement being wrought at a particular historical moment, in order to be true to LDS scripture, he must al-

---

30. Robin Scott Jensen, Robert J. Woodford, and Steven C. Harper, eds., *Manuscript Revelation Books*, facsimile edition, 25–26. The particular pages of the manuscript that apparently contained Doctrine and Covenants 19:15–19 are missing. However, from the remainder of the revelation manuscript the lack of punctuation is clear.

low the possibility that there is an upper limit to the amount of sin that individuals can commit. If this is so, then there is some maximal level of collective sin of which God is aware and for which Christ could have atoned at a particular moment in the past.[31]

Given the scriptures of the Restoration, one can presume that God can anticipate an upper-bound of sin and suffering humans will experience individually and collectively. This does not require God's absolute foreknowledge, but only that God knows where human bounds are set. Christ suffers the maximal amount of human sin. Christ's suffering is not unjust, since his suffering is volitional.[32]

Green's view would require us to reject the standard reading and reinterpret section 19 as follows:

(c) God suffered the pain of these things in Gethsemane for all who have, do now, or may ever become mortal to the full extent they could possibly sin regardless of whether or not they actually commit the sins or repent.

This is a rather amazing suggestion given Green's concern about what she calls the "sadistic" suffering she claims is entailed by the Compassion Theory. This view entails that Christ suffers for sins that are not even committed, and thus suffers to the maximum extent logically possible given the persons who could exist! Such a theory entails that Christ suffers the maximum amount of pointless suffering possible. What could be more sadistic and calculating than this view suggested by Green?

On the other hand, the Compassion Theory of Atonement entails that all of Christ's suffering is redemptive and none of it is pointless. It is all in furtherance of repentance and the gift of new life in union with Christ. The entirety of Christ's suffering is directed toward the purpose of healing relationships and transforming our darkness into light. Christ's suffering is thus maximally redemptive with the Compassion Theory of Atonement and maximally pointless with Green's proposed reading.

Further, Green suggests that Christ suffers the actual pain of "guilt" even though he is innocent and not guilty of anything. She also claims that this needless suffering "is not unjust, since his suffering is volitional." Even if Christ was willing to suffer for sins that are never committed, it is unjust

---

31. Green, 7.
32. Green, 17.

for him to suffer for our guilt. For example, imagine that I have stolen an item from a store. However, the store owner thinks it was my son and punishes him in my place. My son, not wanting to expose my guilt, hides my involvement in the theft. If my son is punished for something that I did and willingly undergoes the punishment to hide my guilt, it seems to me that matters are made doubly worse: the person who should be punished escapes punishment, and the innocent person is unjustly punished. This double problem further plagues Green's suggested view of atonement.

This latter problem of innocent suffering is made even greater because Green insists that if Christ suffers pain for our sins, it is precisely the pain of guilt and moral culpability that he must suffer. She states: "What is the 'pain for our sins' other than guilt? In an LDS view Christ suffers for pains *other than* pains for our sins, and transfer of these pains need not imply moral culpability." She then cites Alma 7:11–13 and concludes, "The 'pain for our sins,' however, seems to be precisely pointing toward the issue of guilt and implies moral culpability."[33] Thus, she also rejects that guilt for sins is personal by its very nature because Christ suffers even though he is not personally culpable for any sins. Yet her own view of atonement violates the innocence principle in the most egregious way possible by having Christ pay the price for sins that are not even ever committed. It also entails, if her argument about pain for guilt being necessarily tied to moral culpability holds any water, that Christ feels the pain of such upper limit of possible sins precisely because he is guilty and morally culpable for our sins and potential sins that were never committed even though he did nothing for which he is guilty. This view seems to be maximally morally reprehensible to me.

Thus, while Green's suggested explanation for Christ's suffering in fact solves the problem of backward causation, it fails to resolve the problem of double punishment and violates the innocence principle three times over. Furthermore, no explanation is given for the pain that Christ must suffer for sins never committed. Sins that are never committed could not be the source of pain, because what does not exist cannot cause anything. Does the Father cause this pain? If so, then the Father is not merely unjust but sadistic by Green's own reasoning. It also follows that to know the supposed upper-limit of sin requires God to have middle-knowledge—which I have

---

33. Green, 4.

argued at length is conceptually incoherent and inconsistent with free will.[34] It is unclear why Green claims that LDS scripture entails an upper-limit to the pain that can be generated by sin or the possibility of a maximum amount or number of sins.

Green nevertheless claims that the Compassion Theory gets the "temporal ordering" of the Atonement wrong because she claims that Doctrine and Covenants 19 shows that Christ already completely suffered and fully completed the Atonement while in Gethsemane. However, that is not what the verses say. Verse 19 states: "Nevertheless, glory be to the Father, and I partook and *finished my preparations unto the children of men.*" Christ finished his "preparations." The Compassion Theory maintains that the extremes of Christ's mortal suffering uniquely prepared him to atone. He completed everything necessary to be able to bear our sins:

> Having ascended into heaven, *having the bowels of mercy; being filled with compassion towards the children of men*; standing betwixt them and justice; having broken the bands of death, taken upon himself their iniquity and their transgressions, having redeemed them, and satisfied the demands of justice. (Mosiah 15:9)

There is an already completely accomplished aspect of atonement in Christ's experiences in Gethsemane, death on the cross, and resurrection. He has completed his "preparations" necessary to be able to atone. However, there is also an aspect of atonement that is ongoing and not yet fully accomplished: union with us through our repentance here and now.

Green also argues that the Compassion Theory adopts a problematic "notion of retributive justice" that ought to be critically assessed. She argues

---

34. See Ostler, *The Attributes of God*, 163–81. An editor to this book argued: "It seems reasonable to me that by your definition of omniscience, God could establish a number that would account for every possible sin, basing this on the absolute maximum number of persons possible to inhabit the earth (which would be a finite number), and the absolute possible number of sins which a person could commit in a lifetime (which would also be a finite number)." But that is, of course, false, because there just is not an upper limit or given number of possible choices and different lives possible for persons; rather, the number is infinite and undetermined. Further, it should be clear that there is no "maximum number of possible persons to inhabit the earth." Thus, the very suggestion rests on a logically impossible calculation. But even if God could do such a calculation, it is morally reprehensible to do so because it requires Christ to suffer for the maximal number of sins that are merely potentially, but, in fact, were never committed.

that my citation of Alma 34 (see also Alma 42) entails a notion of retributive justice where persons must suffer punishment for their violations of law:

> Now there is not any man that can sacrifice his own blood which will atone for the sins of another. Now, if a man murdereth, behold will our law, which is just, take the life of his brother? I say unto you, Nay. But the law requireth the life of him who hath murdered; therefore there can be nothing which is short of an infinite atonement which will suffice for the sins of the world. (Alma 34:11–12)

Green is correct that the Nephite law reflected in these verses assumes a retributive theory of justice—capital punishment for murder. However, I expressly rejected the retributive theory of punishment.[35] The only purpose for which I cite Alma 34 is to establish the innocence principle: it is unjust to punish an innocent person for what a guilty person did. Moreover, I expressly adopted a different view of justice: the Law of Restoration discussed by Alma in Alma 41, where we each receive what we send out and ultimately truly desire. This is the notion of justice inherent in an agape theory of ethics which bases moral judgments on the nature of what is required to establish loving relationships.[36]

3. *Claims of Logical Inconsistencies.*

Green also claims that there are several logical inconsistencies in the Compassion Theory. She claims that the Compassion Theory "appears inconsistent" because it claims that the pain for sins is extinguished in the death of Christ's flesh on the cross. She claims that such a claim is inconsistent with the claim that there is no backward causation or foreknowledge.[37] Green, however, is incorrect. I do not claim that all sins were extinguished in Christ's death on the cross. Rather, only all of the sin that existed at that time were extinguished. I speak metaphorically of how even our sins are extinguished in the cross because, in virtue of Christ's death on the cross, the reign of sin is overcome in the resurrection. He completed his prepara-

---

35. See my discussion in Ostler, 204–16.
36. Indeed, I spend not less than three chapters arguing for this view of justice—so it is unfortunate that Green misunderstood me. However, I am sure that the failure to communicate effectively is mine and not hers.
37. Green, "Got Compassion?," 7.

tions to atone, and thus the sins for which we repent are already healed—in the sense that all we have to do is repent and then Christ is able to do the rest by virtue of his mortal experiences and resurrection. He has already accepted us into relationship—the question is whether we will reciprocate. Green admits: "Ostler may be speaking metaphorically here"; however, she argues that the "metaphor is misleading as it attempts to locate the necessity of Christ's suffering in the historical past." Of course, all metaphors break down at some point, but I suggest that the metaphor is more than appropriate. With Christ's death and resurrection, our ability to repent is assured. The Compassion Theory does not try to locate Christ's suffering for our sins as occurring only in the past—it also occurs in each moment of justification when we enter into a new relationship of shared life in Him.

Green also claims that the theory is inconsistent because it claims that "Christ suffers when we sin, i.e., fail to live the law of love, yet Christ does not suffer until we repent, i.e., succeed in living the law of love by working toward reconciliation and obedience to Christ."[38] To the contrary, I do not claim that God goes without experiencing pain until we repent. Rather, I contend that He suffers the pain of loss when we reject Him. Green's assertion of inconsistency fails to pay attention to the distinction between suffering at the time we choose to breach the relationship and alienate ourselves from God and the compassionate pain that only a God can suffer by sharing our lives with us in indwelling unity. These two kinds of suffering are not mutually exclusive—which of course they must be for Green's argument to work.

There are also claims made by Green (following Ivone Gebara) that are rather misleading in my view. Green joins many feminist theorists in claiming that women suffer in particular as victims of the view that Christ showed love by his sacrificial death. She claims: "What is problematic with lifting up the crucifixion as the ultimate act of love is that it not only validates current suffering, but incites women to seek unnecessary sacrifice."[39]

---

38. Green, 8.

39. Green, 13; citing Ivone Gebara, *Out of the Depths: Women's Experience of Evil and Salvation*, 88. As Kathryn Tanner, another feminist theologian, observed, feminist theologians risk missing the entire point of Christ's Atonement by merely judging the suffering involved as something negative and therefore to be denigrated: "Of course, a feminist and womanist focus on Christ's ministry can itself become

Neither Green nor Gebara provides a shred of evidence for this bold empirical claim. Moreover, it appears to me to be unsupportable, because it seems impossible to know that viewing the crucifixion as an expression of God's love for us somehow "incites" women to seek unnecessary suffering. I believe that this type of rhetoric is not only evidentially unjustified but also devalues and denigrates Christ's gift to us.

Green and I surely agree, however, that there is nothing good *per se* in suffering itself. The horror of Jesus's brutal and violent death on a Roman cross is a reminder of the corruption of imperial governmental power and the depth of human depravity in sin. However, the suffering of Jesus is also the ultimate expression of God's loving choice to be with us sinners in the depth of human despair and alienation. The fact that God himself, the Son of the Father in the Godhead, emptied himself of his glory to descend below all things to experience the most remote depths of such excruciating physical pain and abandonment by the Father—while in the moment of greatest need—expresses a love so great that it shocks us. In this suffering we see perfect obedience to God's will to lay down his life for his friends. Green's suggestion that we should not recognize love in Jesus's suffering because it "validates suffering" misses the entire point of the fact that we have a Savior who suffered both for and with us so that we do not have to. In my opinion, while attempting to recognize the inequality of feminine perspectives in theology, her claims ultimately trivialize the undoubted failure to adequately value women's voices in the past. Christ's suffering ends the need to suffer. The message, not only for women but for all of us, is that we already have a Savior and do not need another. Indeed, the most emphatic point of Christ's atonement is that both sin and continuing to suffer for our own sins are pointless acts. We do not have to suffer for our sins if only we will repent by turning back toward God, who stands with open arms waiting for us to walk into his embrace.

---

one-sided, and therefore susceptible of critique on the grounds . . . that the cross can fall out of consideration altogether except as something simply negative. The usual recourse of feminist and womanist theologians is to dismiss the idea that there is anything saving going on in the crucifixion." See Kathryn Tanner, "Incarnation, Cross and Sacrifice: A Feminist-Inspired Reappraisal," 39.

HEALING EVIL: A CONCLUSION

What then shall we say about our experiences of the amount and kinds of evils that occur in our world? Are they evidence that God does not exist? As I have argued, that all depends on what one means by "God." The problem of evil is decisive, it seems to me, against the all-controlling and meticulous providence views. For those who adopt these views, they must either give up all sense of moral urgency and call to action or the commitment that God is good. Neither alternative is acceptable. There are of course incredibly intelligent people who see it otherwise. However, I believe that we are entitled to conclude that as far as we are capable of grasping and assessing moral issues, the god of these traditions cannot exist. If God leaves us completely clueless as to His goodness and is good no matter what the kinds and amounts of evils that we experience, then it seems to me that terms like "good," "evil," "right," "wrong," "morally allowable," and so forth are vacuous and have no meaning in any discourse about God.

The open view of God fares much better, but in the end it cannot explain the amounts of natural evils and the other better options that God had available to Him in creation. While such a view is feasible with respect to moral evils, it does not have the resources to explain why God did not avail Himself of the much better options available to Him in creating the world—including creation of virtually omniscient beings who could rid the world of so many more natural evils than we can.

The process and finitist views have the considerable merit of simply dissolving the problem of evil. As a result, they remain live options. They also explain the natural world and features such as evolution and the kinds of evils that we experience much better than any view that adopts creation out of nothing. In fact, they have advantages over a naturalistic worldview to explain the order we find in the world and the progress of evolution.

Nevertheless, both the finitist and process views exact a heavy price in terms of belief in God's ability to triumph over evil. For me they remain live options, but it is understandable that for many the price is just too high. The process view seems more feasible to me than the finitist view with respect to the kinds of things persons of faith are wont to say about God. For example, the process view can explain why prayer is efficacious and increases God's power to bring about desired results while leaving it quite uncertain as to whether God can answer any prayer. However, both the finitist and process views explain evil by asserting that God is incapable of dealing with the amounts and kinds of evils that actually occur—even with our cooperation. Whether such a God will eventually triumph is quite uncertain—and it remains uncertain even if we do all that we can to assist God in God's endeavor and plan for the world.

I believe that the most viable position is the plan of agape theodicy that takes advantage of more complete resources of the Mormon faith tradition. The view of God that I have elucidated in the prior three volumes of *Exploring Mormon Thought* explicates what I consider to be the most defensible and inspiring views available in terms of faithfulness to scriptural and other authorities, logical coherence, and explanatory adequacy.

On the view that I have elucidated, God is able to triumph over evil with certainty but controls neither what the natural laws shall be nor what free humans will choose. It places the problem of evil in the more complete vista of God's plan for us, given Mormon faith commitments that include the challenges that God must work with as prior and uncreated conditions to His plan to bring us to share fully in the most complete and fulfilling life possible. The focus is on bringing us to participate in the loving relationship enjoyed by the divine persons of the Godhead. In so doing, God brings us to actualization of our greatest potential to be as God is to realize every glory, power, knowledge, and loving relationship that God possesses. He seeks to share it all with us by giving us an opportunity to learn to love each other as He does.

The plan of agape theodicy has the considerable merit that it makes us co-creators of God's plan through our agreement to cooperate with Him in the endeavor. Moreover, the agape theodicy places God's plan in the more complete panorama of the pre-mortal life in which we had the opportunity not only to consent to or refuse to experience this life—but also to make commitments and agreements with one another to consent to be a part of each other's lives, as well as each other's challenges and triumphs. It makes virtually every person that we encounter a potential angel to further God's plan and to teach us how to love one another. The fact that we consented to confront the amounts and kinds of evils that we encounter in this life has great explanatory power to place God's love for us into context of His purposes and our own person-centered interests. It appears to be the only explanation that respects our dignity as persons and does not render us mere cogs in God's plan and that disregards individual interest to achieve some greater harmony. It is the only theodicy that I know of that does not sacrifice those who do not even get a start on this mortal life to some interest of those who do make it to maturity.

The focus of the plan of agape theodicy is primarily on the gifts given to us by Jesus Christ in his cooperative plan with the Father and his mortality and resurrection to life. The Atonement accomplished by Christ is thus the linchpin to God's plan to heal all evil in the world. The focal point is the human heart. We must change our hearts through repentance and, in doing so, heal the world by being forgiven for our many evils and wrongs and forgiving all others—including those we may perceive as enemies. The problem of evil is found in our own hearts. The solution to the problem of evil is found in opening and softening our hearts to love others and accepting Christ to take up abode in them.

The response to the problem of evil is thus not a logical argument that explains how God's existence is logically and practically compossible with the kinds and amounts of evil that we experience in this world. Rather, the response to the problem of evil is to heal evil: to repent, heal our relationships through repentance, and learn to love with the fullness of divine love. Evil is overcome one human life at a time—that then includes all others in healing the world. The problem of evil is thus the very thing that motivates us, goads us on, challenges us, and becomes an essential part of God's plan to heal the world and to give us the incredible blessing of sharing fully in God's love—if that is what we choose.

God does not sacrifice those who do not have the opportunity to learn through mortal experience, nor would He allow evil if He could accomplish His purposes without it. God invites us to struggle with Him against the evil in our hearts to bring us to the triumph of healing evil and achieving the fullest realization of human potential to participate fully in the divine relationship.

APPENDIX

SELECT BIBLIOGRAPHY FOR PROCESS THEODICY

Altonaga, Francisco A. "An Exploration of Charles Hartshorne's View of Divine Omnipotence in the Context of the Problem of Evil: Uncovering the Aesthetic Venture of God in Process." PhD. Dissertation. De La Salle University, Manila, 2002.

Baldwin, Dalton. "Evil and Persuasive Power: A Response to Hare and Madden." *Process Studies* 3, no.4 (Winter 1973): 259–72.

Baker-Fletcher, Karen. *Dancing with God: The Trinity from a Womanist Perspective*. St. Louis: Chalice Press, 2006.

Barciauskas, Rosemary Curran. "The Primordial and Ethical Interpretations of Evil in Paul Ricoeur and Alfred North Whitehead." *Modern Theology* 2 (Oct. 1985): 64–77.

Barineau, R. Maurice. *The Theodicy of Alfred North Whitehead: A Logical and Ethical Vindication*. Lanham, MD: University Press of America, 1991.

———. "Whitehead and Genuine Evil." *Process Studies* 19, no.3 (Fall 1990): 181–88.

Barnhart, J. E. "Persuasive and Coercive Power in Process Metaphysics." *Process Studies* 3, no. 3 (Fall 1973): 153–57.

Basinger, David. *The Case for Freewill Theism: A Philosophical Assessment*. Downers Grove, IL: Intervarsity Press, 1996.

———. "Evil as Evidence Against the Existence of God: A Response." *Philosophy Research Archives* 4 (1978): 55–67.

———. "Evil: Does Process Theism Have a Better Explanation?" In *Divine Power in Process Theism: A Philosophical Critique*, edited by David Basinger, 55–68. Albany: State University of New York Press, 1988.

———. "Plantinga's 'Free-Will Defense' as a Challenge to Orthodox Theism." *American Journal of Theology and Philosophy* 3, no. 2 (May 1982): 35–41.

———. "Process Theism Versus Free-Will Theism: A Response to Griffin." *Process Studies* 20, no. 4 (Winter 1991): 204–20.

———. "Review: Marjorie Hewitt Suchocki, The End of Evil: Eschatology in Historical Context." *Journal of Religion* 70, no.1 (January 1990): 117–18.

Bellett, Alan J. D. "Evolution, Process and the Tree of the Knowledge of Good and Evil." *Process Studies* 32, no.1 (Spring–Summer 2003): 121–41.

Birch, Brian D. "Mormonism and the Challenge of an Adequate Theodicy: A Response to David Paulsen et al." *Element: The Journal of the Society for Mormon Philosophy and Theology* 6, no. 1 (Spring 2015): 63–69.

Blaisdell, Charles R. "Griffin's Theodicy." *Encounter* 50, no.4 (Autumn 1989): 367–78.

Bracken, Joseph, A. "The End of Evil." In *World without End: Christian Eschatology from a Process Perspective*, edited by Joseph A. Bracken, 1–11. Grand Rapids: Eerdmans, 2005.

———, ed. *World without End: Christian Eschatology from a Process Perspective.* Grand Rapids: Eerdmans, 2005.

Brizee, Robert, and Adrienne Brizee. "Responding to Evil: 'I Just Can't Forgive Him.'" *Creative Transformation* 13, no. 2 (Spring 2004): 20–21.

Burrow, Rufus Jr. "The Doctrine of Unearned Suffering." *Encounter* 63, no. 12 (Winter/Spring 2002): 65–76.

Cargas, Harry J. "Review: The Theodicy of Alfred North Whitehead: A Logical and Ethical Vindication." *American Journal of Theology and Philosophy* 16, no. 2 (May 1995): 226–28.

Case-Winters, Anna. "Endings and Ends." In *World without End: Christian Eschatology from a Process Perspective*, edited by Joseph A. Bracken, 177–96. Grand Rapids: Eerdmans, 2005.

Cauthen, Kenneth. *The Many Faces of Evil: Reflections on the Sinful, the Tragic, the Demonic, and the Ambiguous.* Lima, OH: CSS, 1997.

Chew, Ho Hua. "Process Theism and Physical Evil." *Sophia* 31, no.3 (1992): 16–27.

Clarke, Bowman L. "A Whiteheadian Theodicy." In *The Defense of God*, edited by J. K. Roth and F. Sontag, 32–47. New York: Paragon House, 1985.

Cobb, John B., Jr. "Evil and the Power of God." In *God and the World*, 87–102. Philadelphia: Westminster Press, 1969.

———. "The Problem of Evil and the Task of Ministry." *Encountering Evil: Live Options in Theodicy*, edited by Stephen T. Davis, 181–90. Louisville, KY: John Knox, 2001.

Collins, Marvin A. "God and Evil in the Process Thought of A. N. Whitehead, Charles Hartshorne, and David Griffin: A Question of Theological Coherence." Ph.D. Dissertation. Fuller Theological Seminary, 1986.

Cooper, Burton Z. *Why, God?* Atlanta: John Knox Press, 1988.

Crespy, Georges. "The Problem of Evil in Teilhard's Thought." In *Process Theology: Basic Writings*, edited by Ewert H. Cousins, 283–98. New York: Newman Press, 1971.

Davis, Stephen T., ed. *Encountering Evil: Live Options in Theodicy.* Atlanta: John Knox Press, 1981.

———. "Truth and Action in Theodicy: A Reply to C. Robert Mesle." *American Journal of Theology and Philosophy* 25, no. 3 (September 2004): 270–75.

Deavel, Catherine Jack. "Relational Evil, Relational Good: Thomas Aquinas and Process Thought." *International Philosophical Quarterly* 47, no. 3 (September 2007): 297–313.

Devenish, Philip E. "Theodicy and Cosmology: The Contribution of Neoclassical Theism." *Journal of Empirical Theology* 4, no.2 (1991): 523.

APPENDIX

Faber, Roland. "God's Adventure: The End of Evil and the Origin of Time" In *World Without End: Christian Eschatology from a Process Perspective*, edited by Joseph A. Bracken, 91–112. Grand Rapids: Eerdmans, 2005.
Fiddes, Paul. *The Creative Suffering of God*. Oxford: Clarendon Press, 1988.
Fisher, Loren. *Who Hears the Cries of the Innocent?* Willits, CA: Fisher Publications, 2002.
Frankenberry, Nancy. "Some Problems in Process Theodicy." *Religious Studies* 17, no.2 (June 1981): 179–97.
Garrison, Jim. *The Darkness of God: Theology After Hiroshima*. Grand Rapids: Eerdmans, 1982.
Griffin, David Ray. "Actuality, Possibility, and Theodicy: A Response to Nelson Pike." *Process Studies* 12, no.3 (Fall 1982): 168–79.
———. "Creation Out of Chaos and the Problem of Evil." In *Encountering Evil: Live Options in Theodicy*, ed. Stephen T. Davis, 101–36. Atlanta: John Knox Press, 1981.
———. "Divine Causality, Evil, and Philosophical Theology: A Critique of James Ross." *International Journal for Philosophy of Religion* 4, no. 3 (Fall 1973): 168–86.
———. "Divine Goodness and Demonic Evil." In *Evil and the Response of World Religion*, ed. William Genkner, 223–40. New York: Paragon House, 1997.
———. *Evil Revisited*. Albany: State University of New York Press, 1991.
———. *God, Power, and Evil: A Process Theodicy*. Louisville: Westminster John Knox Press, 2004.
———. "On Hasker's Defense of his Parity Claim." *Process Studies* 29, no. 2 (Fall–Winter 2000): 233–36.
———. "The Rationality of Belief in God: A Response to Hans Kung." *Faith and Philosophy: Journal of the Society of Christian Philosophers* 1, no. 1 (January 1984): 16–26.
———. "Review: Marjorie Hewitt Suchocki, The End of Evil." *Process Studies* 18, no. 1 (Spring 1989): 57–63.
———. "Traditional Free Will Theodicy and Process Theodicy: Hasker's Claim for Parity." *Process Studies* 29, no. 2 (Fall/Winter 2000): 209–26.
Hallman, Joseph M. *The Descent of God: Divine Suffering in History and Theology*. Minneapolis: Fortress Press, 1991.
Hare, Peter. "Evil and Unlimited Power." *Review of Metaphysics* 20 (1966): 278–89.
———. "Review: David R. Griffin, God, Power and Evil: A Process Theodicy." *Process Studies* 7, no. 1 (1977): 44–51.
Hare, Peter, and Edward Madden. "Evil and Persuasive Power." *Process Studies* 2, no. 1 (Spring 1972): 44–48.
Harrison, R. K. "A. N. Whitehead on Good and Evil." *Philosophy* 28 (1953): 239–45.
Hartshorne, Charles. "A New Look at the Problem of Evil." In *Current Philosophical Issues: Essays in Honour of Curt John Ducasse*, edited by Frederick C. Dommeyer, 201–12. Springfield, IL: Charles C. Thomas, 1966.
Hasker, William. "'Bitten to Death by Ducks': A Reply to Griffin." *Process Studies* 29, no. 2 (Fall–Winter 2000): 233–36.
———. "The Problem of Evil in Process Theism and Classical Free Will Theism." *Process Studies* 29, no. 2 (Fall–Winter 2000): 194–208.
Heffner, Philip. "The Problem of Evil: Picking up the Pieces." *Dialog* 25, no. 2 (Spring 1986): 87–92.

Hick, John. "Process Theodicy." In *Philosophy of Religion*. 4th Edition, edited by John Hick, 48–55. Englewood Cliffs, NJ: PrenticeHall, 1990.

———. "Response to Mesle." *American Journal of Theology and Philosophy* 25, no. 3 (September 2004): 265–69.

Ho, Hua-Chew. "Process Theism and Physical Evil." *Sophia* 31, no. 3 (1992): 16–27.

Inbody, Tyron. "Religious Empiricism and the Problem of Evil." *American Journal of Theology and Philosophy* 12, no. 1 (Jan. 1991): 35–48.

———. *The Transforming God: An Interpretation of Suffering and Evil*. Louisville, KY: John Knox Press, 1997.

Kaufman, Peter I. "Daniel Day Williams and the Science of Suffering." *Union Seminary Quarterly Review* 34, no. 1 (Fall 1978): 35–46.

Keller, Catherine. *God and Power: Counter-Apocalyptic Journeys*. Minneapolis: Fortress Press, 2005.

———. "The Mystery of the Insoluable Evil: Violence and Evil in Marjorie Suchocki." In *World without End: Christian Eschatology from a Process Perspective*, edited by Joseph A. Bracken, 46–71. Grand Rapids: Eerdmans, 2005.

Keller, James A. *Problems of Evil and the Power of God*. UK: Ashgate, 2007.

Kropf, Richard W. *Evil and Evolution: A Theodicy*. Cranbury: Associated University Press, 1984.

Kushner, Harold S. *When Bad Things Happen to Good People*. New York: Schocken Books, 1981.

Loy, David R. "Evil as the Good? A Reply to Brook Ziporyn." *Philosophy East & West* 55, no. 2 (April 2005): 348–52.

Madden, Edward H. and Peter Hare. *Evil and the Concept of God*. Springfield, IL: Charles C. Thomas, 1968.

———. "Evil and Unlimited Power." *Review of Metaphysics* 20 (December 1966): 278–89.

Maller, Mark. "Animals and the Problem of Evil in Recent Theodicies." *Sophia* 48, no. 1 (March 2009)

McDaniel, Jay B. "Can Animal Suffering be Reconciled with Belief in an All-Loving God?" In *Animals on the Agenda*, ed. Andrew Linzey and Dorothy Yamamoto, 161–70. London: SCM Press, 1998.

McLachlan, James. "Coercion and Persuasion in Mormon and Process Theologies." *Element: The Journal of the Society for Mormon Philosophy and Theology* 6, no. 1 (Spring 2015): 71–78.

———. "Fragments for a Process Theology of Mormonism." *Element: The Journal for the Society of Mormon Philosophy and Theology* 1, no. 2 (Fall 2005): 1–40.

McWilliams, Warren. *The Passion of God: Divine Suffering in Contemporary Protestant Theology*. Macon, GA: Mercer University Press, 1985.

Mesle, C. Robert. "Does God Hide from Us? John Hick and Process Theology on Faith, Freedom and Theodicy." *International Journal for Philosophy of Religion* 24, no. 12 (JulySept. 1988): 93–111.

———. "Humanism and Hick's Interpretation of Religion." In *Problems in the Philosophy of Religion*, ed. Harold Hewitt, 54–71. Hampshire: Macmillan, 1991.

———. *John Hick's Theodicy: A Process Humanist Critique*. New York: St. Martin's Press, 1991.

———. "The Problem of Genuine Evil: A Critique of John Hick's Theodicy." *Journal of Religion* 66, no. 4 (Oct. 1986): 412–30.

———. "Response to My Critics." *American Journal of Theology and Philosophy* 25, no. 3 (September 2004): 294–301.

APPENDIX

———. "Review: Barry Whitney, Evil and the Process God." *Process Studies* 16, no. 1 (Spring 1987): 57–61.

Miller, Christopher Peyton. "Theodicy for the Sexually Abused." *Creative Transformation* 5, no. 4 (Summer 1996): 19, 223.

Moltmann, Jurgen. "'Deliver Us from Evil' or Doing Away with Humankind?" In *World without End: Christian Eschatology from a Process Perspective*, edited by Joseph A. Bracken, 12–27. Grand Rapids: Eerdmans, 2005), 12–27.

Neville, Robert Cummings. "Eschatological Visions." In *World without End: Christian Eschatology from a Process Perspective*, edited by Joseph A. Bracken, 28–45. Grand Rapids: Eerdmans, 2005.

Noddings, Nel. "Review: David Ray Griffin, Evil Revisited." *Process Studies* 20, no. 3 (Fall 1991): 179–81.

Ogden, Schubert M. "Evil and Belief in God: The Distinctive Relevance of a 'Process Theology.'" *Perkins Journal* 31, no. 4 (Summer 1978): 29–34.

Oord, Thomas Jay. "Evil, Providence, and a Relational God." *Quarterly Journal.* 23, no. 3 (Fall 2003): 238–50.

Paulsen, David, Alan Hurst, Michael Pennock, and Martin Pulido. "Searching for an Adequate Theodicy: David Ray Griffin and Mormonism." *Element: The Journal for the Society of Mormon Philosophy and Theology* 6, no. 1 (Spring 2015): 37–61.

Pederson, Ann. "To Love the Enemy: A Theological Problem." In *God, Evil, and Suffering: Essays in Honor of Paul R. Sponheim*, ed. Terence E. Fretheim and Curtis L. Thompson, 127–35. St. Paul: Word & World, Luther Seminary, 2000.

Peterson, Michael L. "The Problem of Evil." In *Blackwell Companions to Philosophy: A Companion to Philosophy of Reliigon*, ed. Philip Quinn and Charles Taliaferro, 393–401. Cambridge: Blackwell Publishers, 1997.

———. "Recent Work on the Problem of Evil, VI. Process Theodicy." *American Philosophical Quarterly* 20, no. 4 (October 1983): 331–32.

Pike, Nelson. "Process Theodicy and the Concept of Power." *Process Studies* 12, no. 3 (Fall 1982): 148–67.

Pittenger, Norman. "The Fact of Evil and the Concept of God." *Modern Free Churchman* (1971): 28.

———. "Process Theology and the Fact of Evil." *Expository Times* 83 (1971): 73–77.

Polk, David P. "Is God a Power that Loves? A Sermon." *Encounter* 67, no. 4 (Autumn 2006): 417–26.

Quinn, John M. "Triune Self-Giving: One Key to the Problem of Suffering." *The Thomist* 44 (Apr. 1980): 173–218.

Ramal, Randy. "Review: Evil Revisited: Responses and Reconsideration, by David Ray Griffin." *Process Studies* 31, no. 1 (2002): 186–87.

Reichenbach, Bruce R. *Evil and a Good God.* New York: Fordham University Press, 1982.

Roth, John K. "Theistic Antitheodicy." *American Journal of Theology and Philosophy* 25, no. 3 (September 2004): 276–93.

Schilling, S. Paul. *God and Human Anguish.* Nashville: Abingdon, 1977.

Schwarz, Hans. "Evil in Contemporary Theological Discussion." In *Evil: A Historical and Theological Perspective*, ed. Hans Schwarz, 163–98. Minneapolis: Fortress Press, 1995.
Southwick, Jay S. "Job: An Exemplar for Every Age." *Encounter* 45, no. 4 (Autumn 1984): 373–91.
Spencer, Bonnell. *God Who Dares to be Man: Theology for Prayer and Suffering*. New York: Seabury Press, 1980.
Suchocki, Marjorie Hewitt. "As Good as It Gets? Musings on Mortality and More." *Creative Transformation* 11, no. 4 (Fall 2002): 2–8.
———. *The End of Evil: Process Eschatology in Historical Context*. Albany: State University of New York Press, 1988.
———. "Evil, Eschatology, and God: Response to David Griffin." *Process Studies* 18, no. 1 (Spring 1989): 63–69.
———. "Sin in Feminist and Process Thought." In *God, Evil, and Suffering: Essays in Honor of Paul R. Sponheim*, ed. Terence E. Fretheim and Curtis L. Thompson, 143–53. St. Paul: Word & World, Luther Seminary, 2000.
Tang, Yi. "On Process Theodicy II." *Philosophy Investigation* 10 (1995): 69–75.
Vieth, Richard F. *Holy Power, Human Pain*. Bloomington, IN: Meyer-Stone Books, 1988.
Viney, Donald Wayne. "Process Theism." Stanford Encyclopedia of Philosophy. Revised April 3, 2018. http://plato.stanford.edu/entries/process-theism/.
Whitney, Barry L. "An Aesthetic Solution to the Problem of Evil." *International Journal for Philosophy of Religion* 35, no. 1 (Feb. 1994): 21–37.
———. *Evil and the Process God*. New York and Toronto: Edwin Mellen Press, 1985.
———. "Hartshorne and Theodicy." In *Hartshorne, Process Philosophy, and Theology*, eds. Robert Kane and Stephen H. Phillips, 53–69. Albany: State University of New York Press, 1989.
———. "Process Theism: Does a Persuasive God Coerce?" *The Southern Journal of Philosophy* 17 (Spring 1979): 133–43.
———. "Process Theodicy." In *Theodicy: An Annotated Bibliography On the Problem of Evil 1960–1990*, edited by Barry L. Whitney, 181–234. New York: Garland Pub., 1993.
———. "Process Theodicy." In *What Are They Saying About God and Evil?* 47–57. New York: Paulist Press, 1989.
Wood, Forrest, Jr. "Some Whiteheadian Insights into the Problem of Evil." *Southwestern Journal of Philosophy* 10, no. 1 (Spring 1979): 147–55.
Wotherspoon, Dan. "Process Theology and Mormonism: Connections and Challenges." *Element: The Journal of the Society for Mormon Philosophy and Theology* 6, no. 1 (Spring 2015): 79–84.
Yong, Amos. "Possibility and Actuality: The Doctrine of Creation and Its Implications for Divine Omniscience." *The Wesleyan Philosophical Society Online Journal* 1, no. 1 (2001).
Zycinski, Joseph M. "God, Freedom, and Evil: Perspectives from Religion and Science." *Zygon* 35, no. 3 (September 2000): 653–64.

BIBLIOGRAPHY

Adams, Marilyn McCord. "Plantinga on 'Felix Culpa': Analysis and Critique." *Faith and Philosophy* 25, no. 2 (April 2008): 123–40.

Adams, Robert M. "An Anti-Molinist Argument." In *Philosophical Perspectives: Vol. 5*, edited by James E. Tomberlin, 343–53. Atascadero, CA: Ridgeview, 1991.

———. "Middle Knowledge and the Problem of Evil." *American Philosophical Quarterly* 14, no. 2 (April 1977): 109–17.

Alston, William P. "Some (Temporary) Final Thoughts on Evidential Arguments from Evil." In *The Evidential Argument from Evil*, edited by David Howard-Snyder, 311–32. Bloomington: Indiana University Press, 2008.

Anderson, C. Alan. "Immortality in a Process Perspective." In *Religion and Parapsychology*, edited by Arthur S. Berger and Henry O. Thompson, 21–37. Barrytown, NY: Unification Theological Seminary, 1988.

Andrus, Hyrum L. *God, Man and the Universe.* Salt Lake City: Bookcraft, 1968.

Arminius, Jacobus. *The Works of James Arminius*, translated by James Nichols, William Nichols, and Carl Bangs. Grand Rapids, MI: Baker Book House, 1986.

Basinger, David. "Process Theism, Evil, and Life After Death: A Response to Griffin." *Encounter* 53 (1992): 353–63.

Bergmann, Michael. "Skeptical Theism and Rowe's New Evidential Argument from Evil." *Noûs* 35, no. 2 (June 2001): 278–296.

Bergmann, Michael and Michael Rea. "In Defence of Skeptical Theism: A Reply to Almeida and Oppy," *Australian Journal of Philosophy* 83, no. 2 (2005).

Bracken, Joseph A. "Bodily Resurrection and the Dialectic of Spirit and Matter." *Theological Studies* 66 (2005): 770–82.

———. "Subjective Immortality in a NeoWhiteheadian Context." In *World without End: Christian Eschatology from a Process Perspective*, edited by Joseph A. Bracken, 72–90. Grand Rapids: Eerdmans, 2005.

Cain, James. "Free Will and the Problem of Evil." *Religious Studies* 40, no. 4 (2007): 437–56.

Calvin, John. *Bondage and Liberation of the Will: A Defence of the Orthodox Doctrine of Human Choice Against Pighius (Texts and Studies in Reformation and Post Reformation Thought).* Ada, MI: Baker, 1984.

Clark. L. C., and F. Gollan. "Survival of Mammals Breathing Organic Liquids Equilibrated with Oxygen at Atmospheric Pressure." *Science* 152, no. 3730 (1966): 1755–56.

Cowan, Steven B. "The Grounding Objection to Middle Knowledge Revisited." *Religious Studies* 39, no. 1 (2003): 93–102.
De Molina, Luis. *Liberi arbitrii cum gratiae donis, divina praescientia, providentia, praedestinatione et reprobatione Concordia* ("A Reconciliation of Free Choice with the Gifts of Grace, Divine Foreknowledge, Providence, Predestination and Reprobation"). First edition, Lisbon, 1588; Second edition, Antwerp, 1595.
Draper, Paul. "Natural Selection and the Problem of Evil." *The Secular Web*. Updated in 2007. http://www.infidels.org/library/modern/paul_draper/evil.html.
England, Eugene. "How Can God Be Both Good and Powerful?" *Dialogues with Myself: Personal Essays on Mormon Experience*, 93–100. Salt Lake City: Orion Books, 1984.
———. "That They Might Not Suffer: The Gift of Atonement." In *Dialogues With Myself: Personal Essays on the Mormon Experience*, 77–92. Midvale: Signature Books, 1984.
Gale, Richard. "Freedom and the Free Will Defense." *Social Theory and Practice* 16, no. 3 (Fall 1990): 397–423.
Gaskin, Robert. "Conditionals of Freedom and Middle Knowledge." *Philosophical Quarterly* 43 (1993): 412–43.
Gebara, Ivone. *Out of the Depths: Women's Experience of Evil and Salvation*, translated by Ann Patrick Ware. Minneapolis: Fortress Press, 2002.
Geddes, Allsdair M. "The History of Smallpox." *Clinics in Dermatology* 24, no. 3 (May–June 2006): 152–57.
Geirsson, Heimir and Michael Losonsky. "What God Could Have Made." *The Southern Journal of Philosophy* 43 (2005): 355–76.
"Global HIV and AIDS Statistics." *Avert*. February 18, 2020. https://www.avert.org/global-hiv-and-aids-statistics.
Green, Deidre. "Got Compassion? A Critique of Blake Ostler's Theory of Atonement." *Element: The Journal of the Society for Mormon Philosophy and Theology* 4, no. 1 (Spring 2008): 15–16.
Griffin, David Ray. "Creation out of Chaos and the Problem of Evil." In *Encountering Evil: Live Options in Theodicy*, ed. Stephen T. Davis, 101–36. Atlanta, GA: John Knox Press, 2001.
———. *God, Power, and Evil: A Process Theodicy*. Louisville: John Knox Press, 2004.
———. "Life After Death in the Modern and Post Modern Worlds." In *Religion and Parapsychology*, edited by Arthur S. Berger and Henry O. Thompson, 39–60. Barrytown, NY: Unification Theological Seminary, 1988.
———. *Parapsychology, Philosophy, and Spirituality: A Postmodern Exploration*. New York: SUNY, 1997.
———. "The Possibility of Subjective Immortality in Whitehead's Philosophy." *Modern Schoolman* 53, no. 1 (November 1975): 39–57.
Hartshorne, Charles. "The Acceptance of Death." In *Philosophical Aspects of Thanatology*, Vol. I, edited by Florence M. Hetzler and Austin H. Kutscher, 83–87. New York: MSS Information Corp., 1978.
Hasker, William. *God, Time and Knowledge*. Ithaca: Cornell University Press, 1989.
———. "A New Anti-Molinist Argument." *Religious Studies* 35 (1999): 291–97.
———. "The Problem of Evil in Process Theism and Classical Free Will Theism." *Process Studies* 29, no. 2 (Fall/Winter 2000): 194–208.
———. *The Triumph of God Over Evil: A Theodicy for a World of Suffering*. Downers Grove, IL: Intervarsity Press, 2008.

BIBLIOGRAPHY

Heiner, Ronald A. "The Necessity of a Sinless Messiah." *BYU Studies* 22, no. 1 (1982): 5–30.
Henry, Granville C. "Does Process Thought Allow Personal Immortality?" *Religious Studies* 31, no. 3 (1995): 311–21.
Hick, John. *Evil and the God of Love.* New York: Harper & Row, 1978.
———. "An Irenaean Theodicy." In *Encountering Evil: Live Options in Theodicy*, edited by Stephen T. Davis, 38–72. Atlanta: John Knox, 2001.
Hooker, Morna. "Paul." In *The Oxford Companion to Christian Thought*, edited by Adrian Hastings, Alistair Mason, and Hugh Piper, 522. Oxford: Oxford University Press, 2000.
Howard-Snyder, Daniel. "The Argument from Inscrutable Evil." In *The Evidential Argument from Evil*, edited by Daniel Howard-Snyder, 286–310. Bloomington: Indiana University Press, 1996.
Howe, A. Scott, ed. *Parallels and Convergences: Mormon Thought and Engineering Vision.* Salt Lake City: Greg Kofford Books, 2012.
Howsepian, A. A. "Compatiblism, Evil, and the Free-Will Defense." *Sophia* 46 (2007): 217–36.
Huff, Benjamin. "Contingency in Classical Creation: Problems with Alvin Plantinga's Free Will Defense." *Element: The Journal of the Society for Mormon Philosophy and Theology* 1, no. 1 (Spring 2005).
Hunt, David. "Middle Knowledge: The 'Foreknowledge Defense.'" *International Journal for Philosophy of Religion* 28 (1990): 1–24.
James, William. *Pragmatism.* New York: Longmans, Green, 1948.
Jensen, Robin Scott, Robert J. Woodford, and Steven C. Harper, eds. *Manuscript Revelation Books.* Facsimile edition. First volume of the Revelations and Translations series of *The Joseph Smith Papers*, edited by Dean C. Jessee, Ronald K. Esplin, and Richard Lyman Bushman. Salt Lake City: Church Historian's Press, 2009.
Journal of Discourses. 26 vols. London and Liverpool: LDS Booksellers Depot, 1854–86.
King, J. Norman, and Barry L. Whitney. "Rahner and Hartshorne on Death and Eternal Life." *Cambridge University Press* 15, no. 2 (1988): 239–61.
Krafte, Lore E. "Subjective Immortality Revisited." *Process Studies* 9, no. 1–2 (Spring and Summer 1979): 35–36.
Larson, Stan. "The King Follett Discourse—A Newly Amalgamated Text." *BYU Studies* 18, no. 2 (Summer 1978): 193–208.
Langtry, Bruce. "The Prospects for the Free Will Defence." *Faith and Philosophy* 27, no. 2 (April 2010): 142–52.
Lectures on Faith. Salt Lake City: Deseret Book, 1985 printing.
Lewis, C. S. *The Problem of Pain.* New York: Macmillan, 1978.
Mackie, J. L. "Evil and Omnipotence." *Mind*, New Series, 64, no. 254 (April 1955): 200–212.
Madsen, Truman G. "The Meaning of Christ—The Truth, The Way, The Life: An Analysis of B. H. Roberts' Unpublished Masterwork." *Brigham Young University Studies* 15, no. 3 (Spring 1975): 259–92.
Mavrodes, George. "Defining Omnipotence." *Philosophical Studies* 32 (1977): 191–202.
McCann, Hugh J. "Divine Providence." *The Stanford Encyclopedia of Philosophy.* Updated August 1, 2001. plato.stanford.edu/archives/fall2001/entries/providence-divine/.
McLachlan, James. "Fragments of a Process Theology of Mormonism." *Element. The Journal fo the Society for Mormon Philosophy and Theology* 1, no. 2 (Fall 2005), 1–40.

———. "Process Thought and Mormonism." Unpublished manuscript.
McMurrin, Sterling. *Religion, Reason, and Truth*. Salt Lake City: University of Utah Press, 1982.
———. "Some Distinguishing Characteristics of Mormon Philosophy." *Sunstone* (March 1993): 35–46.
Moore, G. E.. *Some Main Problems of Philosophy*. New York: Macmillan, 1953.
Morgan, Jacob. "The Divine Infusion Theory: Rethinking the Atonement." *Dialogue: A Journal of Mormon Thought* 39, no. 1 (Spring 2006): 57–81.
Morriston, Wes. "Is Plantinga's God Omnipotent?" *Sophia* 23, no. 3 (1984): 45–57.
Mosser, Carl. "Evil, Mormonism, and the Impossibility of Perfection *Ab Initio*: An Irenean Defense." *Southern Baptist Journal of Theology* 9, no. 2 (2005): 56–68.
O'Connor, Timothy. "The Impossibility of Middle Knowledge." *Philosophical Studies* 66, no. 2 (May 1992): 139–166.
Oord, Thomas Jay. *The Nature of Love: A Theology*. Nashville: Chalice, 2010.
"Origin of HIV & AIDS." *Avert*. October 10, 2019. https://www.avert.org/professionals/history-hiv-aids/origin.
Ostler, Blake T. "The Absurdities of Prayer to the Metaphysical Absolute." *Inscape*, Brigham Young University (Fall/Winter 1983): 24–38.
———. "The Book of Mormon as a Modern Expansion of an Ancient Source." *Dialogue: A Journal of Mormon Thought* 20, no. 1 (Spring 1987): 66–123.
———. *Exploring Mormon Thought: The Attributes of God*. Salt Lake City: Greg Kofford Books, 2001.
———. *Exploring Mormon Thought: Of God and Gods*. Salt Lake City: Greg Kofford Books, 2008.
———. *Exploring Mormon Thought: The Problems of Theism and the Love of God*. Salt Lake City: Greg Kofford Books, 2006.
———. *Fire on the Horizon: A Meditation on the Endowment and Love of Atonement*. Salt Lake City: Greg Kofford, 2013.
———. "A God Who is Morally Praiseworthy." *Element: The Journal of the Society for Mormon Philosophy and Theology* 4, no. 2 (Fall 2008): 55–78.
———. "The Idea of PreExistence in the Development of Mormon Thought." *Dialogue: A Journal of Mormon Thought* 15 no. 1 (Spring 1982): 59–78.
———. "The Mormon Concept of God." *Dialogue: A Journal of Mormon Thought* 17, no. 2 (Summer 1984): 64–93.
———. "Out of Nothing: A History of Creation ex Nihilo in Early Christian Thought." *Review of Books on the Book of Mormon* 17, no. 2 (2005): 253–320.
Ostler, Blake T., and David L. Paulsen. "Sin, Suffering, and Soul Making: Joseph Smith on the Problem of Evil." In *Revelation, Reason, and Faith: Essays in Honor of Truman G. Madsen*, edited by Donald W. Parry, Daniel C. Peterson, and Stephen D. Ricks, 237–84. Provo, UT: Foundation for Ancient Research and Mormon Studies, 2002.
Packer, Boyd K. "The Mediator." *Ensign* (May 1977). Available at https://www.churchofjesuschrist.org/study/ensign/1977/05/the-mediator.
Patterson, Kristine B., and Thomas Runge. "Smallpox and the Native American." *The American Journal of the Medical Sciences* 323, no. 4 (April 2002): 216–22

BIBLIOGRAPHY

Pereboom, Derk. "The Problem of Evil." In *The Blackwell Guide to Philosophy of Religion*, edited by William E. Mann, 148–72. Oxford: Blackwell, 2004.

Perszyk, Kenneth, ed. *Molinism: The Contemporary Debate*. Oxford: Oxford University Press, 2011.

Plantinga, Alvin. *God, Freedom, and Evil*. Grand Rapids: Eerdmans, 1977.

———. *The Nature of Necessity*. Oxford: Clarendon Press, 1974.

———. "Supralapsariansim, or 'O Felix Culpa.'" In *Christian Faith and the Problem of Evil*, edited by Peter van Inwagen, 1–25. Grand Rapids, MI: Eerdmans, 2004.

———. "Transworld Depravity, Transworld Sanctity, & Uncooperative Essences." *Philosophy and Phenomenological Research* 7, no. 1 (2009): 178–91.

Potter, R. Dennis. "Did Christ Pay for Our Sins?" *Dialogue: A Journal of Mormon Thought* 32, no. 4 (Winter 1999): 73–86.

Pratt, Orson. "The Great First Cause." In *Orson Pratt: Writings of an Apostle*, edited by Jerry Burnett and Charles Pope. Salt Lake City: Mormon Heritage Publishers, 1976.

———. "The Holy Spirit." In *Orson Pratt: Writings of an Apostle*, edited by Jerry Burnett and Charles Pope. Salt Lake City: Mormon Heritage Publishers, 1976.

Quinn, Philip L. "Abelard on Atonement: Nothing Unintelligible, Arbitrary, Illogical or Immoral About It." In *Reasoned Faith*, edited by Eleonore Stump, 281–300. Ithica: NY: Cornell University Press, 1993.

Reichenbach, Bruce R. *Evil and a Good God*. New York: Fordham University Press, 1982.

Roberts, B. H. "The 'Mormon' Doctrine of Deity." *Improvement Era* 6, no. 2 (December 1902): 81–102.

———. *The Seventy's Course in Theology: The Fifth Year: Divine Immanence and the Holy Ghost*. Dallas: L. K. Taylor, 1976.

———. *The Truth, the Way, The Life: An Elementary Treatise on Theology*, edited by Jack Welch. Provo, UT: BYU Studies, 1994.

Robson, Mark Thomas Ian, *Ontology and Providence in Creation: Taking ex nihilo Seriously*. London: Continuum, 2008.

Ross, Floyd. "Process Philosophy and Mormon Thought." *Sunstone* 7 (January–February 1982): 17–25.

Ross, James. "God, Creator of Kinds and Possibilities." In *Rationality, Religious Belief, and Moral Commitment*, edited by Robert Audi and William J. Wainwright, 315–34. Ithaca: Cornell University Press, 1986.

Rowe, William. "The Evidential Argument from Evil: A Second Look." In *The Evidential Argument from Evil*, edited by Daniel Howard-Snyder, 262–85. Bloomington: Indiana University Press.

———. "Evil and the Theistic Hypothesis: A Response to Wykstra." *International Journal of Philosophy of Religion* 16 (1984): 95–100.

———. "Friendly Atheism, Skeptical Theism, and the Problem of Evil." *International Journal for Philosophy of Religion* 59, no. 2 (April 2006): 79–92.

———. "The Problem of Evil and Some Varieties of Atheism." *American Philosophical Quarterly* 16 (1979): 335–41.

———. "Skeptical Theism: A Response to Bergmann." *Noûs* 35, no. 2 (June 2001): 297–303.

Russell, Bruce. "Defenseless." In *The Evidential Argument from Evil*, ed. Daniel Howard-Snyder, 193–206. Bloomington: Indiana University Press.

———. "The Persistent Problem of Evil." *Faith & Philosophy* 6, no. 2 (1989): 121–39.
———. "The Problem of Evil: Why is there So Much Suffering?" In *Introduction to Philosophy: Classical and Contemporary Readings*, edited by Louis P. Pojman, 207–13. New York: Oxford Univ.ersity Press, 2004.
Russell, Bruce, and Stephen Wykstra. "The 'Inductive' Argument From Evil: A Dialogue." *Philosophical Topics* 16, no. 2 (1988): 133–60.
Sennett, James F. "The Free Will Defense and Determinism." *Faith and Philosophy* 8 (1991): 340–53.
Shieber, Joseph. "Personal Responsibility and Middle Knowledge: A Challenge for the Molinist." *International Journal for Philosophy of Religion* 66, no. 2 (2009): 61–70.
Skousen, W. Cleon. *The First 2,000 Years: From Adam to Abraham*. Salt Lake City: Ensign, 1997.
Smith, Joseph Jr. *Teachings of the Prophet Joseph Smith*, compiled by Joseph F. Smith. Salt Lake City: Deseret, 1977.
Swinburne, Richard. *The Existence of God*. Oxford: Clarendon Press, 2004.
———. "Natural Evil." *American Philosophical Quarterly* (1978): 295–301.
———. *Providence and the Problem of Evil*. Oxford: Oxford University Press, 1998.
Tanner, Kathryn. "Incarnation, Cross and Sacrifice: A Feminist-Inspired Reappraisal." *Anglican Theological Review* 86, no. 1 (Winter 2004): 35–56.
Tennant, F. R. *Philosophical Theology*. London: Cambridge, 1928.
Tickemyer, Garland E. "Joseph Smith and Process Theology." *Dialogue: A Journal of Mormon Thought* 17, no. 3 (Autumn 1984): 75–85.
Van Inwagen, Peter. *God, Knowledge, and Mystery: Essays in Philosophical Theology*. Ithica, NY: Cornell University Press, 1995.
———. *The Problem of Evil*. Oxford: Oxford University Press, 2006.
———. "The Problem of Evil, the Problem of Air, and the Problem of Silence." In *The Evidential Argument from Evil*, edited by Daniel Howard-Snyder, 151–74. Bloomington: Indiana University Press, 2008.
Wainwright, William J. *Philosophy of Religion*. Belmont, CA: Wadsworth, 1988.
Whitehead, Alfred North. *Process and Reality: An Essay in Cosmology*, Corrected ed., edited by David Ray Griffin and Donald W. Sherburne. New York: Press Free, 1978.
Widtsoe, John Andreas. *A Rational Theology*. Salt Lake City: LDS Church Publishing, 1915.
Wierenga, Edward. *The Nature of God. An Inquiry Into Divine Attributes*. London: Cornell University Press, 1989.
Wotherspoon, Daniel W. "Awakening Joseph Smith: Mormon Resources for a Postmodern Worldview." Ph.D. dissertation, Claremont Graduate University, 1996.
Yao, Qiwei and Howell Tong. "On Chaos and Prediction in Stochastic Systems." *Philosophical Transactions: Physical Sciences and Engineering Publication* 348, no. 1688 (September 15, 1994): 357–69.
Zimmerman, Dean. "Yet Another AntiMolinist Argument." In *Metaphysics and the Good: Themes From the Philosophy of Robert Merrihew Adams*, edited by Samuel Newlands and Larry M. Jorgensen, 33–94. Oxford: Oxford University Press, 2009.

INDEX

A

agape, 113
agape theodicy, 113–39. *See also* plan of agape.
   and creation, 114
   differences from other theodicies, 113–14
   outline of, 135–39
age of accountability, 150–53.
analogies and examples
   adulterous husband, 212–13
   AIDS, 12–14, 96
   alcoholic father, 165
   Anti-Nephi-Lehies, 175
   Archie and Betty, 146–47
   cancer, 16–17
   car accident, 2, 8–9, 89, 99, 109, 150–53
   child victim, 2, 7–8, 46, 89, 95–96, 108–9, 150–53, 173–74
   Einstein, 53–54
   freezing water, 67–68
   gold atoms, 121
   Groundhog Day, 133–35
   Job, 115–16
   Karate Kid, 117
   marriage relationship, 133
   nuclear weapon, 158–60
   nurse intern, 16
   parenting, 31–32
   prison sentencing, 32–33
   rabies shots, 10
   risky pregnancy, 212
   Rock, 41–43
   smallpox, 2–3, 12–14, 89, 96, 109
   sunlight, 182
   tribesman, 28
   Trolley Paradox, 160–61
   vaccinations, 11
   water molecules, 121–23
Andrus, Hyrum, 192–93
Aquinas, Thomas, 63
Arminius, Jacob, 64
Atonement, 185–222
   compassion theory, 203–22. *See also* compassion theory.
   divine infusion theory, 201–2
   empathy theory, 199–200
   intelligences demand justice theory, 195–96
   moral theory, 196–99
   Mormon theories of, 194–209
   penal substitution theory, 191–93
   requires moral evils, 38
   theory requirements, 186–91

C

Calvin, John, 22–24
Calvinism, 18, 22–24
categorical imperative, 6, 35, 152
coercion, 133
compassion theory, 203–22. *See also* Atonement.
   critiques of, 209–22
   double punishment, 214
   and experiential knowledge, 211–12
   logical consistency of, 220–22
   and sadism, 209–14
   scriptural exegesis, 215–20
   and suffering, 212
compatibilism, 39

consent
  general or specific, 164–69
  in pre-existence, 166–67
  required in plan of agape, 155–71
contra-causal freedom, 39
creation, 34, 41–45
  in agape theodicy, 114
  ex nihilo, 43–45, 63–66
  by evolution, 92
  and finitism, 74–76
  and God's culpability, 109–10
  and God's power, 126
  and natural law theodicy, 66–69
  in plan of agape, 162
  in process thought, 65–66
  in scripture, 105

D–F

de Molina, Luis, 64
defense, 37
disease, 12–14
Draper, Paul, 74
enemies, 175
England, Eugene, 196–99
fall of Adam, 142–43
finitism, 71–72
  and creation, 74–76
  defined, 83
  and miracles, 80–81
free will, 20–24
  and divine foreknowledge, 22–24
  and God's power, 127
  and intelligences, 118
  in Mormon theology, 73
  and omniscience, 64–65
  and relationships, 146
free-will defense, 37–46

G

Gebara, Ivone, 221
Genuine Evils, 19–21
  allowed by God, 110–11
  defined, 20
  and Justified Evils, 21
  and omni-god, 25
God. *See also* finitism, godhead, omni-god.
  adequate object of worship, 127–28
  and foreknowledge, 22–24
  and free will, 22–24
  as godhead, 89. *See also* godhead.
  immanence, 77–78, 83–86, 89, 93
  knowledge of, 128–30
  limits of, 86–87
  material being, 78–80
  miracles, 80–81, 99–100
  and persuasive power, 92–98
  power of, 125–28. *See also* Maximal Power.
  providence of, 117–35
godhead, 71–75
  unity of, 89
Green, Deidre, 209–22
Griffin, David Ray, 97, 106–7

H–L

Hasker, William, 18–19, 97, 108–11
Hick, John, 34, 145, 147–48
Hooker, Morna, 208
human cognitive limitations, 9–18
intelligences, 84–85
  free will of, 118
  natural, 118–19
  nature of, 118–20
  personal, 119–20
intransigent evils, 12–13
  and Skeptical Theist response, 13
James, William, 164–65
Job, 115–17
Justified Evils, 21
Justifying Goods, 6
Kant, Immanuel, 6, 35, 152
King Follett Discourse, 71, 78, 119–20
learning to love, 130–35
Lectures on Faith, 79, 101
Leibniz's Lapse, 39–40
less evil options argument, 47–60
  defined, 49–50
  objections to, 50–59
logical possibility, 122

M

Mackie, J. L., 38–39, 48–49
Maximal Power, 125–26

INDEX

McCann, Hugh, 145
mental disabilities, 132
Meticulous Providence, 18–28, 64
    requirements of, 26
miracles, 80–81
    and coercive power, 99–100
    in process thought, 100
Molinism, 18, 25–26
Moore's Shift, 37–38
moral quietude, 15–28
    and God, 18
    and Meticulous Providence, 18–28
Morgan, Jacob, 201–2
Mormon finitistic theodicy, 71–81
Mormon process theodicy, 83–112
    basic commitments of, 90–91
    criticisms of, 105–12
    differences from process thought, 108
    and God's power, 106
    outline of, 102–4

N–O

natural evils, 176–83
natural law, 63
natural law theodicy, 66–69
natural laws, 121–25
natural regularities, 63–66
no minimum evil defense, 29–35
nomological possibility, 122
omnibenevolence, 4
omni-god
    and creation, 34, 41–45
    defined, 4–5
    and disease, 12–14
    and Genuine Evils, 25
    and natural law, 67–68
    and predestination, 40
    and problem of evil, 15
    and radical evils, 11
omnipotence, 4
    and free will, 64–65
    virtual, 47–49
omniscience, 4
Oord, Thomas Jay, 100
open theism, 65
opposition, 144–45

P

panentheism, 83
penal substitution theory, 191–93. *See also* Atonement.
perfectly good. *See* omnibenevolence.
plan of agape, 141–53. *See also* agape theodicy.
    and children, 150–53
    creation, 162
    the Fall, 142–43
    and free will, 146
    and natural evils, 176–83
    opposition in, 144–45
    and radical evils, 148–53, 173–83
    requires consent, 155–71
    requires Jesus, 160
    soul-building, 147–48
    types of consent, 164–69
    and unevangelized, 170–71
Plantinga, Alvin, 39–44, 155–57
possible worlds, 41–42
Potter, Kelli, 199–200
Pratt, Orson, 84–85
prayer, 98–99
predestination, 40
pre-existence, 119, 131, 158
    consent in, 166–67
Principle of Relevant Similarity, 11–12
problem of evil
    adjusted argument, 7
    and afterlife, 94–95
    basic argument, 4
    and cognitive limitations, 9–18
    and radical evils, 5
process thought. *See also* Mormon process theodicy.
    and creation, 65–66
    and miracles, 100
    and Mormon process theodicy, 108
purpose of mortal life, 72–73

R

radical evils, 2–3
    benefits, 148–53
    defined, 3
    and God, 7–8

and moral obligation, 7–8
and omni-god, 11
and plan of agape, 148–53, 173–83
and problem of evil, 5
rational possibility, 53–54
relationships, 133
and free will, 146
resurrection, 76, 101–2
Roberts, B. H., 85–89
theodicy of, 87–89

S–W

Sermon on the Mount, 174
Skeptical Theist response, 10–11
defined, 10
and intransigent evils, 13
and moral quietude, 15–18
Skousen, Cleon, 194–95
Smith, Joseph, 71, 119–22
soul-building, 147–48
soul-building theodicy, 34–35
theodicy
defined, 37, 61
requirements of, 62
Thomism, 18
total divine control, 63
transworld depravity, 42
unevangelized, 170–71
Unjustified Evils, 6–7
defined, 6
and God, 29–30
van Inwagen, Peter, 29–33
virtual omniscience, 47–49
Widtsoe, John A., 71
world-type, 19

Old Testament

Genesis 1:26–27 — 142
Genesis 5:3 — 142
Genesis 22:10–12 — 7
Joshua 10:12–14 — 76
Job 1:6–12 — 115
Job 2:10–15 — 115
Isaiah 53:4–6 — 189
Daniel 3:15–27 — 76

New Testament

Matthew 5:38–48 — 174
Matthew 9:29 — 101
Matthew 13:58 — 101
Matthew 20:28 — 189
Matthew 26:28 — 189
Mark 5:34 — 101
Mark 10:52 — 101
Luke 8:48 — 101
Luke 22:44 — 189
John 11:38–44 — 76
John 18:11 — 192
Romans 3:21–4:25 — 187
Romans 5:8 — 196
Romans 5:9 — 189
Romans 6:3–11 — 208
Romans 8:19–22 — 208
1 Corinthians 1:30 — 187
1 Corinthians 5:7 — 187
1 Corinthians 13:12 — 117
2 Corinthians 5:17–19 — 189
2 Corinthians 5:18–19 — 187
2 Corinthians 5:21 — 208–9
Galatians 1:4 — 187
Galatians 2:29–20 — 208
Ephesians 1:7 — 187
Ephesians 2:13 — 189
Colossians 1:14 — 187
Colossians 1:15–20 — 208
Colossians 1:20–21 — 187
Colossians 2:15 — 187
Hebrews 9:28 — 189
Hebrews 10:12 — 187
Hebrews 11:3 — 101
1 Peter 2:21–24 — 188
1 Peter 3:18 — 188

Book of Mormon

1 Nephi 3:28–29 — 8
1 Nephi 9:6 — 128
2 Nephi 2 — 200
2 Nephi 2:8 — 200
2 Nephi 2:11 — 142, 144
2 Nephi 2:11–12 — 143
2 Nephi 2:14–16 — 118

INDEX

2 Nephi 2:22–23 — 143
2 Nephi 2:22–25 — 104
2 Nephi 2:25–26 — 144
2 Nephi 2:26 — 202
2 Nephi 9:25–26 — 132
2 Nephi 9:26 — 190
Mosiah 2:38 — 190
Mosiah 3:16 — 132
Mosiah 14:4–6 — 189
Mosiah 15:9 — 190, 206
Alma 7:11–12 — 189
Alma 34 — 200
Alma 34:11–12 — 220
Alma 34:15 — 101, 206
Alma 34:16 — 190
Alma 41 — 206–7
Alma 42 — 200, 207
Alma 42:13 — 194
Alma 42:15 — 190, 196
Alma 42:22 — 194
Alma 42:24 — 190
3 Nephi 7:19 — 76
3 Nephi 11:11 — 192
3 Nephi 19:35 — 101
Mormon 9:19 — 194
Ether 12:12 — 101
Moroni 7:16 — 202
Moroni 7:19 — 202

Doctrine and Covenants

Doctrine and Covenants 18:11 — 190
Doctrine and Covenants 19:15–17 — 215
Doctrine and Covenants 19:16 — 190
Doctrine and Covenants 19:16–17 — 216
Doctrine and Covenants 19:19 — 219
Doctrine and Covenants 29:36 — 141
Doctrine and Covenants 29:39 — 142
Doctrine and Covenants 74:7 — 200
Doctrine and Covenants 76:41 — 190
Doctrine and Covenants 88:6–13 — 76–77, 85
Doctrine and Covenants 88:7–10 — 211
Doctrine and Covenants 88:11–13 — 120
Doctrine and Covenants 88:12–14 — 121
Doctrine and Covenants 88:20–32 — 206
Doctrine and Covenants 88:21–31 — 132
Doctrine and Covenants 88:34 — 121
Doctrine and Covenants 88:34–38 — 77
Doctrine and Covenants 88:39–40 — 201
Doctrine and Covenants 88:41–45 — 77
Doctrine and Covenants 88:43 — 121
Doctrine and Covenants 88:45–58 — 204
Doctrine and Covenants 93:28–40 — 204
Doctrine and Covenants 93:29–31 — 119
Doctrine and Covenants 93:33–34 — 123
Doctrine and Covenants 121:41 — 91, 112
Doctrine and Covenants 122:7 — 169
Doctrine and Covenants 132:20 — 120
Doctrine and Covenants 137:10 — 150

Pearl of Great Price

Moses 4:3 — 141
Moses 5:10–11 — 142
Moses 6:55 — 144
Abraham 3:18–19 — 87, 120
Abraham 3:18–25 — 130–31
Abraham 3:25–28 — 141

Also available from
GREG KOFFORD BOOKS

Exploring Mormon Thought Series

Blake T. Ostler

IN VOLUME ONE, *The Attributes of God*, Blake T. Ostler explores Christian and Mormon notions about God. ISBN: 978-1-58958-003-9

IN VOLUME TWO, *The Problems of Theism and the Love of God*, Blake Ostler explores issues related to soteriology, or the theory of salvation. ISBN: 978-1-58958-095-4

IN VOLUME THREE, *Of God and Gods*, Ostler analyzes and responds to the arguments of contemporary international theologians, reconstructs and interprets Joseph Smith's important King Follett Discourse and Sermon in the Grove, and argues persuasively for the Mormon doctrine of "robust deification." ISBN: 978-1-58958-107-4

Praise for the *Exploring Mormon Thought* series:

"These books are the most important works on Mormon theology ever written. There is nothing currently available that is even close to the rigor and sophistication of these volumes. B. H. Roberts and John A. Widtsoe may have had interesting insights in the early part of the twentieth century, but they had neither the temperament nor the training to give a rigorous defense of their views in dialogue with a wider stream of Christian theology. Sterling McMurrin and Truman Madsen had the capacity to engage Mormon theology at this level, but neither one did."
—Neal A. Maxwell Institute, Brigham Young University

Fire on the Horizon: A Meditation on the Endowment and Love of Atonement

Blake T. Ostler

Paperback, ISBN: 978-1-58958-553-9

Blake Ostler, author of the groundbreaking Exploring Mormon Thought series, explores two of the most important and central aspects of Mormon theology and practice: the Atonement and the temple endowment. Utilizing observations from Søren Kierkegaard, Martin Buber, and others, Ostler offers further insights on what it means to become alienated from God and to once again have at-one-ment with Him.

Praise for *Fire on the Horizon*:

"*Fire on the Horizon* distills decades of reading, argument, and reflection into one potent dose. Urgent, sharp, and intimate, it's Ostler at his best." — Adam S. Miller, author of *Rube Goldberg Machines: Essays in Mormon Theology*

"Blake Ostler has been one of the most stimulating, deep, and original thinkers in the Latter-day Saint community. This book continues and consolidates that status. His work demonstrates that Mormonism can, and indeed does, offer profound nourishment for reflective minds and soul-satisfying insights for thoughtful believers." — Daniel C. Peterson, editor of *Interpreter: A Journal of Mormon Scripture*

Mormonism at the Crossroads of Philosophy and Theology: Essays in Honor of David L. Paulsen

Edited by Jacob T. Baker

Paperback, ISBN: 978-1-58958-192-0

"There is no better measure of the growing importance of Mormon thought in contemporary religious debate than this volume of essays for David Paulsen. In a large part thanks to him, scholars from all over the map are discussing the questions Mormonism raises about the nature of God and the purpose of life. These essays let us in on a discussion in progress." —RICHARD LYMAN BUSHMAN, author of *Joseph Smith: Rough Stone Rolling*.

"This book makes it clear that there can be no real ecumenism without the riches of the Mormon mind. Professor Paulsen's impact on LDS thought is well known. . . . These original and insightful essays chart a new course for Christian intellectual life." —PETER A. HUFF, and author of *Vatican II* and *The Voice of Vatican II*

"This volume of smart, incisive essays advances the case for taking Mormonism seriously within the philosophy of religion–an accomplishment that all generations of Mormon thinkers should be proud of." —PATRICK Q. MASON, Howard W. Hunter Chair of Mormon Studies, Claremont Graduate University

"These essays accomplish a rare thing—bringing light rather than heat to an on-going conversation. And the array of substantial contributions from outstanding scholars and theologians within and outside Mormonism is itself a fitting tribute to a figure who has been at the forefront of bringing Mormonism into dialogue with larger traditions." —TERRYL L. GIVENS, author of *People of Paradox: A History of Mormon Culture*

"The emergence of a vibrant Mormon scholarship is nowhere more in evidence than in the excellent philosophical contributions of David Paulsen." —RICHARD J. MOUW, President, Fuller Theological Seminary, author of *Talking with Mormons: An Invitation to Evangelicals*

Discourses in Mormon Theology: Philosophical and Theological Possibilities

Edited by
James M. McLachlan and Loyd Ericson

Hardcover, ISBN: 978-1-58958-103-6

A mere two hundred years old, Mormonism is still in its infancy compared to other theological disciplines (Judaism, Catholicism, Buddhism, etc.). This volume will introduce its reader to the rich blend of theological viewpoints that exist within Mormonism. The essays break new ground in Mormon studies by exploring the vast expanse of philosophical territory left largely untouched by traditional approaches to Mormon theology. It presents philosophical and theological essays by many of the finest minds associated with Mormonism in an organized and easy-to-understand manner and provides the reader with a window into the fascinating diversity amongst Mormon philosophers. Open-minded students of pure religion will appreciate this volume's thoughtful inquiries.

These essays were delivered at the first conference of the Society for Mormon Philosophy and Theology. Authors include Grant Underwood, Blake T. Ostler, Dennis Potter, Margaret Merrill Toscano, James E. Faulconer, and Robert L. Millet

Praise for *Discourses in Mormon Theology*:

"In short, *Discourses in Mormon Theology* is an excellent compilation of essays that are sure to feed both the mind and soul. It reminds all of us that beyond the white shirts and ties there exists a universe of theological and moral sensitivity that cries out for study and acclamation."
    -Jeff Needle, Association for Mormon Letters

Perspectives on Mormon Theology: Scriptural Theology

Edited by James E. Faulconer
and Joseph M. Spencer

Paperback, ISBN: 978-1-58958-712-0
Hardcover, ISBN: 978-1-58958-713-7

The phrase "theology of scripture" can be understood in two distinct ways. First, theology of scripture would be reflection on the nature of scripture, asking questions about what it means for a person or a people to be oriented by a written text (rather than or in addition to an oral tradition or a ritual tradition). In this first sense, theology of scripture would form a relatively minor part of the broader theological project, since the nature of scripture is just one of many things on which theologians reflect. Second, theology of scripture would be theological reflection guided by scripture, asking questions of scriptural texts and allowing those texts to shape the direction the theologian's thoughts pursue. In this second sense, theology of scripture would be less a part of the larger theological project than a way of doing theology, since whatever the theologian takes up reflectively, she investigates through the lens of scripture.

The essays making up this collection reflect attentiveness to both ways of understanding the phrase "theology of scripture." Each essay takes up the relatively un-self-conscious work of reading a scriptural text but then—at some point or another—asks the self-conscious question of exactly what she or he is doing in the work of reading scripture. We have thus attempted in this book (1) to create a dialogue concerning what scripture is for Latter-day Saints, and (2) to focus that dialogue on concrete examples of Latter-day Saints reading actual scripture texts.

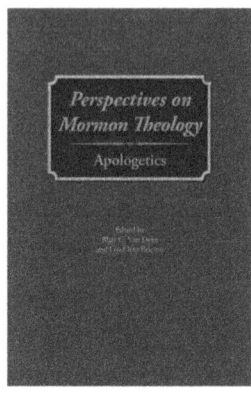

Perspectives on Mormon Theology: Apologetics

Edited by Blair G. Van Dyke and Loyd Isao Ericson

Paperback, ISBN: 978-1-58958-580-5
Hardcover, ISBN: 978-1-58958-581-2

This volume in the PERSPECTIVES ON MORMON THEOLOGY series is an exploration of Mormon apologetics—or the defense of faith. Since its very beginning, various Latter-day Saints have sought to utilize evidence and reason to actively promote or defend beliefs and claims within the Mormon tradition. Mormon apologetics reached new levels of sophistication as believers trained in fields such as Near-Eastern languages and culture, history, and philosophy began to utilize their knowledge and skills to defend their beliefs.

The contributors to this volume seek to explore the textures and contours of apologetics from multiple perspectives, revealing deep theological and ideological fissures within the Mormon scholarly community concerning apologetics. However, in spite of deep-seated differences, what each author has in common is a passion for Mormonism and how it is presented and defended. This volume captures that reality and allows readers to encounter the terrain of Mormon apologetics at close range.

Future Mormon: Essays in Mormon Theology

Adam S. Miller

Paperback, ISBN: 978-1-58958-509-6

From the Introduction:

I have three children, a girl and two boys. Our worlds overlap but, already, these worlds are not the same. Their worlds, the worlds that they will grow to fill, are already taking leave of mine. Their futures are already wedged into our present. This is both heartening and frightening. So much of our world deserves to be left. So much of it deserves to be scrapped and recycled. But, too, this scares me. I worry that a lot of what has mattered most to me in this world—Mormonism in particular—may be largely unintelligible to them in theirs. This problem isn't new, but it is perpetually urgent. Every generation must start again. Every generation must work out their own salvation. Every generation must live its own lives and think its own thoughts and receive its own revelations. And, if Mormonism continues to matter, it will be because they, rather than leaving, were willing to be Mormon all over again. Like our grandparents, like our parents, and like us, they will have to rethink the whole tradition, from top to bottom, right from the beginning, and make it their own in order to embody Christ anew in this passing world. To the degree that we can help, our job is to model that work in love and then offer them the tools, the raw materials, and the room to do it themselves.

These essays are a modest contribution in this vein, a future tense apologetics meant for future Mormons. They model, I hope, a thoughtful and creative engagement with Mormon ideas while sketching, without obligation, possible directions for future thinking.

Rube Goldberg Machines: Essays in Mormon Theology

Adam S. Miller

Paperback, ISBN: 978-1-58958-193-7

"Adam Miller is the most original and provocative Latter-day Saint theologian practicing today."

—Richard Bushman, author of *Joseph Smith: Rough Stone Rolling*

"As a stylist, Miller gives Nietzsche a run for his money. As a believer, Miller is as submissive as Augustine hearing a child's voice in the garden. Miller is a theologian of the ordinary, thinking about our ordinary beliefs in very non-ordinary ways while never insisting that the ordinary become extra-ordinary."

—James Faulconer, Richard L. Evans Chair of Religious Understanding, Brigham Young University

"Miller's language is both recognizably Mormon and startlingly original.... The whole is an essay worthy of the name, inviting the reader to try ideas, following the philosopher pilgrim's intellectual progress through tangled brambles and into broad fields, fruitful orchards, and perhaps a sacred grove or two."

—Kristine Haglund, editor of *Dialogue: A Journal of Mormon Thought*

"Miller's Rube Goldberg theology is nothing like anything done in the Mormon tradition before."

—Blake Ostler, author of the EXPLORING MORMON THOUGHT series

"The value of Miller's writings is in the modesty he both exhibits and projects onto the theological enterprise, even while showing its joyfully disruptive potential. Conventional Mormon minds may not resonate with every line of poetry and provocation—but Miller surely afflicts the comfortable, which is the theologian's highest end."

—Terryl Givens, author of *By the Hand of Mormon: The American Scripture that Launched a New World Religion*

For Zion:
A Mormon Theology of Hope

Joseph M. Spencer

Paperback, ISBN: 978-1-58958-568-3

What is hope? What is Zion? And what does it mean to hope for Zion? In this insightful book, Joseph Spencer explores these questions through the scriptures of two continents separated by nearly two millennia. In the first half, Spencer engages in a rich study of Paul's letter to the Roman to better understand how the apostle understood hope and what it means to have it. In the second half of the book, Spencer jumps to the early years of the Restoration and the various revelations on consecration to understand how Latter-day Saints are expected to strive for Zion. Between these halves is an interlude examining the hoped-for Zion that both thrived in the Book of Mormon and was hoped to be established again.

Praise for *For Zion*:

"Joseph Spencer is one of the most astute readers of sacred texts working in Mormon Studies. Blending theological savvy, historical grounding, and sensitive readings of scripture, he has produced an original and compelling case for consecration and the life of discipleship." — Terryl Givens, author, *Wrestling the Angel: The Foundations of Mormon Thought*

"*For Zion: A Mormon Theology of Hope* is more than a theological reflection. It also consists of able textual exegesis, historical contextualization, and philosophic exploration. Spencer's careful readings of Paul's focus on hope in Romans and on Joseph Smith's development of consecration in his early revelations, linking them as he does with the Book of Mormon, have provided an intriguing, intertextual avenue for understanding what true stewardship should be for us—now and in the future. As such he has set a new benchmark for solid, innovative Latter-day Saint scholarship that is at once provocative and challenging." — Eric D. Huntsman, author, *The Miracles of Jesus*

"This is My Doctrine": The Development of Mormon Theology

Charles R. Harrell

Hardcover, ISBN: 978-1-58958-103-6

The principal doctrines defining Mormonism today often bear little resemblance to those it started out with in the early 1830s. This book shows that these doctrines did not originate in a vacuum but were rather prompted and informed by the religious culture from which Mormonism arose. Early Mormons, like their early Christian and even earlier Israelite predecessors, brought with them their own varied culturally conditioned theological presuppositions (a process of convergence) and only later acquired a more distinctive theological outlook (a process of differentiation).

In this first-of-its-kind comprehensive treatment of the development of Mormon theology, Charles Harrell traces the history of Latter-day Saint doctrines from the times of the Old Testament to the present. He describes how Mormonism has carried on the tradition of the biblical authors, early Christians, and later Protestants in reinterpreting scripture to accommodate new theological ideas while attempting to uphold the integrity and authority of the scriptures. In the process, he probes three questions: How did Mormon doctrines develop? What are the scriptural underpinnings of these doctrines? And what do critical scholars make of these same scriptures? In this enlightening study, Harrell systematically peels back the doctrinal accretions of time to provide a fresh new look at Mormon theology.

"This Is My Doctrine" will provide those already versed in Mormonism's theological tradition with a new and richer perspective of Mormon theology. Those unacquainted with Mormonism will gain an appreciation for how Mormon theology fits into the larger Jewish and Christian theological traditions.

The End of the World, Plan B: A Guide for the Future

Charles Shirō Inouye

Paperback, ISBN: 978-1-58958-755-7

Praise for *End of the World, Plan B*:

"Mormonism needs Inouye's voice. We need, in general, voices that are a bit less Ayn Rand and a bit more Siddhartha Gautama. Inouye reminds us that justice is not enough and that obedience is not the currency of salvation. He urges us to recognize the limits of the law, to see that, severed from a willingness to compassionately suffer with the world's imperfection and evanescence, our righteous hunger for balancing life's books will destroy us all."
— Adam S. Miller, author of *Rube Goldberg Machines: Essays in Mormon Theology* and *Letters to a Young Mormon*

"Drawing on Christian, Buddhist, Daoist, and other modes of thought, Charles Inouye shows how an attitude of hope can arise from a narrative of doom. The End of the World, Plan B is not simply a rethinking of the end of our world, but is a meditation on the possibility of compassionate self-transformation. In a world that looks to the just punishment of the wicked, Inouye shows how sorrow, which comes from the demands of justice, can create peace, forgiveness, and love."
— Michael D.K. Ing, Assistant Professor, Department of Religious Studies, Indiana University

"For years I've hoped to see a book that related Mormonism to the great spiritual traditions beyond Christianity and Judaism. Charles Inouye has done this in one of the best Mormon devotional books I've ever read. His Mormon reading of the fourfold path of the Bodhisattva offers a beautiful eschatology of the end/purpose of the world as the revelation of compassion. I hope the book is read widely."
— James M. McLachlan, co-editor of *Discourses in Mormon Theology: Philosophical and Theological Possibilities*

Re-reading Job: Understanding the Ancient World's Greatest Poem

Michael Austin

Paperback, ISBN: 978-1-58958-667-3
Hardcover, ISBN: 978-1-58958-668-0

Job is perhaps the most difficult to understand of all books in the Bible. While a cursory reading of the text seems to relay a simple story of a righteous man whose love for God was tested through life's most difficult of challenges and rewarded for his faith through those trials, a closer reading of Job presents something far more complex and challenging. The majority of the text is a work of poetry that authors and artists through the centuries have recognized as being one of--if not the--greatest poem of the ancient world.

In *Re-reading Job: Understanding the Ancient World's Greatest Poem*, author Michael Austin shows how most readers have largely misunderstood this important work of scripture and provides insights that enable us to re-read Job in a drastically new way. In doing so, he shows that the story of Job is far more than that simple story of faith, trials, and blessings that we have all come to know, but is instead a subversive and complex work of scripture meant to inspire readers to rethink all that they thought they knew about God.

Praise for *Re-reading Job*:

"In this remarkable book, Michael Austin employs his considerable skills as a commentator to shed light on the most challenging text in the entire Hebrew Bible. Without question, readers will gain a deeper appreciation for this extraordinary ancient work through Austin's learned analysis. Rereading Job signifies that Latter-day Saints are entering a new age of mature biblical scholarship. It is an exciting time, and a thrilling work." — David Bokovoy, author, *Authoring the Old Testament*

Whom Say Ye That I Am? Lessons from the Jesus of Nazareth

James W. McConkie and Judith E. McConkie

Paperback, ISBN: 978-1-58958-707-6

"This book is the most important Jesus study to date written by believing Mormons for an LDS audience. It opens the door for Mormons to come to know a Jesus most readers will know little about—the Jesus of history." — David Bokovoy, author of *Authoring the Old Testament: Genesis–Deuteronomy*

"Meticulously documented and researched, the authors have crafted an insightful and enlightening book that allows Jesus to speak by providing both wisdom and council. The McConkies masterfully weave in sources from the Gospels, ancient and modern scholars, along with Christian and non-Christian religious leaders." — *Deseret News*

The story of Jesus is frequently limited to the telling of the babe of Bethlehem who would die on the cross and three days later triumphantly exit his tomb in resurrected glory. Frequently skimmed over or left aside is the story of the Jesus of Nazareth who confronted systemic injustice, angered those in power, risked his life for the oppressed and suffering, and worked to preach and establish the Kingdom of God—all of which would lead to his execution on Calvary.

In this insightful and moving volume, authors James and Judith McConkie turn to the latest scholarship on the historical and cultural background of Jesus to discover lessons on what we can learn from his exemplary life. Whether it be his intimate interactions with the sick, the poor, women, and the outcast, or his public confrontations with oppressive religious, political, and economic institutions, Jesus of Nazareth—the son of a carpenter, Messiah, and Son of God—exemplified the way, the truth, and the life that we must follow to bring about the Kingdom of Heaven.

The Lost 116 Pages: Reconstructing the Book of Mormon's Missing Stories

Don Bradley

Paperback, ISBN: 978-1-58958-760-1
Hardcover, ISBN: 978-1-58958-040-4

On a summer day in 1828, Book of Mormon scribe and witness Martin Harris was emptying drawers, upending furniture, and ripping apart mattresses as he desperately looked for a stack of papers he had sworn to God to protect. Those pages containing the only copy of the first three months of Joseph Smith's translation of the golden plates were forever lost, and the detailed stories they held forgotten over the ensuing years—until now.

In this highly anticipated work, author Don Bradley presents over a decade of historical and scriptural research to not only tell the story of the lost pages but to reconstruct many of the detailed stories written on them. Questions explored and answered include:

- Was the lost manuscript actually 116 pages?
- How did Mormon's abridgment of this period differ from the accounts in Nephi's small plates?
- Where did the brass plates and Laban's sword come from?
- How did Lehi's family and their descendants live the Law of Moses without the temple and Aaronic priesthood?
- How did the Liahona operate?
- Why is Joseph of Egypt emphasized so much in the Book of Mormon?
- How were the first Nephites similar to the very last?
- What message did God write on the temple wall for Aminadi to translate?
- How did the Jaredite interpreters come into the hands of the Nephite kings?
- Why was King Benjamin so beloved by his people?

Despite the likely demise of those pages to the sands of time, the answers to these questions and many more are now available for the first time in nearly two centuries in *The Lost 116 Pages: Reconstructing the Book of Mormon's Missing Stories*.

www.ingramcontent.com/pod-product-compliance
Lightning Source LLC
Chambersburg PA
CBHW031432160426
43195CB00010BB/708